*Melanesian
Cargo Cults*

Friedrich Steinbauer

Melanesian Cargo Cults

New Salvation Movements in the South Pacific

Translated by Max Wohlwill

University of
Queensland Press

© Friedrich Steinbauer

First published as *Melanesische Cargo-Kulte: Neureligiöse Heilsbewegungen in der Südsee* by Delp'sche Verlagsbuchhandlung KG, München, 1971

First published in English by University of Queensland Press, St Lucia, Queensland, 1979.

Typeset by Academy Press Pty Ltd, Brisbane
Printed and bound by Hedges & Bell Pty Ltd, Melbourne

Distributed in Europe, the Middle East, Africa
and the Caribbean by Prentice-Hall International,
International Book Distributors Ltd, 66 Wood Lane
End, Hemel Hempstead, Herts., England

National Library of Australia
Cataloguing-in-Publication data

Steinbauer, Friedrich.
    [Melanesische Cargo-Kulte. English]
    Melanesian Cargo Cults.
    Index
    Bibliography
    ISBN 0 7022 1095 1

    1. Cargo movement. 2. Nativistic movements — Melanesia. 3. Melanesia — Religion. I. Wohlwill, Max Emil Heinrich, 1934–, tr. II. Title.

299.9

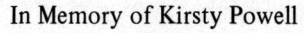

In Memory of Kirsty Powell

Contents

Illustrations

Figures

Acknowledgments

Acknowledgment is made to *Das Wort in der Welt* (*The Word in the World*), and Neuendettelsau Missionwerk; and Professor Peter Lawrence and Manchester University Press for permission to reproduce illustrations which appeared in the original German edition. Acknowledgment is also made to B.A.L. Cranstone and the British Museum for the map of Melanesia.

Translator's Foreword

This book on Melanesian cargo cults, their record, history and assessment of their significance for the people of Melanesia, their governments and religious institutions was written by Dr F. Steinbauer, an anthropologist and a member of the Lutheran Mission in Papua New Guinea.

Peter Lawrence and M.J. Meggitt in their introduction to *Gods Ghosts and Men in Melanesia** explain that cargo cults are new social formations based on a belief that through religious ritual white man's material goods would be provided.

It may initially seem to be a very specialized text, yet it is a fascinating book. I found a copy of the original German edition in the home of a missionary in Wantoat, an out-station of the Lutheran Mission at the foot of the Finisterre Ranges. No Europeans were living there in 1972, apart from the district officer, the missionary, his wife and their child. My wife and I could walk where we wanted. We met native children on our scrambles on bush tracks, we attended the Sunday church service, visited the school and enjoyed the extraordinary artwork of the children; the liveliness and the eager sparkle in these children's eyes were wonderfully exciting. We made purchases in the village co-operative shop; in a more distant village we saw preparations for magic rain-making ceremonies intended to end the terrible drought. The beauty of the wilderness made us happy. We had found human beings with the usual human needs. We felt like their friends.

The book seemed to open our eyes and helped us understand the situation of the Melanesians. It became apparent that cargo cults were a response to an emergency, an effort to understand a new situation and to adjust to it. The cults apparently dealt with problems which, under totally different aspects, concern all

* Melbourne: Oxford University Press, 1972.

human beings. To change the structure of society in order to obtain greater wealth, a better distribution of worldly goods or happiness; to change one's way of thinking in order to release fresh energies in new endeavours, are familiar undertakings to the Western reader.

Western experiments in new communities and communes test new life styles just as the Melanesians attempted to alter their traditional ways of dealing with property, or regulating marriages through cargo cults.

Here was a colourful mirror reflecting modern man and woman. If readers can see this, they may gain closer relationships with other peoples in the world. Barriers between races might be removed, or at least a way be shown to that end. The Melanesian readers in particular may find their own traditions can make an essential contribution to the Western world and to their own adjustment to the impact of a strange civilization. It is not difficult therefore to find the reasons for translating *Melanesische Cargo–Kulte: Neureligiöse Heilsbewegungen in der Südsee.*

It is not difficult to understand why the author, Freidrich Steinbauer, at first, suggested calling the English edition of his book "The Dream of Happiness". The never-ending elusive search for happiness is like a dream, the driving force and energy of the search often being supplied by dreams or dreamlike experiences reflected in fairy-tales, myths, and sacred writings of all people.

With the permission of Dr F. Steinbauer, the author, the text of the second part which presents an analysis of the cults has been shortened. Results of a statistical analysis and the discussion of them have been fully reported. Yet a chart presenting the computation of data has been eliminated. The computation has been checked and the reader can assess the validity of the author's approach to his problems with the help of a table in appendix 6. A section sketching the situation of the missions in Melanesia about ten years ago has been reduced to a short summary. Theological discussions have been severely shortened. But the serious student will still find the challenge by which the author wants to stir the reader of any denomination or belief to seek for new ways of thinking and changing.

The bibliography has been adapted to the needs of the English speaking reader and it has been enlarged by selected items from the full bibliography of the unabridged thesis upon which this book is based.

Notes with references to relevant literary sources have been added to the first section of the book with Dr Steinbauer's help. The illustrations present a selection from the original.

All alterations of the original text as indicated above and additions are my responsibility.

I have to thank Dr Steinbauer for his help with the bibliography and in clarifying some of his sociological terms and also for his readiness to make pictures and diagrams available to the publisher of the English translation. The Reverend John Kuder, D.D., bishop of the Evangelical Lutheran Church of New Guinea at the time, very kindly allowed me to make use of a draft of an incomplete translation of the first section, which he could not continue because of pressure of official work. I am particularly grateful to the editorial staff of the University of Queensland Press who made the publication of the translation possible.

I am especially indebted to Maggie Weidenhofer of EdInk for her conscientious care in preparing the text for publication. I have enjoyed the supporting advice of Professor Peter Lawrence of the University of Sydney. Dr Sabine Willis of the History Department of Macquarie University and my wife, Erika Wohlwill, helped me with proofreading.

Max Wohlwill
1978

Introduction

Melanesia is a part of the Third World. Its influence is growing. The cargo cults significantly determine the spiritual climate of Melanesia. They are for this region what the spiritistic movements of the Umbanda are for South America, what the innumerable independent churches and sects are for Africa, what the welfare religion of the Soka Gakkai is for Japan and what is manifest as materialism and social trends in the Western world.

The cults provide problems for the missions, the indigenous churches and the governments. Those who have turned back from Christianity and participate in these cults number many thousands. The influence of their members as political revolutionaries is so great that the administration is growing restless and nervous. A sense of helplessness overcomes those who have to cope with this phenomenon.

These pages explain how the cults began, how they operate and how we may understand them. We cannot remain silent if we face the facts. Like cultural earthquakes they shake not only a few small South Sea Islands, but they affect indeed the worldwide political, intellectual and religious spheres in which we all are involved. What takes place today in the Pacific is of greater importance than was once thought. Besides, the cults raise questions which are familiar to all who long for justice and a meaningful, happy life.

This book is the abridged and revised version of a religio–historical and missiological thesis.* The scientific, accessory detail with its notes and references has been omitted. The complete thesis will supply all required information and references which have not been mentioned here. This edition presents a valuable sample of almost two hundred cults. It is not the purpose of this publication to suggest premature solutions. Rather, it is the desire to circulate the material to enable the reader to make his own judgement.

* Presented at the University of Erlangen, West Germany, 1971.

The first section of the book presents the history of cults; the second part attempts an analysis and explanation. The conclusions reached may help readers to develop an increasing sense of responsibility for the lives of their fellow men. The numbering of the cults corresponds to that in the complete thesis. The cultic movements are classified according to their chief tendency: magico–mechanistic, religio–spiritual, and politico–social. A catalogue of the cults which are reported in the complete thesis is added to the text of this book as Appendix 3. It should help the reader to gain a better picture of the full scope of the investigation. Some identifications of cults or movements by specification of locality and by the years of their activity follow the complete thesis which quotes more details and may slightly differ from the headings in this abbreviated text. But such differences do not distort the meaning.

Much of the material reported in this book was collected during six years when I was living in New Guinea and travelled extensively through Melanesia. In the complete thesis, four hundred publications are used as sources.

I wish to thank my teacher at the university, my wife and family, and the parishes of the Evangelical Lutheran Church in Bavaria for giving me time to write while carrying out my parish duties. I would like to acknowledge the work of the typists, and help from my publishers and especially the grant of funds from the church. I would like to give special recognition to the assistance I received through my friends in Melanesia. They let me share life and experiences with them. They helped me to gain some understanding of their thinking. I wrote for them and I hope and wish that courage and equanimity may not fail them in the future.

Friedrich Steinbauer

PART 1

The History of the Cults

1

West Irian Jaya

MANSREN–KORERI MOVEMENT (1ST PHASE), 1857–1901

Cult Nos. 1–3, 7
Scene of action: Geelvink Bay, Biak
Leaders: Korana Baibo and other konors (magicians, heralds, forerunners)
**Character of movement: Magico-mechanistic: Expectations of goods with
    messianic signs**

All the known cargo cults of West Irian Jaya are derived from
the same myth and are thus interrelated. West Irian Jaya is
that part of Melanesia from which the earliest cults were
reported, and accounts were collected early in their history.
There were forty different movements in that area alone over
the past hundred years. During this period some changes of the
cult myth occurred, but its fundamental character remained
unchanged and infiltrated all concrete cultural manifestations.
 It is necessary to know the original myth of Mansren
Manggundi in order to understand the subsequent movements.
The Evangelical missionaries from Utrecht who began their
work in Dutch New Guinea in 1855 heard a "strange story"
for the first time in 1857. However, it may be confidently
assumed that the Mansren myth had been known to the
indigenous people long before 1857. The office of konor indicates
that it is highly probable that, even in earlier years, manifestations of the cult had already occurred. A konor is a herald
or forerunner or a bringer of salvation, and his role was to
establish the koreri, an all-embracing time and state of well-
being and salvation through prosperity. The existence of konors
is related to the living conditions and the resultant longings of
the West Irianese people. There is no cult without a need. The
Dutchman F.C. Kamma strongly emphasizes the connection
between the difficult battle for existence of West Irianese people

who are involved in a bitter struggle for survival, and the religious ideal of an eternal, perfect, future state, the so-called koreri. The koreri state of expectation is an expression of wishful thinking, of the desire for unity, abundance, peace and harmony.

The myth on which these movements are based always revolves around a central figure. This person is the hero, Manarmakeri. He wrests his secrets from the morning star, gains great wealth and finally experiences the resurrection of the dead and the coming of the great time of salvation. But the people would not accept salvation without doubt. Because of their unbelief they aroused his anger. He therefore left them and went away to the West, where according to one version of the myth he brought the people there great abundance and eternal life so that they became wealthy and built factories; all progress is due to him.[1] But he will return again to West Irian Jaya. Then the koreri, the day of salvation will dawn. His departure to the West, which was considered to be the mythical centre of power, made the people receptive to everything that came from that direction. The geographical west was seen against the mythical west. For this reason it was later possible for the technical progress of the West to be accepted as self-evident.

This is the myth in detail:[2]

In time immemorial there lived on the islet of Meok Wundi (near Wiak) an old and ugly man named Manarmakeri (a name denoting an infectious skin disease). Being unmarried he had no offspring and therefore lived in the house of his sister. Near the village he occupied himself with tapping palm trees to get swan (palm-wine). He made a careful cut in the blossoming part of the tree-top and each morning enjoyed the taste of the juice which had, during the night, dripped into a piece of bamboo. Once he found the bamboo empty and, becoming very angry, decided to keep watch in order to catch the thief who was stealing his precious wine.

For a whole night he lay hidden near the foot of the tree, and towards dawn he saw a great light coming from heaven. It was the morning star, Sampari, who seated himself upon the top of the tree and changed into a youth. Before he could get hold of the bamboo the old man climbed the tree and seized hold of him. Manarmakeri, very angry, accused Sampari of making considerable trouble by stealing away the only comfort left to him. Sampari, in danger of death because of the coming dawn, asked Manarmakeri what he would take to set him free. "I am poor and have nothing to eat, but make me as you are, or I hold you till dawn", replied Manarmakeri. So Sampari told him to spring into a fire of ironwood and he would become the equal of Sampari himself.

Not yet satisfied, the old man also received a piece of wood with magic power: whatever he wanted, he had only to draw it on the sand of the beach with the piece of wood and he would get it. But still the old man did not loosen his grip until he had a third gift: a fruit which he had only to cast in the direction of a maiden if he wanted a child. Then he set the youth free.

Seeing a young virgin taking a bath, he resolved to test the power of the fruit, and succeeded. The girl became pregnant and bore a son, a fact which caused much quarrelling in the family of the girl, who did not know who was the child's father. The child grew fast but cried continually and drove the family nearly mad. "He is crying for his father", they concluded and arranged a dancing-party, so that the child himself might identify his father. After the young men had passed by, dancing and springing, the older men came along, but still the child cried. At last the very old ones were prompted to take part, and behold; the youngster called "Father, father", pointing to Manarmakeri, who stumbled by leaning on his stick.

The dancing-party came to a sudden end. The family, outraged with anger at this humiliating union, left the three of them on the islet, after destroying the houses, gardens and canoes. But thanks to the gift obtained from Sampari, they were able to survive in the now deserted place. However the young wife Ninggai and her son complained of loneliness. So the family set sail in an outrigger canoe (called forth by the use of the magic piece of wood).

In the middle of Geelvink Bay, Manarmakeri called the island Mufor into being, and they went ashore. Once when Manarmakeri was walking in the forest, he saw himself mirrored in a shell filled with water. He became ashamed of his appearance and understood his wife's disgust with him. Remembering Sampari's promises, he lit a big fire of ironwood, sprang into the flames and suddenly his old skin fell from him and he was miraculously changed into a brilliant youth, while his old skin turned into gongs, bracelets and porcelain. Seeing in the shell mirror that his skin was white, he sprang for the second time into the flames. Now his skin became a nice dark brown colour and, very content, he adorned himself with the bracelets and walked in the direction of his house. His young wife, seeing a stranger coming, hid herself as is the custom, but her son Konoor cried: "Father is coming".

Notwithstanding the fact that Ninggai enjoyed the new appearance of Manarmakeri, who now called himself Mansren Manggundi (the Lord Himself), she still had no one to talk to. She prompted her husband to draw houses in the sand. So the four houses of Mufor came into being. Later they formed the four main divisions of the tribe—the Er. Here Mansren Manggundi reigned over his people, settled customs and tabus, cured the sick and raised the dead. They never lacked food, because he provided them with all they needed. But when a woman whose child had died lost confidence in his power, most of the other inhabitants revolted against him, and he took his departure. Some people believe that he has gone to the West, others that he has settled on the shore of the great Mamberamo river. But he will come back. The golden age—the Koreri—will begin.

The end of this story remained concealed from Europeans for a long time. Only much later the relationship between myth and cult practices was understood. The history of a few of these numerous cults is outlined here.

In 1867 one of the many konors had a vision. Following it, he taught the people new songs. These were the so-called "*do mamun*" (cult no. 1)—songs of bloodshed in which hatred against the enemies is aroused. A list of opponents who were to be killed was drawn up. The routine of daily work was interrupted. For a whole month people came together at night to sing and dance. At the same time the stories of the lord Mansren were more or less intensively enacted and dramatized.

In 1883 a new konor, *Korano Baibo of Mokmer* (cult no. 2), gained influence beyond his own district. He had seen a comet over his village, Meok Wundi, on the south coast of Biak and concluded that he himself was called to be the messenger of the "Highest". From the Rajah of Tidore he officially obtained the title of konor. From this office he derived personal gain. He demanded wives and gifts for himself and sought to benefit his own family. His teaching emphasized increased fertility. The revolutionary features of his predecessors were lacking entirely. After about twenty years his influence waned. Even the marriage of one of his daughters to the Chinese official Lan Sen could not save his status. Yet his reputation as having been a dangerous, influential, although very egotistical leader was still evident seventeen years later when in 1910 he visited the German physician Moszkowski at the Mamberamo River to determine the latter's possible identity with Mansren.

It was in 1886 that a konor amplified his prophecies for the first time by including a *cargo ship* motif (cult no. 3). A great many people, even inhabitants of other islands, came to see the ship bringing the goods. Several gatherings were held at which prayers were offered for the early arrival of the blessings. These assemblies were kept secret from the Europeans.

Warlike manifestations quickly assumed unusual forms. The islanders held parades, carried out military exercises and sang songs such as "Lord, we wish to come to you, but we cannot; the strange Dutch birds are closing the door".[3] The fact that at the same time a seaman was killed on a Dutch steamer is generally recognized as having had a connection with the agitation of this leader.

A whole series of such "messengers of the king of peace" appeared in those years. All of them proclaimed the advent of the golden age. S. Kooijman[4] writes that *the Advent nights* (cult no. 7), spent in singing and dancing in anticipation of the return of Manggundi, give the impression of an atmosphere of serious religious tension. The centre of the festival is the village of the konor towards which the faithful stream from all directions. The konor's house is the religious focus. The realization of the koreri begins in a closed room in this house. This sacred room is the country of the souls. All beings who sit there are different and all things belong already to the world of the koreri.

In certain dances, and particularly in those which are believed to be a prelude to the resurrection of the dead, the people fall into an ecstatic state. Often masses of people are involved and drawn into the dances against their will. After several nights spent in this manner without the appearance of the koreri, the people again disperse. The non-appearance of Manggundi and of the welfare state do not undermine the faith of the participants, who believe that the unbelief of the non-followers is responsible for the failure.

KORERI MOVEMENT OF THE ANGGANITA, 1939–1942

Cult No. 14
Scene of action: Biak; Supiori; Rani; Insubabi Islands; Sowek village
Leader: Angganita
Character of movement: Religio–spiritual: Messianic syncretism with political
    accents

When the Second World War began in 1939, an old woman lived on the off-shore island of Supiori, near Biak. Her name was *Angganita Menufaur* (cult no. 14). She was married and had three children. Since she was afflicted with a leprosy-like disease, she was cast out and forced to live on the desolate island of Insubabi.

At one time she was believed to be a gifted woman, and she had been known as a poetess well beyond the boundaries of her home village of Sowek. When her husband and one of her children died she became gaunt and weak. One day during this affliction Mansren appeared to her. She had been near death five times, but had always recovered, these miraculous recoveries being attributed as a matter of course to Mansren. Finally he healed her completely and sent her back to her village.

Angganita was chosen to be a prophetess and to teach the people the plans of the Lord of Koreri. The reign of peace was about to begin. Countless masses of goods were to be brought by ship. At first only her relatives listened to her message. But soon people flocked to her from near and far to marvel at the wonder woman whose prophecy was so evidently substantiated by her physical healing.

Mansren, who had nourished, healed and blessed Angganita, commissioned her to proclaim the "never-ending life". From the whole Schouten Islands area the faithful hastened to the movement's centre, Biak's off-shore islands of Rani and Insubabi. No-one doubted the sincerity of the prophetess nor of her message. She continually saw new visions and heard voices.

At her request many place names changed in the progress of the universal renewal. Biblical names were preferred. Rani became Gadara; Insubabi was changed to Judea; the village of Sowek was renamed Bethlehem. Some years later Angganita herself was renamed "the golden virgin" or Maria. Soon it was believed that Mansren Manggundi was actually hidden in Jesus Christ. Meok Wundi, where once the old Manarmakeri had lived, was the messianic island upon which Christ had come into the world. Bit by bit Biblical expressions were applied to the Koreri myth. The people apparently had little difficulty in merging Christian teaching with the cults.

Initially, Europeans thought the Koreri movement was simply a somewhat enthusiastic application of the Gospel. But soon the movement accused the churches of deliberately withholding decisive Biblical passages which asserted the link between Jesus and Mansren. A growing enmity was the result. The colonial authorities were also accused of deceit and they were attacked. Corrective measures were greatly hindered by the outbreak of the Second World War and the invasion of Holland in May 1940. The two police constables at Biak did nothing.

When a few Indonesian police moved against Angganita, cleared the island of Isubabi of many hundreds of cult adherents and took the prophetess before the court, suddenly so many witnesses came to her defence that the court proceedings were stopped. Angganita considered this to be a great victory. In fact she believed that through her secret powers she could change all police into stone. The trial in Serui on the island of Japen only increased her prestige. Following the trial, many dance festivals were held at which biblical psalms were sung. In the sanctuary on Isubabi special mixtures were drunk which induced a state of trance and finally speaking in tongues. Towards the end of 1940, strong political manifestations began to appear, resulting in Angganita's arrest for the second time. Her arrest resulted in violent resistance; a man by the name of Stefan Dawan, who became prominent in the movement in later years, killed a policeman, wounded another and put the district officer to flight. Angganita was gaoled at Biak. In the Biak area the waves of the movement rolled ever higher. The people danced and sang day and night. Reports circulated that Holland had been destroyed in the war because Mansren had forsaken that country and was finally returning to his birthplace via Germany and Japan. Huge sea-going canoes were built and the people lived in daily expectation of an earthquake. New konors arose and gained many followers. The movement grew markedly until the Japanese occupied the country and other cult leaders took over.

MANSREN REVOLTS OF THE STEFANUS, 1942–1947

Cult no. 15
Scene of action: Geelvink Bay; Manswam on Biak; Japen; Numfoor
Leaders: Stefanus Simopiaref, Stefanus Dawan and wife Tedora, Jan Simopiaref,
    Korinus, Boseren and others
Character of movement: Politico-social: Messianic nationalism

Successor to the prophetess Angganita was a murderer who had been released from prison when the Japanese marched into New Guinea. He was *Stefanus Simopiaref* (cult no. 15). He later insisted on only being called General Stefanus. His movement was more strongly political than the others had been. Under his leadership the movement reached a militant climax, but soon faded away.

In July 1942, while Stefanus was still in his home village of Manswam on Biak, people came by canoe from the nearby island of Japen to be initiated into the secrets of the new cult. Gradually a full-scale pilgrimage to Manswam developed. Stefanus claimed to be a konor. He also took as a second title "Dewa" (God) and claimed to be an incarnation of Mansren. All those schooled by Stefanus were, in turn, allowed to go home with titles. One respected title was "damai" (peace, or man of peace), which distinguished those who proved their worth as peacemakers. One could also become an "officer" or a "commander". Since the movement considered it was a military organization, these titles were very pertinent.

The movement claimed to establish the political independence and unity of West New Guinea under the koreri banner in the name of its sovereignty. To what extent the figure of Mansren still played a role cannot now be determined. Angganita, for whose rescue from prison Stefanus had gathered the army, was the sovereign of the new and unified state, and Stefanus was her general. The army was structured like a secret society, and would number 8888 men. In its ranks discrimination against the indigenes was often discussed, and fires of hatred were fanned against the foreigners. Stefanus's message was:[5]

> We are Christians, but now we see it all in a new and truer light. The missionaries have deceived the Papuans on purpose. They have torn out the first pages of the Bible, where it is clearly stated that Jesus was one of our own race, a Papuan, and not a white foreigner as the missionaries wanted us to believe. From the moment the foreigners arrived we had to obey orders and were no longer free people in our own land. But our time is coming, the masters will be slaves and the slaves become masters.

It is clear that these words were intended to incite hatred and violence. However, this was in accord with the circumstances of the time, when many Europeans were interned by the Japanese, and the people believed that the great reversal of all values had begun. The Europeans had lost their master status; it seemed as if an all-Asiatic prosperity together with the Japanese was a possibility.

The state of world politics blended in well with General Stefanus' magical understanding of his own intellectual horizon. It was only necessary to dance a couple of hours daily, according to a strict ritual, in order to acquire invulnerability, power and long life. Everywhere Stefanus's followers sold the so-called "air kabal", the holy water. Rubbing one's body with "air kabal" conferred invulnerability against the enemy's arrows and bullets. Water was also mixed with oil and used as "airunur" to assure long life. The forehead was anointed with the mixture as protection against accidents and sickness. In the General's house was a box in which the "secret of health" was thought to be hidden. On the day of Mansren's arrival, this box would open and reveal that for which the people had longed. All believers would exchange their dark skins for white ones and receive eternal life. As a foretaste of the glories of the koreri salvation, a rare glass prism was passed around which had mysterious properties and, if held in a certain way in the light of the sun, showed marvellous colours. In their dances people often became ecstatic. The speaking-in-tongues was claimed to be in English, Dutch and Chinese. People who would not join the dancing were threatened with a curse and were warned that they would be turned into stone.

The revolutionary element of the movement became ever more pronounced, and the expulsion of the foreigners was demanded with increasing vehemence. The more the movement gained in strength, the more Stefanus felt under pressure to respond with action. He first moved to Numfoor. From there he sent out instructions to burn down churches and schools, and to begin to massacre all opponents of the movement. Even Japanese military patrols were attacked and killed when the people failed to obtain the expected blessings and rewards from the "liberators". The Japanese had difficulty catching up with the movement's ringleader. On one occasion a perfectly harmless Papuan was surrendered to them, whom they beheaded in the belief that he was Stefanus.

New confrontations occurred repeatedly. In September 1942 an Ambonese tax official, as corrective action, ordered a whole village to be flogged. As a result an ambush awaited him as he approached the next village and four men of his company were shot. Then, in April, 1943 Stefanus planned a full-scale army operation. First two canoe loads of his "officers" went to Biak to organize the army. The roads were patrolled day and night so that none of the hated foreigners could escape. Ships were carefully checked. The first attack was on the island of Kurudu. However, most of the foreigners had made a timely escape to safety. Stefanus's followers could only lay waste the land and kill a few people.

Soon after this outbreak of violence the koreri army disintegrated, although some acts of terror were perpetrated later. Schools, government and mission stations especially were the objects of the released fury of believers. In their wild dances associated with these attacks, the people sang again and again "Jesus menang! Menang Jesus!" (Jesus conquers). By Jesus, of course, Mansren was meant. When the number of secret murders began to mount the Japanese took action. They burnt down a whole village and shot thirty people by machine-guns on the island of Japen on 13 July 1943. In the meantime Stefanus had conquered the village of Sowek and also stopped a police patrol, disarming them and deporting them to Rani. There Stefanus was surprised by Japanese troops and guns and taken prisoner. He was probably beheaded.

How strongly the leaders of these movements believed in their invulnerability is evidenced by a report about one leader who, when going into the attack, had a bottle of "air kabal" water hanging from his neck and a New Testament tied on top of his head.

2

East Irian Jaya

SIMSON'S CEMETERY CULT, 1940–1944

Cult no. 20
Scene of action: Tanah Merah, near Djajapura (formerly Hollandia)
Leader: Simson
Character of movement: Magico–mechanistic: Expectation of goods with
    nationalistic accent

In 1940, between Tanah Merah and Lake Sentani, the tradition of a group expecting salvation was strengthened by a man called Simson (cult no. 20). Foreign rule by the Dutch and Japanese triggered events that bordered on revolution. The people of Djajapura were dissatisfied with decisions made by foreigners. The Japanese occupation was felt by many to be intolerable.

The rise of messianic expectations was caused by the people's longing for freedom and independence. Simson, therefore, could reckon with sympathetic hearers when he began to speak to his people in Tanah Merah about the golden era. He was a baptized Christian who had lived for several months in the house of a European settler. Occasionally the latter had spoken about "spiritual books". The existence of such secret writings was combined in Simson's mind with the remembrance of the ancestral cults practised to commemorate the dead. Usually he imparted his knowledge in gatherings among the graves in the cemetery. There he also communicated with the spirits of the ancestors.

His sermons gave a simple but consistent message. The Papuan Messiah had prepared great wealth for the people of New Guinea. This wealth did not reach its proper destination however, for the European businessmen changed the addresses on the packing-cases to their own advantage. But it was unjust that all these goods went to the Europeans, after having arrived through underground channels from the Cyclops mountain where they had been manufactured.

Simson said that the Papuan Messiah lived in Holland, where he created all kinds of goods. His presence in Holland accounted for the wealth of the colonial masters, but soon the Messiah would come to expel the fraudulent Europeans and the Japanese, and would ensure that the goods reached the Papuans. Once the foreigners were expelled, a happy and carefree time would begin.

Simson was also able to explain how the Papuans had been deceived for so long regarding their wealth. The Europeans had many books, and these books contained the truth. Part of the truth was kept from the Papuans, who were taught only what was harmless and unimportant. The real secret of how to become wealthy or the secret of a full life was strictly concealed. However he, Simson, had fathomed the mystery and would now reveal the way to obtain freedom, happiness and riches.

The cemetery cult of Simson developed strictly along the lines of the old cargo magic. The cult came to a sudden halt only through the arrival of the Japanese occupation forces. The Japanese could not tolerate large sections of the people preparing themselves for the coming of a Messiah. It was a troublesome nuisance to be eliminated. In 1944 Simson was executed without fanfare on the landing field at Lake Sentani. With the death of its prophet, the cult collapsed. Later others were to revive it.

MUYU UNITY MOVEMENT, 1942–1955

Cult no. 23
Scene of action: Irian, South Coast; Merauke; Muyu tribal area
Leader: Karum
Character of movement: Politico–social: Political Messianism with expectation
    of wealth

On the south coast of Irian, near the Papua New Guinean border, lies the town of Merauke. In the areas behind the town lives the Muyu tribe. During the Second World War this tribe had experienced a period of strong opposition against European rule. A Netherlands police officer was murdered in 1942. In 1945 Muyu bands attacked several government stations. It was a time of hostile acts against the colonial administration. These were expressions of a desire for cultural and political emancipation.

The movement towards unity had its origin in a "spirit" visitation experienced by the labourer *Karum* (cult no. 23) at Merauke in 1953. He was told how the Papuans could obtain freedom from European oppression and gain great wealth. This was to be part of a completely new world order. All mankind should work together, and establish unity and well-being for everyone. God would reign over all in a kingdom of peace in which each would have what he wished. The people imagined this paradise as it would really exist. A new city would arise, with factories, a mint for coining money, and all the trappings of the modern world would be available in abundance. Taxes and also offerings to the Christian churches would be abolished. The dead would arise and the coconut palms begin to walk.

The accumulation of wealth was a part of the old traditional value system of the Muyu people, who needed great quantities of goods in order to celebrate their customary feasts, for bride prices and for prestige. Their whole social life was based on the exchange of goods. It was a plutocratic and hierarchical society. The more a man possessed, the greater was his influence, and the more valuable he considered his life to be. It was, therefore, tremendously important to acquire wealth and increase it continually. Not surprisingly, the acceptance of Christianity also became a feature of the acquisition of more power. However, one of Karum's adherents said quite frankly that Christianity would be abandoned as soon as the movement succeeded in acquiring the wealth and well-being of the Christian world.

Karum's prophecies were qualified by certain conditions. One of the taboos was to refrain from all sexual relations with native and Indonesian women, for only then would it be possible one day to obtain beautiful American and Australian wives. This prescription was coupled with a strong expectation of an American occupation. Queen Juliana of the Netherlands would be rendered powerless; subsequently America, symbolized by the figure of "Marianne", would come as a liberator and unite with New Guinea. To hasten the coming of this future kingdom of happiness, voluntary saving of funds began in 1955. Each person laid aside a portion of his wages as a step on the road to wealth. At the same time spirit seances were held. Communion with the spirits would hasten the realization of the new era.

Since the Karum cult took no hostile stance against Europeans, hardly any action was taken against it. Open enmity was shown only towards Indonesians and Eurasians, as these people were felt to be competitors for the native markets. For many years hopes for a unified state, welfare and peace were nourished from underground sources.

3

Papua

BAIGONA CULT, 1912–1914–1920

Cult no. 30
Scene of action: North-east Papua; Mt Victory (Keroro); Massim; North Gira;
    Kumusi River
Leaders: Maine, Gaiaribari, Eroro, Kaipa, Sinemi, Aede
Character of movement: Magico–mechanistic: Magico-curative blessings

The first years of the twentieth century were relatively quiet
in Papua and generally free from religious cults. All the more
noticeable therefore were the many cults which appeared shortly
before and after the First World War. In 1912 an administration
officer named Hogan died at Joma under mysterious circumstances. Shortly afterwards a certain Aede, a practicing adherent
of the *Baigona cult* (cult no. 30), declared himself responsible
for Hogan's death. An investigation concluded that Aede had
not actually had anything to do with the death, but had merely
wanted to acquire the reputation of being a sorcerer. Only later
did the Europeans gradually learn the kind of sorcery he
practised.

Many inhabitants of the district were inspired and became
followers of the Baigona cult. A.C. Haddon[6] comments:

> The natives of the Kumusi, and more especially of the Mambare
> Divisions, must be in an excited condition . . . An awakening of
> religious activity is a frequent characteristic of periods of social
> unrest. The weakening or disruption of the older social order may
> stimulate new and often bizarre ideals, and these may give rise to
> religious movements that strive to sanction social or political
> aspirations. Communities that feel themselves oppressed anticipate
> the emergence of a hero who will restore their prosperity and
> prestige. And when the people are imbued with religious fervour
> the expected hero will be regarded as a Messiah. Phenomena of
> this kind are well known in history, and are not unknown at the
> present among peoples in all stages of civilization.

In the Kumusi region, on the peak of Mt Victory (Keroro), the spirit of the great serpent Baigona is said to dwell. Once it killed a man and made many others ill. Soon after it chose a man by the name of Maine from Okena as the prophet for its cult. When Maine was on the mountain, the serpent cut out his heart, dried it in the sun, roasted it at the fireplace, smoked it and after his initiation, returned it in a little basket. Maine carried it to his village and hung it from the verandah of his house. According to the secret lore revealed to him by Baigona, Maine was now able to heal all illnesses and thereby exercise influence over life and death. Obedient to instructions he initiated others into the cult. These people were subordinate to him in a hierarchical order of ranks and were required also to pay fees accordingly for their instruction.

Small circles of initiated Baigona men began to appear in each village. They constituted a kind of priesthood and exercised great power, gradually changing the people's social life. The initiation into the cult included anointing the novices with a certain ointment, prepared from material from the forest, which later had to be removed in a ceremonial "washing". The washings were the constitutive element of the movement, and after them the cult members had the power to heal people by using leaves and ointments. Many were actually healed. The Baigona men used, among others, two plants which had often been used as a medicine by the early Australian settlers. One of the plants was burned and the ashes mixed with other additives and then used as an ointment. In other instances the leaves were chewed and laid on the painful area. In other cases something had to be eaten or drunk. The body was also massaged, and the illness was drawn out of the affected part by calling, "Baigona, come forth!". During his ministrations the healer was assisted by several young men who sang and danced. The fee was always paid in advance, but it was returned if no cure had been effected. In one instance it was said that a tuberculosis patient was a hopeless case, because his illness had been transmitted by Europeans and thus Baigona was not effective. This seems to have been the sign of a hostile attitude towards Europeans.

Clearer evidence of hostility was provided when medicine tendered by an Australian doctor was rejected by a whole group of people, who instead experienced cramp-like seizures. Incidentally, these seizures were an integral part of the cult and were deliberately fostered as gifts of the spirits. Speaking in other tongues and epileptoid cramps were thought to be desirable, and assisted in the spread of the cult into the interior. People were proud of this religion. They told one European:[7] "Yes, you cure people's legs—we cure their bodies."

Maine's gardens were worked by his followers. He drank only coconut milk and despised plain water. He spent much time in ornamenting and grooming himself. The healer had to observe certain taboos. For example the eating of sugar-cane was forbidden, and above all no reptile must be injured. The latter taboo is not surprising, since the whole Baigona cult was based on an ancient serpent cult. However, the extension of the taboos to other animals, such as crocodiles, sharks and tree bears was new.

On one of his trips an officer had a crocodile shot. Immediately the people accompanying him were terrified, and the next day several of them were ill. They assumed the illness was a punishment for violating the commandment of the serpent Baigona.

The experience of a Mr Oates was considered to be especially significant and a divine judgement. He had killed a snake one morning. The Baigona followers were startled, but he tried to joke and said, "Oates, now you have killed the Baigona." At 7.30 that evening rain began to fall very heavily, so that the river rose a metre above its banks. At 9.30 all Mr Oates's possessions were swept away into the sea, but none of the other houses was damaged. Baigona's followers were convinced that a supernatural power had intervened. "Be not deceived, Baigona is not mocked."

Among Maine's followers was the old Eroro of Ombeia. He was influential and like many others he was suspected of profiting personally from the credulity of his fellow members in the movement. He claimed to have received his initiation from the hands of a certain Gaiaribari. He assured the people that he had the power to make or prevent rain. Following up his suspicion, the village constable Barigi used an opportunity during a feast to arrest Eroro, and charged him with dishonest practices. Barigi pointed to the twenty pigs and two dogs which, he was convinced, were gifts from the villagers for his services. He also knew that one of Eroro's patients had died, perhaps because the cure had been reversed by the villagers' counter-sorcery which was more powerful than Eroro's craft. During the argument which followed the constable accused Eroro of fraud and said: "You ask for payment and live from exploiting your poor neighbours. You should go to the Mamberamo River and get your goods directly from the ancestors' spirits." Eroro, quickly and cleverly, retorted: "Why don't you go up into your Christian heaven and obtain pigs instead of living off your friends and fellow-believers?" Obviously Eroro was not impressed by plain, moral lecturing. As a matter of fact the charges had to be dropped for lack of evidence.

The confrontation between Eroro and Barigi had an unexpected result: Eroro left the cult and said he would no longer observe the taboos, would drink plain water again, and also work himself in his gardens. The constable, however, had come under the influence of the cult by his meeting with Eroro. He gradually became convinced that the Baigona cult and its teaching were serious and true. Barigi was firmly persuaded that suffering is always caused by an "evil smoke" and that Baigona would provide help against it.

Knowledge of the awe in which people held the snake cult could be abused. It is reported that an old policeman named Tai-imi, profiting by what his travels afield had taught him, set up as a sorcerer on the Gira River and had his snakes invisible to ordinary eyes, but nevertheless very deadly and real to any who obtained the illwill of the sorcerer.

European culture played no part in the Baigona cult, nor did Christianity. The cult was a result of indigenous, magico-curative needs, and developed solely within the limits of traditional, cultural changes. It was not a cargo cult in the sense of expectation of wealth to come; rather it was a salvation movement directed toward power and health, dominance and well-being, seeking deliverance from personal suffering. Messianic features were missing. To this extent it was different from many other movements.

Nevertheless, the administration considered that the cult was dangerous because the secret lore of the cultists was beyond its control. The systematic suppression of the cult seems to have been successful. For example in 1914 at the Gira River fifteen Baigona leaders were brought before the court. Soon no one referred openly to the Baigona cult, but underground it may have been active for much longer.

VAILALA MADNESS, 1919–1931

Cult no. 36
Scene of action: Gulf of Papua; Vailala
Leaders: Evara, Kori, Ua Halai, Biere, Harea, Hairi
Character of movement: Magico–mechanistic: Syncretistic expectation of wealth

The best-known cult of former years is the so-called *Vailala Madness* (cult no. 36) of the south coast of the Gulf of Papua. This cult originated in the village of Arihavu near Kerema in 1919. It spread far and wide. People called it Vailala–kavakeva or Orokolo–kavakeva; in Pidgin: *het i go raun.* This meant that the head moved sideways, that people experienced ecstasy and that they were out of their minds. It is perhaps not insignificant that these manifestations occurred at the end of the First World War, that the ecstatic speaking of the "possessed" was claimed to be German, and was possibly a sign of increasing anti-British sentiment.

The followers of the movement were, to a large extent, former contract labourers who manifested a strong political concern. The movement spread like a grass fire. The chief witness and chronicler of these events was F.E. Williams, the Government Anthropologist, who spoke about mass hysteria and confusion of the mind as a reaction against the influence of Western ideas. The practising cult members were seized with unusual feelings, lost control over their bodies and danced with eccentric steps on the village commons. Young people and children were not immune from the power of this "possession".

Three classes of involvement were recognized:
1. Those who did not consciously want to participate, but were drawn in the wake of the movement.
2. Those who were actively interested in the movement and who stimulated or even simulated the manifestations of the unusual behaviour.
3. The group of deliberate organizers who used and channelled these happenings. Cult leaders came from their ranks. One leader built himself a European-style house and was very much interested in the administration's agricultural development projects. Another, Kori from Nomu village, had been with the Papuan constabulary for twenty years, acted as an interpreter, and had connections with several European traders. He was considered to be a strong personality and also to be the "Papuan cult apostle". Biere also belonged to this group.

The cult founder, however, was an old man by the name of Evara. According to his son, a government interpreter, Evara had had epileptic seizures in the years prior to the first appearance of the Vailala Madness. In addition, he seems to have been very nervous, anxious and sometimes even under internal pressure. As a boy he avoided the men's house. During fighting he often hid himself in the forest for days. He could not look at a corpse without becoming faint. However at his marriage he became completely "hardened" within.

When he related to his fellow villagers his experiences during the times he went into a trance, he awakened in them the desire for similar experiences which "broadened the consciousness". More and more people fell under Evara's influence, especially so since his sensitive nature and his seizures enabled him to communicate rather concrete revelations.

Evara predicted the arrival of the steamer *Sisima*, which was to have on board the departed ancestors as Europeans, and also a great many cargo treasures. At the beginning, expectations also included firearms, as well as the usual trade store articles. As time went on the dreams of material wealth superceded all other thoughts. Only a short time later a few adherents "heard" the ship dropping its anchor. They ran to the shore in crowds. They "saw" lights, "heard" the rattle of anchor chains and the noise of the ship's engine. Ever new hallucinations of hearing and sight were experienced. In the coastal village of Kerema the spirit ship was "seen" repeadedly. One convinced another, saying, "Don't you hear it? Don't you see it? I can clearly perceive it. Out there it is!" One night they were all frightened by the report that the ship had entered the Vailala River. The prophet Evara immediately paddled out to the steamer in his canoe. He returned wearing a victory medal around his neck. A spirit had tossed him the medal from a three-masted ship with a red funnel as a sign of fellowship. From 1919 Evara wore the medal as a sign of his supernatural powers. The ship itself, however, did not come. Allegedly it was delayed due to "insufficient preparation".

Evara's message comprised additional elements. Moral purity and bodily cleanliness was emphasized in the villages. His followers adopted a puritanical attitude towards the observance of Sunday, and introduced a system of general confessions and payments for offences committed. Stealing and adultery especially were severely punished. On the other hand, sexual taboos were swept away. Equality of the sexes was advocated. All heathen ceremonies were abolished. The old masks were burned and the old bull-roarers which had been used to create the spirit voices were openly revealed to the women and so rendered valueless. The men's houses were torn down. Reverence for the ancestors however was generally fostered.

An excited "telegraphic communication" began to take place. Middlemen, as interpreters of strange noises, provided ever new announcements from the spirit world. Since the cargo could be obtained only from the ancestors, who were delaying the coming of the cargo ship, it was most important not to neglect any message from the other world.

Again and again traditional beliefs were mixed with half-understood Christian teachings. The adherents of the Vailala Madness were called the "Jesus Christ people". Heaven was known as Jehovah's country and was in all respects an improved version of this world. Jesus was occasionally used simply as a term for "the good place", but was sometimes confused with a portrait of George V.

Evara had also prophesied the coming of an aeroplane. At that time no one in Papua had ever seen a plane. One can imagine the exultation when shortly afterwards a plane piloted by Captain Hurley actually flew over the Gulf of Papua and the cult villages. This event only created more confusion.

About 1920 an event occurred which served to strengthen the movement even more, but which in European eyes appeared to be outright deception. In the village of Arihava a certain Ua Halai had complained one day of not feeling very well, and several hours later he "died". Before his "death" however he had given instructions that no one was to come near his body. His friends should wait to see what would happen. They were not to dig a grave. At noon on the third day he "rose from the dead". For the followers of Ua Halai, the proof of his actual death was the fact that his ears had been chewed by rats. (F.E. Williams later confirmed that the man's ears were deformed.) The resurrection was therefore an evident miracle. Ua Halai arose from his bier and in a thunderous voice began to preach in "German". He was carried around in the village, where he announced that he had been in the land of the dead and had received new directions for the introduction of the cult practice. His vehicle had been the steamship of the ancestress Lavara. The new message, however, was nothing more than a confirmation of the existing rites.

Another occurrence was less successful. Among the followers of Biere, a cult leader from West Vailala, a massive spirit appearance had been staged. Maivake, who had recently died, was to appear. Biere's collaborators selected two young men, Aita and Karoa who, hidden behind fantastic masks and costumed completely in cloth, took turns at playing the role of Maivake. First sacrificial gifts were brought. However only a few women were allowed to enter the cult house and communicate with the spirits. Singing and dancing followed, and finally at night the masked spirit appeared. The magic was willingly believed by most of those present. But the spirit appearance came to an abrupt end when Kaiva dared to touch the spirit and, perceiving flesh and blood, to unmask him. The astonishment of the bystanders was overwhelming, and their anger fell upon the charlatan. Nevertheless this was not enough to check the movement.

Many tribes who neglected their gardens soon experienced a period of hunger. The appearance of cases of malnutrition and the anti-British attitude of some of the leaders caused the authorities to carry out a number of arrests. The driving spirits of the movement were brought to the government stations, were adequately fed, and given sufficient work. Thus their psychological balance was restored. By November 1923, when the most violent ecstasies were a thing of the past, eighty-six cult leaders were in prison. Naturally only a few could be truly convinced of the futility of the cult's beliefs and activities. Their stereotype answer to all reproaches and accusations was: "I do not know, God knows." Frequently reports appeared in the press that the Vailala Madness was over. But this was true only of a few places; in others the cult continued to be practised. Only in 1931 could it be said that the cult's activities had ceased and there were no new outbreaks or ceremonies.

The years 1912 to 1919 left some remarkable memories in the minds of those people who had been affected. Williams had an opportunity once more to survey the whole area in 1934 and to speak with the people. He was surprised to find they were not grieving for unfulfilled hopes, but were firmly convinced they had had a wonderful experience, a time in which extraordinary things had happened.

For the Vailala people most of the prophecies had been fulfilled. In retrospect, supernatural events had taken place. In their recollection, the wishes of the past had been realized. They had experienced an enraptured era of the unusual and an aura of happiness; as one spoke about it this faith was further glorified. For them the earth had really quaked. The trees had actually swayed in a peculiar way just as it had been predicted. Flowers had come to bloom in a single day. The air had been filled with a pleasant perfume. The spirits of the dead had appeared. They had seen the footprints of the ancestors, and heard their voices in the forest at night. The ancestors had had lanterns and had been there on visits. The aeroplane and the ship had definitely been seen. Evara could produce his medal. It had been a happy time. They had had a foretaste of the end of time. Now they could be certain that something still greater awaited them. True, a delay had occurred, an inexplicable fate had intervened so that the dream faded away prematurely, but now it was merely a matter of time until the shadowy precursor would be replaced by total reality. Looking back the historical happening had been converted into a mystery. In other words: history became salvation history. The historical happenings released a "community mythos" which subsequently obscured the facts.

Within a few years a change in their self-understanding took place which can be compared with a kind of cultural metamorphosis. In 1935 the cult houses were reduced to kindling wood. Sacred relics were no longer needed. The growth of legends had succeeded the actual cult practice.

FILO CULT, 1940–1941–1947

Cult no. 40
Scene of action: Central District; Mekeo; Inawaia
Leaders: Aisa Piau or Filo, Keama Gnu'u, Konio Gnu'u, Kavo Ipame, Ikuvu Evi
     and others
Character of movement: Magico–mechanistic: Expectation of goods by means
     of religious revival with a tendency to fight

The greatest Papuan movement between the two world wars took place in the vicinity of Mekeo. It began with a seventeen year old school girl *Filo* (cult no. 40), who lived in the village of Inawaia. Its course included two phases and was supported by a group of friends and relatives of the prophetess. In Melanesia it is rare for a young woman to be the driving force behind such a movement.

The prophetess of Inawaia was originally named Aisa Piau. Prior to 1940 she cherished the thought of marrying Keama Gnu'u who, however, was in an uncle-niece relationship to her. Such a tie was, according to local law, considered endogamous and forbidden. Filo therefore developed an antipathy against the whole traditional social system, and the later results of the developing cult presented a fulfilment of her most secret personal wishes. Yet her subjective sincerity and conviction should not be questioned.

One morning in February 1940 Filo, through a vision, was lifted out of the monotony of garden work, which she had always detested. A figure appeared in whom she recognized A'aia, the creator spirit and cultural hero of her tribe. He directed her to prepare changes in the social order. Everyone should cease working immediately. The fathers and sisters of the mission told the people lies. The ancestors would care much more for the living and pour out blessings if people only had more trust in them. Clouds would fall upon the earth and cause a great darkness. The people of Inawai were bad people and should repent. Instead of working they should erect altars, sing and pray more, and the pigs should all be slaughtered and eaten. Those who did not believe nor obey would perish.

When Filo reported this message to her parents they were not convinced. Beating her with sticks they sent her back to work. Soon afterwards however sixty people died from influenza within a few days and their deaths were looked on as a sign from heaven. Now people recalled Filo's vision and quickly spread the new teaching abroad. The command against work pleased many of them. Altars were erected and decorated with gorgeous bird-of-paradise plumes and flowers. At 9 o'clock in the evening the people assembled to pray for the heavenly gifts. Filo's parents were clever enough to collect money from the assembly. Severe punishments were announced for all who did not want to participate in the movement. It was said that anyone persisting with garden work would change into a weed, anyone hunting would be changed into a pig or cassowary, and those going out in canoes would take on the shape of a fish. The old morality was abrogated. The marriage of Filo was authorized by a special revelation. Theft, lies, and sorcery were forbidden. Planes were to bring tinned food, tobacco, cloth, tools, books, cars and, most importantly, guns and ammunition. Europeans were to be driven out as quickly as possible.

The nearby Catholic mission station was to be the first object of attack. After several nights of singing and dancing the attack on the mission station took place. The excitement had grown into mass hysteria. Three women went to the cult altars and preached from there to the people, who began to run back and forth shouting insanely. Several hundred people marched on the mission fathers. A nun saw them coming and just had time to barricade her schoolchildren and herself in the church. Iova Eko was the first to climb over the fence and attack the approaching Father Coltre. Only with difficulty was the attacker subdued. That night the authorities were informed. When the government cars drove up early in the morning, police and government officers, to their great astonishment, were received and welcomed heartily by the cultists. The confused crowd believed the trucks and the armed men were an answer to prayer and a fulfilment of Filo's vision. Weapons were awaited, now they had arrived. When the real situation was explained, the disappointment was all the greater. Iova Eko was sentenced by the Supreme Court to seven months' imprisonment and Filo was gaoled for three months.

During their absence other leaders came to the fore. Enthusiasm for the cult had not diminished by the end of 1940. At times two thousand people from near and far gathered in Inawaia. Leadership remained, however, in the clan of Filo, who was given the title of "queen". Konio Gnu'u, a brother of Filo's paramour, declared himself to be God, and his person untouchable. Anyone who accidentally touched him had to pay or he would risk being changed into a dog or losing his place in heaven. Konio's cousin Kavo Ipame was said to be Jesus. In order of rank he followed directly behind Konio. Common to both was that they healed the sick. When the "queen" was released from gaol, a mysterious horse was to be made available for her triumphal entry into Inawaia. However since the horse, which just at that time was missed at the mission station, was not properly fed and cared for, it was too weak to walk and was not available for the noble purpose. Later several police constables returned Filo to her village. The planned feast did not take place for there was insufficient food and people were suffering from hunger. Nevertheless the prophetess was able once more to arouse the masses to a state of excitement. She threatened to convert all her opponents into blocks of wood and serpents. "Radio stations" and storehouses were built. Hostility against the government and the mission grew. A second imprisonment of Filo was the result, after which the movement went underground.

For three more years prayers for goods were said at secret places. Only when hunger and the weakness of the diehards became too great did their zeal wane. It is astonishing that, just as with the Vailala Madness, the past was wonderfully embellished in the recollections of the older people. The essential truth of Filo's prophecy was not doubted. The people had been unfortunate; the good fortune did not prove constant. The hope for a change in their manner of living remained firmly in the thinking of the Mekeo society.

TOMMY KABU CO-OPERATIVE MOVEMENT, 1945–1947

Cult no. 42
Scene of action: Purari Delta
Leader: Koivi Aua or Tommy Kabu
Character of movement: Politico–social: Social–economic reform

The *Tommy Kabu Co-operative Movement* (cult no. 42), which came into existence in the Purari Delta in 1946, was not interested in achieving prosperity by magical means. The "new men", as they called themselves, were concerned chiefly about economic reforms. They sought to realize their social and economic aims through a sober and planned development and through a solid process of work and a spirit of enterprise. But there were also some irrational tendencies.

Originally the society's founder was known as Koivi Aua. As a boy he attended a mission school for a brief period. After a time of unsettled seeking, during which he was indentured to several Europeans as a labourer, he entered the native police force. In 1942, while fleeing from the Japanese in a small boat, he reached Cooktown in northern Queensland. During this voyage he took the name of Tommy. In Australia he worked as an orderly to a naval officer in a staff office, and was at that time the first and only Papuan member of the Royal Australian armed forces. During the following years he saw something of Sydney and Brisbane. Tommy returned to the Purari Delta towards the end of 1945.

In 1946 a general stirring in the cultural interests of the people began. Increasingly the tribes in the Purari Delta began to see their own culture as imperfect. Tommy had returned to the village of his tribe with a sense of dissatisfaction. A desire for a change in the structure of society swept through the young people. Tommy experienced it more than anyone else. He had become a wanderer between two worlds. He had interests in both, but he accepted neither uncritically. For a man in his mid-twenties the post-war years provided a time of ferment, yet at the same time a constructive and creative period. During this time Tommy adopted the second name which, according to ancient Purari custom, should have been the patronym. But he chose the name Kabu, which means "He who possesses the goods". From then on his life's goal was to obtain access to the Australian world of wealth and comfort.

The European world of values was taken as the model for the new society. Kabu started by collecting financial contributions from the various Purari tribes. It was his aim to reorder the economy of the whole delta. Everyone should co-operate in a communal effort to produce sago and copra. The co-operative aimed to find markets in Port Moresby and manage the business. One part of the profits would flow to the producers, another part would be used to set up stores and smaller trading centres in tribal areas. Resettlement took place on higher grounds which were drier and healthier. A spirit of brotherliness became evident.

Many young men joined the movement, but Kabu was the undisputed leader. He always understood how to take full advantage of the respect shown to him. Once a rumour spread that Tommy had, whilst in Australia married the daughter of the English king, and had had two children by her. He never officially denied this rumour although of course he did not confirm it either. In this manner his authority grew and with it also the prestige of the "new men".

Gradually they proceeded to form their own police force and to erect little village gaols everywhere. There was a trend to free themselves politically from the Australians in the degree to which they tried to imitate them economically and culturally. The society had its own flag and practised military exercises. Kabu dressed in the European style and had offices constructed in every village for his lieutenants and himself. Wherever he happened to set up headquarters, he furnished a room as his "office", which he decorated with a mass of forms and papers and publications. The content of the papers did not matter. The impression they made upon his followers was of greater importance. Among them were communist pamphlets distributed by Brisbane dock-workers, and also old issues of the *Reader's Digest*. The main thing was that they looked "official".

The aim of the society was a cultural synthesis. A common denominator with other cargo cults was scarcely in evidence with Tommy Kabu's movement. His concern was chiefly to build up a rational modern society, to achieve equality with the Europeans and to provide the necessities of life. But he could not completely exclude an admixture of utopian concepts.

Considering the lack of transport, one can realize that it was of prime importance for the Tommy Kabu movement to possess its own ship. In April 1946 he succeeded in purchasing an old 30-metre freight barge, the *Ena*, for two thousand Australian pounds. The ship was forty-seven years old and was in dire need of repair. Before this could be carried out a fire on the *Ena* in May 1946 brought to an end all the dreams for the future. Subsequently the government compensated the people for part of the loss.

Kabu was deeply affected by the blow. He wanted to buy a new vessel immediately, but the government refused to permit this. It wanted to distribute the funds only to the small shareholders, who however remained unanimously behind Kabu and refused the compensation. Finally the money was paid out and Kabu had to begin gathering funds all over again.

From then on it was the fate of the society's members to be involved continually in unfortunate business enterprises. They lacked trained personnel, particularly technicians, business- and seamen. Europeans either could not or would not help since the work of the society could not easily be supervised from without. Only ten years later the first government adviser was sent to the delta. Much went awry in the meantime. Above all, confidence in Europeans sank more and more each year. Large amounts of sago were frequently spoilt because of the poor transport connections. The money collected by Kabu to buy a new ship never sufficed. All he managed was to turn up with an outboard motor attached to a canoe one day in 1955. That was at least a kind of self vindication. He finally had his ship, but it was useless for the work or any profitable activity.

Kabu's centre of administration in Port Moresby became too demanding and costly. Each economical disappointment, however, increased the danger that the movement would develop magico-cultic characteristics. Eventually this led to an underground activity with nationalistic tendencies.

Nevertheless it was to the lasting credit of Kabu that he united the Lower Purari tribes and showed the way to a modern, indigenous, economic development. The cause for its failure lay to a large extent in the absence of qualified persons able to manage the details of business enterprises.

After fifteen years there was little activity in Tommy Kabu's business organization. He made attempts to set up tea shops, laundries, bakeries in an effort to find new sources of income. It seems that the movement had broken up into smaller units. But the original drive had vanished. Shame, disappointment or resignation succeeded certainty of success and aim. The movement was a failure but the positive contribution of the Tommy Kabu movement lives on and is today an integrating factor of modern life in its development of a Western style. Towards the end of 1969, Tommy Kabu died of tuberculosis aged about fifty.

4

Sepik District

FOUR PROPHETS MOVEMENT, 1931

Cult no. 47
Scene of action: Aitape to Wewak; Sumup; Wau
Leaders: The so-called Four Prophets or Four Black Kings
Character of movement: Magico–mechanistic: Expectation of wealth

Along the whole north coast of New Guinea many mystical figures are known, sometimes referred to as kings or prophets. At the beginning of 1931 four men appeared at Aitape who claimed to have supernatural powers. At first only one appeared in the bush at Kep, and called himself "king". Soon three other adventurers followed and likewise claimed the power to work miracles. As the *four prophets* (cult no. 47), they began to travel together and proclaim to the people the coming of a glorious time. Their message spread quickly over large areas along the coast. The four miracle-workers said they were able to effect the growth of crops and the making of pots and pans by miraculous means. The people should confidently destroy all their old vessels. Soon newer and much better ones would appear. Everything would grow out of the ground without assistance. Canned goods and kerosene for lamps would likewise emerge. They told the people that Europeans shared the same under-standing—they too extracted their kersosene from the ground. One prophet announced that his long dead mother lived in the Kep mountain. There she was busily preparing all kinds of things for the village people. Up to the present, however, the Europeans had blocked the way for the arrival of the goods.

The prophets also had remedies against sickness. Whoever took their medicine would never again become sick and need never die. The Europeans would soon leave the country and then their possessions could be divided up among the people. The government need not be feared, for the four leaders were not subject to an earthly police force.

In Aitape the doctrine soon assumed concrete form. The naive natives of Walman were credulous and consequently broke all their clay vessels. Before their potshards, they longingly awaited the replacements. When a missionary wanted to interfere and enlighten them he was confidently assured, "You will see, the government station will be swallowed up by the sea and all will be drowned."[8] Others said, "Be careful not to speak against the four. They hear everything and then you may fare badly, During the night your face will be turned around, so that you must look to the rear."

Since the prophets spoke aggressively against the government and declared that paying taxes was unnecessary, an officer had them arrested by the police. They were exiled to the little island of Hasamatia for three years. However their followers did not desert them. Many people were prepared to purchase their leaders' freedom with money, but of course this was not possible. The sentence had to be served to its end. In the meantime the situation calmed down. Since the originators of the unrest could no longer influence the members, initiative was lacking. The movement gradually faded from memory, until some years later it flared up in another form and under a different leadership.

MOUNTAIN KING MOVEMENT, 1935.

Cult no. 50
Scene of action: Wewak; Ulingan; Alexishafen
Leaders: Anonymous enthusiasts
Character of movement: Regligio–spiritual: Escatologism caused by earthquake

East of Wewak, near the boundary of the Madang district, lies the village of Ulingan. In 1935 it was the centre of a king movement which had unsettled many people. It is likely that the four prophets' movement from Aitape also exercised some influence here. The four men had been released from Hasamatia and had created a new variant of their former expectation of goods. At the same time the movement penetrated to Madang and, there likewise, had evoked similar activity.

The population had previously been frightened by several rumours. Two earthquakes had occurred only shortly before; they expected an even greater earthquake in the near future. A devastating calamity would be brought about by the Catholic bishop of St Michael after the completion of the cathedral. He would show how strong and mighty the church was. He would let the earth quake from midnight until morning, so that everything would collapse and no one remain alive. Only his church would stand victorious among the ruins, together with all who sought shelter in it. According to another interpretation the church too would fall and crush the inhabitants—even those who lived far away.

Somewhat different was the novelty that whenever anyone crossed himself fire would spring forth from his forehead and ignite clothing and houses. For fear of possibly perishing in the flames, many people no longer came to places of worship. In one village the school had been torn down because the people felt themselves endangered by this "pious" building. The sign of the cross had become magical and caused fear and anxiety.

One result was the rumour of the *Mountain King* (cult no. 50), who was reputed to be an uncanny, horrific being. The mountains of the back country were believed to be the place of origin of all mysterious things. Nobody had ever seen the "black king", as he was sometimes called, but they all knew what he looked like: "a skin of iron and stone as a symbol of his might, many hands indicating the extent of his power, and with all this the face of a man. He made all things and heard all things through his messengers, the flying foxes." Naturally this king also reckoned with the great earthquake of the Catholic bishop, in whom he saw a hated adversary. He therefore gave instructions to build houses along the river banks. In order to repay the faithful Christians for the damage done by their earthquake, he in turn announced another earthquake, in which only his own followers would be spared. This announcement resulted in an anxious movement into the river valleys. At the same time taboos against certain foods were introduced. Eels, crayfish, and also cassowary eggs were forbidden. By the observance of such eating regulations a kind of cult fellowship developed spontaneously, which again could easily spread cult ideas. The leaders of the movement were kept secret and remain unknown. The cult finally ended in a mass-psychotic condition. Confidence in living returned and displaced anxiety, since after a lapse of time nothing happened. So the myth of the Mountain King was forgotten.

BOUNDARY STONES OF YELIWAN, 1971

Cult no. 53a
Scene of action: Sepik River Delta; Yangoru; Mt Turu
Leaders: Yeliwan, Hawina, Kowae
Character of movement: Magico–mechanistic: Messianic expectations of
happiness

Matthias Yeliwan (or Aliwan), born in 1930, was a man of little formal schooling. After the third grade, having worked in different jobs, he joined the police and served three years in Goroka and two in Madang. Then he joined the Roman Catholic mission in Wewak, a coastal town west of Madang. During this period he learnt to read the New Testament fluently. One night he dreamt that God was appointing him to great deeds, through which he would be able to help his fellowmen and mediate to them the world of cargo goods.

Cargo is the expectation of salvation. He accepted as a basic premise that the attainment of this goal depended on certain technical knowledge. Salvation is something hidden. The right key has to be found to reveal it. Yeliwan believed he had discovered the key when, one day on Mount Turu, 1300 metres above the Sepik River valley where the river leaves the mountains, he found four cement blocks which had been placed there by surveyors. From that day, 15 May 1971, Yeliwan began to mobilize his countrymen. He asked them to remove the blocks and thus clear the way for an era of salvation. He gained several thousand followers. A big event was announced for 7 July 1971. The date had a special significance since it was the seventh day in the seventh month of the seventh decade in this century. Wild rumours began to spread. There were rumours of human sacrifices, of the expulsion of all Europeans from the country. Money was collected. The promotion of the movement jumped to other parts of New Guinea. Men from the Sepik valley who were working on neighbouring islands were summoned home to share in the expected blessings.

Yeliwan kept himself in the background. He disappeared a few days before 7 July. People said he was sacrificing himself for his people and would rise again on the third day. He returned on the day of revelation and led a procession of more than six thousand people up Mount Turu. Europeans, even members of the press, had been invited to come and take photographs. Two of the four cement blocks were dug out. Nothing happened. The Europeans were blamed for blocking the blessing, the reaction of the ancestors and the arrival of goods. The blocks were taken down the mountain and dumped on the property of the Australian government official of the district of Yangoru.

Daniel Hawina Wavingan, then forty-one years old, an energetic follower, raised $A8,000 and requested the Roman Catholic bishop, Leo Arkfeld, to distribute it among the ancestors to make them more generous. The bishop declined to take the money. The government officer would have nothing to do with this request. Yeliwan commented that God could do everything. All further development depended on Him and He would certainly find a new way.

At the same time, a new political party, the Peli Association, was formed in the Sepik district. It made use of the cult movement for political purposes. Elections were held at that time and Yeliwan, who had run for office unsuccesfully in 1969, became the representative in parliament. People said he was the only true leader of New Guinea, and only those who voted for Yeliwan had the prospect of a better life. They belived that the government and the churches were unsuitable leaders for the country.

Yeliwan had a secretary, Peter Kowae, a young semi-intellectual Papuan, who supported him in the legislature and who later became the leader of the Peli Association, which through Kowae's efforts developed into a fanatical political party.

Yeliwan was not a successful parliamentarian. He seemed to become less enthusiastic and eventually he resigned from his office. But his influence was still considerable some years later. Government agencies found it difficult to engage Yeliwan in conversation. Their aim was to break his influence. Not all people in the Sepik district believed in Yeliwan and some very outspoken criticism of Yeliwan and his ideas was made public.

Yeliwan withdrew to a kind of country estate where he had several huts surrounded by a very high barbed-wire fence, and at some distance a second fence had been provided. Loyal followers, acting as bodyguards, kept unwanted visitors away. In front of the huts a monument of cement and steel rods had been erected. It was unveiled on Independence Day in 1975 as a reminder to later generations of the beginning of salvation.

In 1976 the author and nine other Europeans on a study tour visited the prophet here. He had been away in the bush for meditation. But finally he seemed quite pleased to see the Europeans, whose interest seemed to emphasize his significance.

He conversed with great dignity like a true prophet. All evils in the world, the crisis of the world economy, the problem of inflation, strife between parties, political arguments, the failure of education, increasing delinquency and other problems were due to neglect of his teachings. But, he said, he was only the obedient messenger of God, only the bearer of salvation, and the time was near when the signal would be given from Mount Turu for the beginning of a new world.

European "cargo" travels the New Guinea Highlands roads. One must pay to acquire these goods. But where do the Europeans obtain them?

Practical development aid in agriculture here in Banz in the Highlands.

The people of Yalimotal, West New Guinea (Irian Jaya) met white people a few years ago. They now expect a share in European wealth.

Villagers live on the fruits of the field. Hard work is women's lot.

Bearers in port earn some money by contract labour.

A New Guinean bush church with cross and frontal of wool from Tarabo.

Typical mountain village in the inland of New Guinea.

Electioneering in New Guinea.

Kaum, a follower of Yali in the Madang District.

Polelesi, founder of a cult in the Madang District.

5

New Guinea:
Madang District

KILIBOB–MANUP EXPECTATION, 1900–1914

Cult nos. 55–57
Scene of action: Madang; Rai Coast; Sek to Bongu; Yabob; Bogati; Bilibil
Leaders: Unknown
Character of movement: Magico–mechanistic: Messianic cargo expectations

In 1897 two indigenous prisoners with weapons had broken out
of prison. In an attempt to recapture them, the German
governor, von Hagen was shot in the vicinity of Madang. Three
years later two Europeans and a Chinese were killed in a fight
with native police south of Madang. These events strengthened
the people's belief that they were not defenceless against the
foreign rulers. The hostility against the Germans culminated in
a well-organized revolt in 1904. In this planned *Madang Revolt*
(cult no. 55) all male Europeans were to be killed. The European
women had been designated for certain native leaders on the
Rai coast. A warning which reached the Lutheran missionary
at Bongu was not taken seriously. Nearly all the Madang coastal
tribes participated in the plot, which took the form of a secret
cult.

Hans Wagner wrote about it as follows:[9]

> It was a natural reaction against all the new teachings and customs
> of the Whites . . . The New Guineans . . . did not like the laws
> . . . They wanted to be "free men" . . . They wanted to restore the
> old order of vendetta, the Secret Cult and the customs connected
> with it. They wanted to be free of the continuous admonitions and
> suggestions from the missionaries . . . Some Siar men told Mis-
> sionary Weber (of Siar) what they really thought: "We are tired
> of hearing about Jesus. Why should we always listen to the
> missionaries and obey them? We want to do things our own way,
> and be ourselves. We are sick and tired of all this talk of Jesus."

The Madang revolt of 26 July 1904 was evidence of the people's desire not merely to accept life passively, but to participate creatively in the course of history. At the last moment information as to the planned massacre was nevertheless revealed. The leaders were received with gun salvos, taken prisoner and then convicted by a court martial. Six were immediately shot, in September three more were shot. The village of Bilibil was burned down and the people settled elsewhere. The Europeans had won, but the feelings of the Madang people were affected for generations.

In the background of the people's thinking was the myth of *Kilibob and Manup* (cult no. 56). The myth revealed the following: Kilibob and Manup were brothers. Kilibob was light-skinned; he represented the Europeans. Manup was dark; he represented the New Guineans. One day Kilibob went fishing. During this time his wife, Rorpain, went into the bush to collect fruit. Suddenly an arrow landed beside her. She picked it up and hid it. Shortly afterwards Manup approached her. He said, "I shot my arrow at a bird. It fell near here somewhere. Didn't you see it?" Rerpain answered, "No, I haven't seen an arrow."

Manup left and searched farther away for his arrow. Rorpain was sorry he had to look so long, so she said to him, "Manup, I did find your arrow. It is beautifully decorated. I will give you the arrow if you will tattoo a similar pattern on my pudenda." Manup agreed; he was glad to have found his arrow. With a bamboo knife he cut the desired pattern into Rorpain's body. It was the same pattern as the one on the arrow. As a result of these incisions, Rorpain bled profusely. Manup tried to stanch the blood with a leaf, which he then threw into the sea. Then he took bow and arrow and left.

The wind drove the blood-stained leaf to where Kilibob was fishing. Kilibob wondered at this. Towards evening when he returned home he found his wife and his brother as well. But one thing caught his attention. He noticed that when Rorpain was pulling up the canoe she pressed her legs together unnaturally. "I will see what the matter is" he thought to himself. Rorpain at first did not wish to tell him. Only later at night was the reason obvious.

The next morning Kilibob called together all the men in the village and said to them, "Help me to build a new house. Each of you bring me a post and decorate it with good carving." After a few days the men brought their decorated house posts to Kilibob, who examined each one carefully. Among them he found one bearing the same design as he had seen on his wife's body. Kilibob asked, "Who brought this fine, carved post?" Suspecting nothing, Manup acknowledged he had brought it. From then on Kilibob was firmly determined to kill his brother. Manup perceived his intention; besides he had been warned by Rorpain. He succeeded in eluding all his brother's attempts to kill him, but the quarrel grew in intensity.

Finally Kilibob and Manup decided to separate. Each brother made himself a canoe. Manup sailed with his friends to the north-west, while Kilibob and his friends sailed south-east toward the Dampier Straits. When the first Europeans came from the south through the Dampier Straits the Yabob people believed Kilibob was returning with his friends.

The people believed that Kilibob was superior to his brother, and that he created cargo and gave it to the Europeans. According to some traditions the Whites and Blacks were allowed to choose what they wished. He made firearms and iron ships and placed them beside the traditional weapons and canoes. The Blacks chose the latter because they were familiar with them. Their choice forced them to stagnate. The Whites, however, chose the advanced, technical implements and so became superior to the Blacks. Only when Kilibob returns and shows the Blacks the way to technological mastery over the world will equality between the two be established.

Another movement of the same period was the result of a vision. People expected the arrival of the Lamp–tamo, a mysterious "*Man from Heaven*" (cult no. 57) in the very near future. From the Finschhafen area little baskets were sent along the coast towards Madang. They contained broken weapons, articles of the secret cult practices and of sorcery. Men searched for a "renewal of life" by these means and spoke about "the fruits of the new order". A man was said to have come from heaven and to have brought these "fruits" to earth. The movement had a relatively conciliatory character and also propagated peace with the Europeans. The "man from heaven" revealed himself in a basket as the "Christmas Child"—an indication of a syncretistic mixture with the biblical Christmas story. Along the coast a brisk traffic in these baskets developed. A kind of mystery enshrouded the contents, which were carried from village to village, causing great excitement each time a message came. Lacking any organized leadership, the movement quickly came to an end.

AS-BILONG-KAGO MOVEMENT, c. 1933-1935

Cult no. 60
Scene of action: Madang Coast; Bogadjim-Buged/Bongu
Leaders: Various Roman Catholic and Lutheran mission workers
Character of movement: Magico-mechanistic: Syncretistic-millenial expectation
   of wealth

Early in the 1930s, rumours of the return of Jesus spread in the region behind Madang, from the Rai coast to the Ramu valley and Bagasin area. In 1932 an Australian officer dissolved a large assembly of people who had met to pray for the "second coming of the Lord" and to plead for the arrival of cargo. The missionaries began to take notice and re-examined their work.

The New Guineans were asking—Where is the source of well-being? Who will solve the mystery of the cargo? Where is the cargo made? How is it obtained?" They wanted to raise these questions at the elders' conference at Bogadjim Beach in July 1934.

Long before the conference, missionary Roland Hanselmann, who had a better understanding of the movement than the other missionaries, told his colleagues that the people wanted the opportunity to act out their concern about the origin of cargo.

Hanselmann and two trusted New Guinea friends, Koto and Gamit, erected a platform of boards under a large tree. As soon as the cargo theme was introduced at the conference the people would be able to enact a play dramatizing their needs.

Missionary Welsch questioned Hanselmann, and told him that the people were not coming to the conference to view "a monkey show".[10] The boards used for the platform belonged to the mission and could not be used for such nonsense. Missionaries Welsch and Fliehler tore down the platform and the conference agenda, concerning organization and doctrine, was followed.

Later the people told fantastic tales about the conference. They accused the missionaries of desecrating the "altar", and suppressing the revelation of the secret of the cargo. When Hanselmann failed to return to the district after his furlough in the USA the people accused his superiors of preventing his return. Even today many of the people are still convinced that the missionaries deliberately suppressed their way. On 12 July 1963 a well-known village chieftain said in a tape-recorded interview: "At that time this Hanselmann wanted to show us the way, but the conference prevented him and shoved him aside and so the way is now closed to us forever."

Distrust increased in the months following the conference and for many years the opportunity for mutual understanding was lost. Participation in congregational life declined visibly.

At the next conference, in 1935, some of the missionaries drew attention to the disunity. They drew a bush vine along the length of the church to demonstrate the obvious separation between the Europeans and the New Guineans. The missionaries maintained that they were not to be blamed for the non-arrival of the blessings of goods. Then they removed the vine in the hope that all their problems were solved.

The people repaid the action of the Europeans at the conference in 1936 at Sangpat when they drew a line of separation themselves—a length of wire, used as a symbol of the technical world of the Europeans to show who the real separatists were. A heated discussion was the result and each side accused the other of insincerity.

Again the missionaries reacted by suspending the sacraments and appealing for unity, but it was too late to achieve their object by church discipline. The New Guineans simply could not accept that their search for "as bilong kago" was in vain. Christianity in the Madang district no longer meant formal church membership. The Rai coast became a melting pot for all kinds of syncretistic cult attempts, the people making ever new moves to reach out for the cargo phantom. The belief in cargo was like a net cast out in the hope of capturing Utopia. The Christian church became marginal in the area.

MAMBU MOVEMENT, 1937–1939

Cult no. 64
Scene of action: Bogia-Banara; Madang Hinterland
Leader: Mambu
Character of movement: Religio–spiritual: Social-revolutionary syncretism

Mambu belonged to the large village of Apengan, north of Madang. The population was under the influence of the Catholic mission, but at the same time it felt, ever increasingly, the weight of the European domination. A man from the nearby island of Manam expressed this feeling of depression and resignation in the following words:

> You see, we do not understand. We are just in the middle of nowhere. First the Germans came—and the Australians pushed

them out. Then the Japanese pushed out the Australians. Later the Australians and the Americans forced the Japanese to go. It is beyond us. We can do nothing. When a kiap [administrative officer] tells us to carry his baggage we have to do it. When a German told us to carry his baggage we had to obey. When a Japanese told us to carry his baggage we had to do it. If we did not we might be killed. All right, there it is. Take it or leave it. Nogat tok. I didn't say anything, that's just how it is, that's life.[11]

It is therefore not surprising that every report of delivery from this situation fell on fertile ground. *Mambu* (cult no. 64) was absent from his village for a number of years as a contract worker in Rabaul. In 1937, when he was about thirty years of age, he returned home. He was still unmarried, and as this is rather unusual for a New Guinean of that age, it has been suggested that some of his later actions could be explained as sexual perversion. As a baptized Catholic he had a positive relation to the church. For a while there were plans to send him to Ulingan as a catechist.

Mambu began to show an extraordinary religious enthusiasm. Before 5 o'clock in the morning he was praying in church. He relieved the sister sacristan of all her work; he prepared the altar for the mass; his behaviour was willing and pious. After the missionaries' morning prayers he continued his own devotions in the church until the schoolchildren appeared at the mission at 6 o'clock.

Mambu's actions began to be noticed. At the ringing of the angelus he alone knelt with both knees on the road and remained there until the ringing had finished. One night when a man appeared in the room of one of the nuns, suspicion fell on Mambu. This was the catalyst to effect a change from an eccentric piety to an anti-Christian cult movement. Mambu no longer came to the mission station. Soon new rites were reported from the villages in the back regions—rites practised under his leadership.

An entirely new era was announced. Mambu began with an attack upon exploitation by the Europeans, and demanded an end to submission to them. The black man should refuse to depend on the strangers, said Mambu, after which the ancestors who lived in the volcano on the island would send ships loaded with goods. Soon a new harbour would be formed, fronting directly on Gawat village so the ships could be unloaded there. Labour and toil would then be ended.

To substantiate his message and as a foretaste of the coming paradise, Mambu distributed rice and canned meat to some of the faithful followers. Hatred of the foreign rulers expressed itself in Mambu's demand to cease paying taxes to them, and to pay the tax of ten shillings per head to him. The people should rely only upon him; he had so ordered it. He was the "black king" or the "black master". Obedience and respect were due only to him. Attendance at church and school was forbidden under severe penalties; those who disobeyed would be outlawed and excluded from the future prosperity. Official prayers for money were offered in the cemeteries.

Mambu declared that he—like the nuns—would not marry. He "baptized" men and women at an empty house, always two at a time segregated according to sex. He cut off their grass skirts or groin cloths and sprinkled or washed their genitals with water. The discarded clothing was ceremonially buried under a cross, after which the people wore European clothing. All objects were blessed with a crucifix and then covered with earth. Many pigs were butchered to symbolize the dawning of the time of salvation. Mambu ordered cult houses to be built in the centres of the movement. These were little sanctuaries four metres square without walls, but with two and a half metre high side-posts, a pointed, cone-shaped roof, and a flagpole several metres high to which a red flag was attached.

Mambu had little success in his own village. With the Tangu people who lived farther inland, however, he had great influence. He spread his cult in the neo-Melanesian language, Pidgin, because the neighbouring tribes did not understand his own tongue. As the "founder of his religion" he made regular propaganda trips to every place where he had followers. In these villages Christianity, which had only recently been established, began to decline more and more.

At first the cult amused the Europeans. Trade-store owners were highly pleased with the vogue for European clothing which increased their business. But when anti-European agitation increased, Mambu was arrested. In March 1938 he was sentenced to six months in chains, after he had just predicted the imminent outbreak of war.

His arrest did not seriously affect the movement. It was said that the prophet had agreed to go to Madang to recruit more followers. There he would strengthen the movement and hasten the dawn of the time of salvation. In May 1938 a wave of enthusiasm swept through the area and all were waiting for the arrival of something extraordinary. Simultaneously the *Letub cult* (cult no. 66) arose and took over many groups of former Mambu adherents.

PRE-YALI CULTS, c. 1946

Cult nos. 73–75
Scene of action: Madang; Bagasin; Garia; Rai Coast
Leaders: Uririba, Kasan, Pales, Polelesi, Kaum and others
Character of movement: Magico–mechanistic: Religio-syncretistic expectation
of wealth with social renewal

After the Second World War many new movements occurred in the area around Madang, and were quickly suppressed. However 1946 marked the beginning of a new epoch. New leaders came to the fore. Kaut from Kauris had left the scene; Tagarab had died; Kaum of Kalinam was in prison. Yali, who was well known as a war hero, had not yet begun his movement, and in the months before he took over as the new prophet, smaller local leaders became active. They prepared the way for Yali.

One of these local leaders was *Kasan* (cult no. 73), a man of superior intelligence and clear, persuasive powers. He was an elder at Biliau and known as a collaborator of the Japanese. At first he developed syncretistic concepts and carried on several cultic enterprises on his own. Later he began to indoctrinate Yali with cargo cult ideas. He urged Yali to divorce his heathen wife in favour of a Christian woman, and to let himself be baptized. Intellectually he was far superior to the illiterate Yali and was able to pass on his own ideas to the latter and to make propaganda in Yali's name for projects which would facilitate the coming of cargo. The following may illustrate this:

A deputation arrived in Sor from the Letub village of Kurog near Madang. The leaders of the deputation, Son and Bul'me, claimed immediate access to Yali on two counts: indirectly they were trade partners of the Rai Coast people, and Son had served with Yali in the Allied Intelligence Bureau in Australia during the Second World War. Son and Bul'me brought with them two rolls of money [five pounds each in shillings], and two red laplaps decorated with designs of ships, aircraft, and various types of European goods—which they called flags. They presented these gifts to Yali, and told him that the people of Kurog claimed that God had sent them through the spirits of the dead to the local cemetery in his name. They asked him for his opinion on the matter. He himself tried to remain neutral and predicted in oracular words: "These things —I did not get them from the Europeans during the war. I was given army documents, rank and number—but not these things. They are something belonging to you people.[12]

Kasan was not satisfied with this somewhat half-hearted support of his aims. He wanted a definite and open support for his nightly gatherings in the cemeteries. Yali wished to withdraw from these religious affairs, but Kasan succeeded in undermining Yali's firmness with sexual temptations. During Yali's visits to villages he was given young girls to sleep with, and a second marriage with Rebecca of Matokar was arranged. Through Kasan's planned sexualization of the movement new impulses were introduced. Reports of the brothels in Queensland had filtered through and something similar was planned.

In 1946 a Lutheran missionary advocated sports as an outlet for youthful energy. Kasan was the first to take up the suggestion —using it for his own means. He arranged moonlight swimming parties, which were followed by sexual license between all unmarried participants. As Yali himself—in a different context —had urged the women to bear more children in order to solve the problem of a declining population, his words could be interpreted as approval for Kasan's parties. Yali was able to delay the establishment of the "girl houses" by pointing out the lack of physicians who could examine the girls. In 1948 however a man named Pales decided to establish the project without Yali's blessing.

Before the war *Pales* (cult no. 74) had been a Lutheran evangelist. He lived in Komisangel village on the Rai coast, and had fought on the side of the allied forces. His movement was based on the belief that God and Christ would soon come to New Guinea with much wealth in order to establish here his kingdom. Food offerings for the ancestors, prayer meetings, and regular singing of hymns were fixed parts of his movement. The reasoning behind the system of free love which he established was completely incomprehensible to Europeans. Pales recognized that the concept of legal ownership of property was responsible for the never-ending marital quarrels that frequently led to village disturbances. He believed that every woman should belong to every man, without ownership rights.

The Garia people abhorred Pales's scheme because promiscuity was unknown in their past, so he went further inland to propagate his ideas in Dumpu. There he also said that he had been sent by Yali and the Lutheran mission in order to baptize the people and show them the true way to God. The people accepted him. An extensive system of woman exchange soon became established in the hope of fostering harmony and hastening the cargo's arrival. The cult continued until far into 1948 and spread to the border of the Garia country.

At the same time a young woman drew attention to herself. Her name was *Polelesi of Igurue* (cult no. 75) whose sphere of activity was chiefly in the Garia area. She was married to an evangelist. In a dream, an angel had announced to her the coming of a second deluge. Only the elect would be saved if they held to Polelesi and assembled on Mount Igurue. Houses were erected there in which the prophetess received several messages from God. People began to "root out Satan" (old culture articles) and to purify life from all heathenism. Those who were not prepared to break with the past would be devoured by crocodiles.

A considerable number of her followers destroyed their gardens, slaughtered their pigs, and repeated the prayers prepared by the leader. When rain fell at the time of a cult observance it was looked upon as the beginning of the deluge. The elect, to whom a ship with goods and a full warehouse had been promised, had to remain in the rain in order to be consecrated by baptism for their new life. After a few weeks zeal began to flag considerably, since her predictions were not fulfilled. People were embarrassed and returned to their own villages.

YALI MOVEMENT, 1946–1955

Cult no. 79
Scene of action: Rai Coast; Bagasin area
Leaders: Yali, Gurek, and many others
Character of movement: Magico–mechanistic: Revivalistic expectation of goods

Yali (cult no. 79) was born in 1912. The son of a well-known warrior, he attended the mission school at Sangpat, but ran away. As a young man he sought the proximity of Europeans. At the age of sixteen he was a plantation labourer and a barkeeper at Wau. There, for the first time, he heard about the cargo movement from a fellow villager, Constable Tagarab from Milguk. Yali did not become interested at first because he favoured the old traditions of his people. He returned home in 1931 and was made the tultul (official) of Sor.

At the time, the Lutheran missionaries' attitude towards heathen customs was more strict than that of the Catholic priests, so the population was more sympathetic towards Catholics. Yali was indifferent towards the Roman Catholics and, indirectly, he influenced the people's sympathies by remaining loyal to old traditions.

Yali gave up his office as tultul after the death of his first wife, and at the age of twenty-five he enlisted in the police force. In 1942 he arrived in Port Moresby with a Captain Harris and then went to Queensland. The journey impressed him deeply. He saw the cities of Brisbane and Cairns, the wide streets and large buildings, the bridges and vehicles, the great cattle herds, the factories. The experience of order and hygiene was overwhelming. Yali compared this world with his own country and felt ashamed. He understood very well that the Europeans had to work hard for all these blessings. Nevertheless, thinking of his own culture, he could never shake off a feeling of humiliation.

In 1943 he was transferred from the police to the Allied Intelligence Bureau in Queensland. A talk given by a European officer made an unforgettable impression on him. The officer said: "In the past you were backward. But now, if you help us to win the war against the Japanese, we shall help you to obtain houses with good roofs and walls, to acquire electric light, cars, boats, good clothing and good food. After the war your life will be completely changed." Yali was deeply moved by this prospect. He took the officer's promises literally and believed them.

As a sergeant major he returned to New Guinea and to the war in the jungle. In an exciting partisan existence, he became a war hero of whom others spoke with enthusiasm. The flight from the Japanese, in which he was the only survivor, reads like a New Guinean's odyssey.

Yali maintained his loyalty to the old, inherited religion. He admitted that the Europeans produced their goods in lengthy processes, but he believed that in times of emergency their gods came to their assistance with extraordinary means. This was his explanation for the sudden appearance of fleets of ships bringing supplies and the great number of fighting reinforcements. Scientific methods, he believed, worked only so long as one could depend upon supernatural assistance. Requested to speak to his people in a Brisbane radio broadcast, Yali encouraged them by promising them support and help from the Europeans. The people interpreted his words in the light of their cargo beliefs.

In 1945 Yali began to make many similar speeches along the Rai Coast. From the people at Bogia he learnt about missionary Hanselmann, of whose good intentions many were still convinced. Yali said often and clearly, "I myself have seen the manner in which the Europeans produce their food (kaikai). It requires real work." But the believers of the cargo cult twisted his words, and along the coast they repeated how the Europeans produced their goods (kago).

Yali, the hero of the people, quickly became a messiah who would open the access to the sources of wealth. Wherever he went he was subject to such expectations, and in the long run he could not resist the temptation to use the power connected with such a situation. His best intentions were continually corrupted by such men as Kasan. The boundless adulation accorded Yali in the meeting houses which sprang up everywhere turned him into a cargo demagogue after a short time. Already in 1947 he was called king and people looked for his cargo ships in Port Moresby. The villagers in Biliau called him simply "The Lord". In the villages through which he passed with his escort of disciples and admirers he was hailed, "The great one, the Lord is coming". He was acclaimed as an ancestor spirit raised from the dead, who possessed supernatural powers.

The development took its natural course. The Europeans who had wished him well over the years gradually withdrew their sympathies. Thanks to the records of Yali's main secretary, Kasan, who kept an exact diary, it is possible to follow the various stages of the movement quite closely.

At the height of the crisis Yali planned a trip to Port Moresby to collect the cargo which he believed the Europeans held for him. A whole staff of co-workers journeyed with him. The result of this visit was a shock to Yali. All confidence in the government was destroyed. Yali was told that the administration would indeed provide great sums for education, for public health and for the agricultural development of the country, but there was no thought of any substantial reward for their assistance during the war.

The delegation wandered around confused and resigned. Yali himself alternated between shame and anger. The authorities assured him of an annual allowance of £48 [$A96] if he remained loyal to the administration. He returned home.

At that time no one in the administration foresaw that Yali would become an outspoken enemy of all Europeans, due to his belief that he had been betrayed. His only comment, an expression of contempt, was: "The officials of Brisbane have lied to us and betrayed us in the most shameful manner. Their promises are just bullshit. We are finished with them." Yali remembered the zoo he had seen in Brisbane. Suddenly it was clear to him that the Europeans depended on totems in the animal world. Christianity was the purest and most exquisite falsehood. "How was it possible that we were deceived for such a long time," he wondered. Now both roads to cargo were blocked. The administration denied help and the missionaries were always lying. There was no escape but to revive the traditional veneration of the ancestors. Yali decided to be a whole-hearted "pagan" and to encourage all others to abandon the Christian "superstition".

In 1948 Yali developed his own religion. At this stage Gurek was most influential. He was a Roman Catholic catechist and a prophetically gifted assistant. Gurek was able to make use of mythology. He became the chief ideologist and based his teachings on the saga of Manup. The whole coast between the villages of Matokar and Saidor joined the new cult. In principle the new ritual was not very different from other movements, but peculiar to it was a strict organization transcending regional borders.

Yali also acquired the role of a miracle worker. The enthusiastic crowds greeted him with: "Oh God, Oh Jesus, Oh Yali, give us the blessing which you have prepared for us." The well-known features of the cargo cults reappeared: the cargo ship, which was due to arrive at Port Moresby; the return of the ancestors; a joyous, dissolute life and a unified people freed from the foreign master. It was Yali's strength that he coordinated the longings for material goods in a "military junta" which he organized.

In about 1950 Yali reached the zenith of his power. Europeans in the vicinity reported chaotic conditions. Yali, on his own authority, exercised full police powers on the Rai Coast and even acted as a magistrate. His followers were responsible for many abuses. In Kasan's area in particular assaults and sexual promiscuity were no rarity. Yali not only tolerated this, but even promoted it.

Finally the administration intervened. Yali's trial began on 3 July 1950. The charge was that he had established his own prisons and disposed of his opponents in them. He was sentenced to five years' imprisonment. His organization slowly dissolved, but it exists today to some extent. After his release from gaol in 1955, Yali seldom appeared in public. His ideology, however, continued to be effective and again and again created local secondary movements which were started in his name. He had become an intrinsic part of the cargo mythology. Even in his absence the mythos remained viable. It is sometimes said that Yali's power was broken in 1955. That is only true with many qualifications. On the Rai Coast people still place great hopes in the cargo ideology which is linked to the name of Yali.

VARIOUS POST-YALI CULTS, 1950–

Cult nos. 83, 91, 94
Scene of action: Rai Coast; Sarang to Saidor; Ramu Valley
Leaders: Local Yali admirers
Character of movement: Magico–mechanistic: Revivalistic-syncretistic
    expectations of wealth

On a December night in 1950, all chickens and dogs were suddenly butchered at Bongu. The order was: "Kill these animals or you will all lose your heads!" *Gogol* (cult no. 83) who came from Bogati, operated in the wake of the great Yali. He adopted the title of major and gave orders for a very large house to be built in which all cult followers could take refuge during the deluge he predicted. It was known as Noah's Ark or "haus tambaran" after the old ceremonial houses of the ancestral spirits. Around the outside of the house a deep ditch was dug. When the people sat around the fireplace, episodes from the life of the "king" were reverently recited, and ever more fantastic promises made for a utopian future. At Christmas all Christians were to be beheaded because they were against the cargo cult.

On 25 December Nenegi, Gogol's wife, received in a dream other instructions, which upset all plans. In Yali's time Nenegi had been a medium for Yali and acted as his "radio". From time to time she had brought him new revelations from the realm of the ancestors. Now she had a surprising message from the Messiah: "Leave the haus tambaran, carry everything you have quickly into the jungle. Do away with everything or your heads will be lopped off." The refuge was hurriedly demolished and destroyed. Even the church bells were thrown into the deep jungle. Nothing was left behind in this exodus. From that time people avoided the mission and by every possible means prevented anyone from attending meetings, church services, or school.

One day an indigenous evangelist discovered in the bush a cult house in which innumerable bones (especially jaw bones) were heaped up. They had been collected from dug up graves, and the ancestral spirits were venerated through them. On the other hand, this return to the past meant a pact against all Europeans. In 1952 the Reverend Paul Schulz, at that time a missionary at Bongu, wrote:

> Thousands of people in the Mindjeng River valley have sworn an anti-white pact. None of the young men dare leave to work for

Europeans. Each individual must concentrate upon the worship of the ancestors. Bones are continually being disinterred. No effort is spared at the feasts as they strive to please the departed spirits with dances and sexual indulgences.[13]

Another leader was *Ku of Kaliku–Boimbe* (cult no. 91), a luluai (village headman). In 1956 he founded a movement which was carried through with great drive. He claimed to have died and gone to heaven where he had visited God and King George. He had returned to earth where he now represented the interests of all coloured people as the "Black Jesus". In his cult he used Lutheran prayers and allowed his followers many sexual liberties. All villagers with the exception of two elders of the congregation took part. Missionary Dollinger listed the characteristics of this cult and its leader, Ku, as follows:

(a) The leader regards himself, and is looked upon, as a prophet. When I had the honour to see him on the station he said there are "men" (Papuans and Europeans) in him who talk to him.
(b) The seances can take place everywhere when he is in a house by himself. As a matter of fact, they are more and more concentrated on the back room of a trade store which is managed for a European by a notorious cargo man.
(c) People believe that the spirits talk in English. However at his visit here the prophet said it sounds like it but is not real English. (Beyond Pidgin he knows not one word of English.) What the Administration propagates is here translated into the native's world of thinking. The knowledge of English is not regarded as the key to acquiring other knowledge and the development of skills, but it is the mystical key for all the goods that are in the hands of the white man—and consequently the ancestors, white and black, have to talk in that tongue. Everything that the prophet proclaims in his imitated English gets the character of absolute truth.
(d) This point became a very efficient decoy, which gathered most of the new believers, besides the fear that broke much resistance. The beginning of a war is expected in January. Everybody whose name is not written in the prophet's exercise book will have his throat cut.
(e) In other respects the movement shows the usual organization, membership fee, village leaders (Kaunsil or kuskus), bodyguard, young girls as personal servants.
(f) The abuse of girls nearing the stage of development when they are eligible for marriage is propagated and the exchange of women (an old heathen custom there) has been re-enacted at least at one large meeting to speed up goods to come.[14]

For about six months Ku's cult remained secret. Then the administration intervened in Madang and prevented further activities.

The most sensational event of the following years took place in 1961 in *Garegut* near Sek (cult no. 94). Lagit, the luluai of Sek–Abar and an ex-catechist of the Roman Catholic mission there, planned a sacrifice in honour of the ancestors. The Catholic Bishop Noser was invited to the ceremony. At first a rooster was brought—presumably it was to be slaughtered. Suddenly a man named Lagundemi stepped out of the crowd, knelt down and was beheaded by Lagit with a large bush knife. The public was shocked. However this deliberate sacrifice was consistent with Yali's repeated statements that Jesus had died for the Europeans, that they only had been redeemed.

Lagit was convinced that at the moment when the blood of the sacrifice touched the ground the world would be wonderfully transformed. He was surprised when nothing happened as a result of the voluntary sacrifice. The action had been based on the argument that blessings are possible only through sacrifice. Europeans are blessed; Christ was their sacrifice. Brown people are not blessed; hence they needed a sacrifice too.

6

Morobe District

MONEY MAGIC, 1922–1938

Cult no. 97
Scene of action: Huon Peninsula; Finschhafen to Sattelberg
Leaders: Tutumang, Mutali, Tikombe
Character of movement: Magico–mechanistic: Fraudulent wealth magic

Tutumang and Mutali, two young contract workers from the
Finschhafen area, came into contact with a Chinese in the labour
quarters at Rabaul. He told them about a variety of ways for
increasing money. Aware of their naivety, he sold them a wooden
case with which they would be able to conjure money out of
the air. In 1922 they had begun to ponder over the origin of
goods. They saw that Europeans simply wrote on paper and
obtained their supplies; they saw that Europeans had banks in
which money increased. Now at last they had such a bank, and
with it they would *make money* (cult no. 97). In all secrecy
they tested their costly purchase. It was not a success.

The two labourers now began to try their luck by cheating
others. At first they attempted a kind of alchemy. They heated
shilling pieces over a candle flame. They prepared different
mixtures of liquids. From chalk they made small coin-sized discs,
concealed them in cartons and hoped that their products would
turn into genuine money.

It would not be quite fair to condemn the two as outright
deceivers. A deeply religious and magical faith permeated their
thinking and determined their actions. Only after the failure of
all their efforts did they choose another way. They imitated the
European banks to gain by interest. They soon found credulous
followers who gave them money. It was obvious that money was
needed to attract more money, and they collected more and more
for their enterprise. Under threat of punishment, no one was

to reveal any of this to the Europeans. Nevertheless the swindle was soon exposed and Tutumang and Mutali were punished for their deceit and imprisoned. Some of their followers "wept like little children" when they became aware of the deception. It had been a serious attempt for many of the people to increase their possessions.

After a while the magic was revived. Tutumang and Mutali had heard of the Australian mint, and a money machine was to be the answer. Another large sum of money was collected and was used to purchase a variety of machines, such as old air-operated tapping bells. With these they proposed to try their fortune.

Many years later the money magic was finally abandoned. A great service of repentance was held. A pit was dug and implements which had been used for the magic were thrown into it. The elders even erected a plaque over the pit with the inscription: "In God's presence we buried here all articles of the money magic on the 3rd of July, 1938."

MARAFI SATAN'S CULT, 1933–1936

Cult no. 102
Scene of action: Markham Valley at Bunki
Leader: Marafi
Character of movement: Magico–mechanistic: Nativistic-oriented expectations
      of goods

Communications from spirits and money-making had become fashionable. Near Bunki, at the lower course of the Leron River in the Markham Valley, a man by the name of *Marafi* (cult no. 102) introduced a cult which added a few new features. He was not only concerned with participating in the wealth of the Europeans. He had made up his mind to reverse the order of ranks for the two races, to devalue the European culture and to offer a world view instead, in which the Blacks should set the pace. Marafi saw in Satan, the great "anti-figure" of the Christian faith, the redeemer of the coloured people and a symbol of the old traditional culture. He saw Satan as saviour, helper and friend of the New Guineans.

Wherever he went, he told the villagers that he was in touch with Satan and received supernatural powers from him. He allegedly made a trip with Satan to the interior of the earth. The deceased had assured him they would like to return to the living, but Satan would agree to their return only if Marafi's people would renounce the Christian God and acknowledge Satan as the highest authority. Marafi was to make propaganda for this purpose and he was to be permitted to collect taxes for his "mission work". At first he prophezied a catastrophe of nature: the sky would become dark, the earth would quake and a fire would consume all opponents of the cult. However a huge communal house would provide shelter for all good people who obeyed Satan. The morning following the storm the dead would arise and, laden with tinned food, would appear in the village. Above all, weapons were expected.

On one occasion Marafi left a meeting after telling the people he was going to visit Satan. Climbing secretly to the roof of his house, he called from a safe hiding-place that he was now flying through the air in the shape of a bird. On another occasion he summoned a young man to his hut where he had asked the latter's deceased father to materialize. Father and son were said to have shaken hands. All of the practices made a deep impression on the population.

Marafi's closest co-operators took care that the teaching was spread and that no mistrust developed. Marafi was no doubt gifted as an organizer. He was served and he received gifts wherever he went. Upon his master's instructions he also demanded a number of women and girls for himself and his establishment.

He protected himself by threatening the people that Satan would pierce with his pointed spear-like fingers the abdomen of all who spied on him. Satan would open the earth and cause any officer of the administration suddenly to disappear if he tried to interfere. When the administration accepted this test of strength, however, it soon became apparent how vain these boastings were. After official intervention, the frightened girls whom the prophet had so generously distributed were returned to their homes and the originators of the cult led off to prison. The cult houses were torn down. This ended the episode of the Satan cult.

UPIKNO CULT, 1933–1938

Cult no. 103
Scene of action: Huon Peninsula; Kalasa; Finschhafen; Gitua
Leaders: Upikno or Lazarus, Zorika and others
Character of movement: Religio–spiritual: Semi–Christian vitalism

One day at Gitua near Kalasa a man named *Upikno* (cult no. 103) started to preach repentance.[15] He had heard a voice which told him that the people were all evil and despised the word of God. His place of prayer was under a palm tree. He bowed before God and asked for forgiveness for his village. The voice which came to him again and again was like a "mighty spring gushing forth from the ground". At first the missionary, Wacke, was in favour of this call for repentance.

Soon, however, strange subsidiary manifestations were noted. The daily devotions, the petitions for forgiveness and the avoidance of all evil suddenly was supplemented by Upikno's miracles. For example when he bathed himself and left the water "his body was not wet at all"; he let a dog fall dead and later revived it. The voices he heard multiplied, but each time they ended with the admonition: "Don't tell the missionary about this."

Upikno, who had chosen the name of Lazarus, proclaimed a new era. He accused the Christian missionaries of bad work and said they were expendable. In the future they would not be needed. God would be with them, the dead would return; that would suffice. Soon the moral renewal acquired political features. Then a ten year old boy, Zorika, heard voices. Zorika promised new houses, fine clothing, good food and a "new skin". But first one had to become poor. Only he who possessed nothing could receive gifts, so the destruction of all possessions was the logical consequence. Upikno selected five elders who helped him with his task. One who was blind was promised he would recover his eyesight as a reward. His adherents were first of all to be baptized with the water of the River Jordan, which God would divert through the Kalasa area.

Later, in visions, the ancestors were seen wandering around heavily laden with gifts. People even spoke in tongues. Upikno and his friends composed a whole series of new hymns. The themes of these hymns were often about Jesus and the Cross on Golgotha, but were interspersed with prayers for the blessings of material goods. A new gospel came into existence.

A scapegoat had to be found when, in spite of all the prayers, the desired goods failed to appear. Missionary Wacke was declared to be the chief evil-doer. Some prayed that Wacke's house might burn down. "O Lord, since Wacke is always in the way when you want to give us your good gifts, let him die", one woman prayed.

Upikno's wife burnt all her clothing and put on her old grass skirt again. Some of the people began to cut down their best trees. A destructive madness obsessed the people. They desired to be poor by any possible means in order to qualify for the new and better world. If we discard everything then the "real goods" will come to us, they said.

This cult persisted about five years. Then the religious energy was evidently exhausted.

MANGZO MOVEMENTS, 1946–

Cult nos. 109–12
Scene of action: Huon Peninsula
Leaders: Various enthusiasts
Character of movement: Magico–mechanistic: Chiliastic-syncretistic expectation
    of wealth

Since the end of 1946 the hinterland of Hube and the Komba (Ulap) has been in the grip of cargo expectations, which were followed by ecstatic manifestations. The cultists were seized with a strong trembling. They felt a burning in the abdomen like an "inner fire"—for this reason the movement was also called *Mangzo* (cult nos. 109–12).

Eyes were turned inward and some had visions. The dead were seen and heard to say: "Why do you neglect our graves? Keep them clean, confess your sins and look out for the goods which we shall send you from God!" The pastors were accused of repeating only book knowledge, while the cultists were enlightened and communicated God's voice directly. The young boys especially were frequently possessed by the spirit. Sometimes the elders tried to subdue the seizures by sprinkling cold water over the possessed, but this did not always help. Even critical observers were said to have been affected as though in the grip of an invisible power. A teacher named Sela from Hube declared that at first he had not been convinced that they had heard God's voice, but later during public confessions the truth had come over him. Darkness had fallen before his eyes and he had seen a great number of people dressed in white clothes pass before him, followed by an equally large number of people dressed in filthy clothing. Three winged men had come towards him and one had said, "I am Assaria, the protector of the church. I admonish you to be faithful in giving your lessons." Then the vision had faded. When later a fellow-teacher named Weniong had spoken of different revelations Assaria had appeared again to Sela, and had said, "Now the church is taking the wrong direction. Now I shall leave you and go."

Between 1946 and 1948 the Kalasa population wished to introduce a new order. At secret meetings the members resolved that they would no longer accept a government official at Kalasa, as they had Yali; would not accept missionaries; and would use only English in Kalasa schools because the Kâte language had brought them nothing and English was the language of knowledge, progress and wealth.[16]

Parents refused any association with the Kâte missionaries. Instead they prayed for the "heavenly mana" and for blessings on their new society. At one time the feelings were so intense that a massacre nearly took place. All the inhabitants of a bush village were to be killed. One murder actually did take place. The dwarf-sized luluai Ginu of Binge had promised the people goods and motor cars, but first he wanted to make a sacrifice. After having had intercourse with a girl named Mawawe, he declared, "If I kill her and her blood flows the goods will come." Then he took an axe, beheaded the girl and buried the body. An administration officer arrested Ginu, who had been sure of success and could not believe that his sacrifice had been in vain.

Expectations connected with the trade store affair of 1954 were of a different nature. Radical price reductions had won the sympathies of everyone and provided a foretaste of the world of cargo.

Kalasa mission station had been unoccupied for a year. During this period the store fell deeply into debt because of the manner in which it was conducted. People did not understand why all the goods should be so expensive and why the whole business of buying and selling should involve such tiresome calculations. The storekeeper introduced a system of "good prices"; for example be bought a netbag of coconuts for three shillings and sold it for one shilling to his customer, so both parties were satisfied. He gave a high price for garden fruit and sold at a lower price. He did the same when he bought and sold coffee. Other trade wares were also sold at acceptable prices. Nobody was to be made unhappy, and the store enjoyed increasing popularity. Here was evidence of how smoothly business activities could be run if only the New Guineans took over the management. Here was proof for the exploitation practised by the Europeans. The people were not mistaken after all in expecting cargo. Naturally it was a European, a missionary, who spoiled things by discovering the debt at the annual stocktaking.

NEO-MANGZO CULTS, 1958–

Cult nos. 114–19
Scene of action: Huon Peninsula
Leaders: Various enthusiasts
Character of movement: Magico–mechanistic: Syncretistic expectations of goods

At Dedua, from 1963 to 1965, there was a cult called *Hape hehe* (cult no. 118) or "setting the pots" or "digging in the pots" or a new money magic. The Wemarum population in the Finschhafen-Sattelberg mission circuit had excavated pits, put paper money and coins into pots, and buried them ceremonially. The Ten Commandments, the Creed and the Lord's Prayer were then spoken over the pots, and bananas were planted on the "money graves". The blood of pigs was poured over the graves and the pastor was requested to administer communion. The idea behind these rites was a kind of modernized fertility cult. The "money seeds" or "cuttings" would multiply, according to an old myth. Lukas, the leader of the cult, related this myth as follows:

> In pagan times there lived in my Wemarum country a serpent. The people killed it and hacked it to pieces. But from its blood a hunger period arose in my country. When there was nothing more left to eat my ancestors brought dogs' teeth, put them into a pot and closed it. They dug a pit, poured pigs' blood into the pit and then buried the pot. On top of the pit they planted taro and bananas. That ended the period of hunger. Now there was a plentitude of wealth. People could eat and "life appeared". Since now (here among us) the European missionaries and government people have robbed us of the entire produce of the land, there is again hunger. So we also put pots into the ground, poured pigs' blood over them, so that New Guinea could arise and have money and goods to the full.[17]

An administration officer intervened and ordered the pots exhumed and broken. However, with foresight, Lukas had appropriated a sum of money and escaped to Rabaul.

Again in 1966 reports of money magic were rife in the Finschhafen area. The careless and negative religious attitude of many Europeans often made the problem still more complicated. For example a European once declared, "Your missionaries are idle babblers who understand nothing . . . What they tell you is all a swindle. Do as I do! Earn yourself money and obtain the good life. This is the simple truth."

At *Kaiapit* (cult no. 119), toward the end of 1969 a new cult leader arose and restored the worship of the ancestors. A number of groups combined in an association in which they prayed for the help of the spirits of the dead. Every fortnight each member had to contribute two dollars to the leader, who promised to take the money to the ancestors in Port Moresby in December. In return the people would receive aeroplanes, cars, money and many goods. Sessions were held every night. The leader also announced the forgiveness of sins to his followers through the use of water blessed by him. In addition, he recommended that the people pray to the nature spirits who lived in rock, trees, mountains and streams.

Christians in the area met to try to end the cult, but there is no likelihood of an end to it yet.

7

New Guinea Highlands

GHOST WIND MOVEMENT, c. 1945

Cult no. 121
Scene of action: Eastern Highlands; Kainantu South
Leaders: Anonymous visionaries
Character of movement: Magico–mechanistic: Ecstatic expectation of goods

In the mid-1940s unusual manifestations appeared in the region between Kainantu and Okapa. The people had heard about the European settlement in Kainantu, and products such as newspaper, cloth, matches and so forth. They heard that the Europeans travelled through the air in aeroplanes as in the bodies of huge birds. It was quite feasible to see the Europeans as the reincarnations of the spirits of the dead. The first fear gave place to wild rumours. Tales were told of serpents sent by the Europeans to cause death in the bodies of pregnant women. All kinds of things were tried as protection against these threats.

Suddenly it was rumoured that all black swine would die. It was agreed to kill them before this could happen. A mass butchering of these animals began and the people feasted on them. Excitement, like a kind of mass psychosis, was widespread. A "cold wind", it was said, went through the villages. The mysterious *fever wind* (cult no. 121) affected them like a grass fire. Witnesses described the seizures as similar to fever chills. Hardly anyone was free of the symptoms. People began to tremble, lapse into convulsions and stumble around the village commons. Children were not immune to the fever. People were even asked by their neighbours to sell them the "fever", which was like a shudder of enlightenment, a way to happiness, a kind of rapture or a trance of blessedness. The excitement did not persist for very long. After a short time the shivering stopped and life went back to normal. Only the hope for material blessings remained. People lived in the daily expectation of the cargo and many warehouses were built to receive it. The village commons were cleaned up. Smaller trees were dug up to be replanted at certain other locations. Holes were made at various places in the hope of finding cargo. Directions for these activities were derived from dreams and visions.

Originally the movement was a reaction against the modern world, an opposition to influences from without. Later it changed into a search for the wealth of the Europeans, and fell into the control of speculators who could see an opportunity for personal gain. The deception, however, did not really effect the intrinsic credulity of the people. They explained their lack of success by saying that certain procedures had not been properly carried out, or that outside disturbances had interfered. The Europeans especially were accused of being the cause of the failures—their presence caused the projects to miscarry. Belief in the truth of cargo was not much weakened. It was always a matter of experimenting with the environment, which remained mysterious, dangerous and unpredictable. Different possibilities could be tried. The correct road to the desired goal would be found. Cargo was the goal. Any means of obtaining it were legitimate.

The Fever Wind movement lasted only a short while, but the basic yearning for a better world remained and nourished the belief in cargo. Twenty years later the author met older people who, in all seriousness, said that during the movement deceased ancestors had actually arrived in Kainantu, visited their kinsfolk and wanted to provide all their fellow tribesmen with great treasures. Through some misfortune their intentions had been frustrated.

SPORADIC HIGHLANDS CULTS, 1950–

Cult nos. 130–34
Scene of action: Eastern Highlands; South of Goroka/Kainantu
Leaders: Various enthusiasts
Character of movement: Magico–mechanistic: Expectation of wealth

More than a dozen villages were affected by a cargo cult in the Asaro area in 1962. There were thirty *cargo houses* (cult no. 130). Tables made from woven cane were placed in them, and on the tables people put potatoes, onions, tomatoes, fish, tinned meat and other gifts for the dead. Among the young people American-style parties were fashionable, at which they drank tea and ate biscuits. Why shouldn't the ancestors also have a part in these celebrations? Surely they would soon show their gratitude.

At the same time meetings were being held near *Awigusa* (cult no. 131) at the foot of Mount Kenebi in the Tarabo circuit. The people collected money and butchered fowls and pigs for a feast. A man from the Gimi area was hired to kill someone from among the neighbours of the Awigusa people who had refused to participate in the cargo cult. Fortunately the murderer was seized before he was able to poison the food of the intended victim. The authorities at Henkanofi stepped in, punished those involved and quickly put an end to the movement. But the problem itself was not solved.

Missionary H. Bammler reported in 1963 that a man from Rihona had come forward and stated that he had miraculous experiences with a *Share Certificate* (cult no. 133) which he had obtained from the business firm Namasu. This certificate had magically produced money in his home, so he built a special house where he laid it on a table. Shortly afterwards he had a vision: the neighbouring villages would fall into eternal condemnation, whereas his own village would be spared. He began to hold sessions with his followers and to read and to explain to them the Revelation of St John. Many elders actually believed they were on the threshold of a new revival movement.

Soon remarkable things began to happen in secret. The prophet claimed to be the chief administration officer and wanted to set up his own constabulary. At the same time religious services were held in which highly arbitrary practices were introduced, for example a communion service in honour of the ancestors. The elements were whisky and biscuits, and the words "Take and eat, then your eyes will be opened and you will see!" were spoken.

The need to see and to recognize the "dimension of the super-empirical" is shown as the great primeval longing. The means to acquire this knowledge may come from old fertility cults or may be borrowed from Christian practices. Always they are means of gaining secret powers.

In 1964–65 there was a similar movement in the Kanite area. A man known as Weworuya from Tirokave, who had previously been involved in spreading cargo ideas, introduced a novel movement of *Gathering Suitcases* (cult no. 134). The people were commanded to put their money into small red wooden cases and to deposit them in a specially erected house which was in this leader's care, and the money would multiply. Weworuya took the collected sum of money through all the villages, held nightly meetings and collected still more money. After six months some people became suspicious and demanded the return of their money. The cult leader refused to refund the money, and the result was a crisis. The movement was unmasked as a fraud and its perpetrator was gaoled for a time. It is unlikely that the people became any wiser through this experience.

8

Bismarck Archipelago

BATARI MOVEMENT, 1940–1942

Cult no. 143
Scene of action: New Britain; Galilo near Talasea
Leaders: Batari and others
Character of movement: Magico–mechanistic: Politically-accented expectation
   of wealth.

The Batari Movement is representative of a series of similar
movements which originated independently of each other in New
Britain.

For example, in the hamlet of Sumel the catechist *Varan* (cult
no. 142) came before the public as a prophet and gathered
around him one hundred young, strong men. First of all they
burnt down the huts. Then they led the people to the seashore
to wait for the promised cargo ships. Unnoticed, however, the
police landed behind them and took the ringleaders to prison.
On another occasion several unexploded bombs were discovered,
brought to the shore and celebrated as a gift of the ancestors.
Suddenly one of them exploded and tore a number of those
present to pieces. The missionary was blamed for this. He was
able to escape from the raving mob only at the last moment.

In Talasea a man called *Batari* (cult no. 143) saw a wooden
case marked with the word "battery". He believed the case was
intended for him and requested it, but was refused. This
strengthened his suspicion that cargo had not arrived because
the Europeans seized for themselves all shipments from the
realm of the dead. Batari was encouraged by an interview with
the adventurous Zyganek, a Czechoslovakian who arrived in a
canoe in New Britain at about that time. The two spoke about
their personal fortunes and about the future of the country.
Zyganek is supposed to have said to Batari, "Now I have finally

found in you a leader for the indigenous population; only you have the qualifications for it."[18]

Batari organized his fellow clansmen and placed them under military discipline. He trained "soldiers" and announced that arms would soon arrive. He himself would be king over his people. The flight of the Australians in 1942 and the coming of the Japanese must have seemed like a fulfilment of his prophecy. Batari claimed that all war material belonged to him. He imprisoned the missionary of the area. The Japanese soon realized that Batari was seeking his own ends and hardly suited their purposes. They seized him and incarcerated him in a military prison. The missionary was also put into a prison camp. The movement ended and Batari was not heard of again.

PALIAU MOVEMENT, 1945–

Cult nos. 147–50
Scene of action: Admiralty Islands; Manus
Leaders: Paliau, Maloat and forerunners
Character of movement: Politico–social: Social reform

The Second World War left an overwhelming impression on the Manus population. The friendliness of the Americans was a particularly happy experience for them. That dark skinned soldiers helped win the war was a real revelation and gave hope to the islanders that they would have a better future. More and more young people began to seek a reform of the social structure. One of the numerous forerunners of Paliau was *Samol* (cult no. 147), an ex-catechist and tribal leader from Peri. He sought to introduce a new life-style, and actively opposed certain prevalent taboos. Formerly it had been shameful for a woman to meet her husband in public; nor could she eat with him. Samol succeeded in breaking down these barriers so that Christian marriage could be observed. Thanks to him married couples can now go to church together and share a common life.

Another pioneer of the modern society was *Lukas* (cult no. 148) from Monk. Lukas came to this conclusion: "God made man, but when I look at the natives I do not believe He did. Europeans are people like us. They have two hands and two feet. But what is wrong with us natives? Europeans fly in the air and sail over the seas, but we remain where we are."[19] Lukas held meetings and said the ways of the past were "deadly poison". He demanded that everyone should produce more goods. He did away with the ceremonial barter system because it exhausted the people instead of producing food. He had no use for the old culture which was only an obstacle on the way to good fortune. Also he considered the people's striving for a store and for a modest rise in living standards trivial aims. A small business with a little profit was not enough for him. He strove for an entirely new cultural order, but this was beyond his ability. His plans were shattered and he waited for new impulses. These were supplied by Paliau.

Paliau (cult no. 150) had realized that all evil in the world derived from false thinking and that therefore a new type of thinking was necessary. He was concerned about a broadly-based revision of culture, individual changes to which would be only stages and the instruments of development. He therefore established two offices through which new thinking could be disseminated by instructors and groupleaders (pesmen), whose duty it was to instruct the people. The new thinking was expressed in, for example, regular hours of working, eating, bathing and devotions in church. Life became austere and regulated almost like a military establishment.

Open confessions served as a relief of psychological pressures and achieved a certain liberation from inhibitions experienced against co-operation in common work projects. Paliau felt that the traditional sense of shame was restrictive, so bathing in the nude was also fostered to ease tensions and soften aggression. At the same time there was a strict code of morals. Paliau envisaged model villages offering everything the heart could desire: houses would be arranged in straight lines; cars would be available in great numbers; Europeans and New Guineans would live peacefully side by side, eating and working together.

The cult developed its own concept of history, which cast an interesting light on the past. Tjamilio, a close co-worker of Paliau, explained:

The Germans taught us nothing. They were here for many years. Who could find them out? Now God said: "They must get out. They must go back. They have used men as if they were trucks. Men are men." But the Germans used men as if they were trucks, so God sent them back. All right. Now He turned his thoughts towards Australia. Australia came and replaced Germany. They went on and on, but didn't teach the natives anything. The Australians treated the natives like oxen. Now God said they must get out. Then God considered Japan. Now the Japanese came in the war and took Manus. The Japanese did not show us the road; instead they killed many men. God told them to clear out. "All right", God thought, "each country that I tried was inadequate. They didn't show the real road to Me, God. Why? Because all the men of earth are only human. I made three loaves of bread. One was brown, one was white, and one was black. The pay for two of the loaves has come. I have seen it. The pay for the black bread has not arrived . . . Did they throw it into a hole or what?" Now the Man who made the bread thought about it. "I will go take a look. Did the bread all burn up, or is some of it left?" All right, the Man who was boss over this bread saw that part of it still remained. Part had fallen upon America. Now Jesus said: "You must go. I want to try you, America. I have already tried all other countries. Take my flag, take all this food and all these ships and go. Never mind Japan; you can defeat them. This flag of mine is the flag of the black man, you will fight under it."

Jesus came ahead of them. He came as lightning and as an airplane marked with a cross. Now he came to Paliau in Rabaul. First he had searched all over Manus without finding a single man whose mind was straight. He came down now to Paliau in Rabaul. America came after Jesus. America wanted to bring all these things straight to us, the natives of Manus. America wanted to show us the road that would make us all right. They kept in mind the words of Jesus. But the Australians blocked them. The Americans returned to their own country. Everything they left the Australians took. Now God watched. These men who are with us now [the Australians] will they help us or not? We are watching. If they do not help us, but continue to keep us down, then there will be another country that will come. Why? Because God has not forgotten the Territory of New Guinea. Soon He will get rid of them all.[20]

Soon a third of the population of 13,000 people were under the influence of Paliau's movement. It was said that the Garden of Eden would appear if everyone would forsake sin. The biggest sins were seen to be in anti-social conduct, clinging to the old burial customs, the old dogs' teeth currency and bride prices. Special value was given to hygiene, peacefulness and economic progress. Reserves of finance were created, communal gardens were cultivated. Marriage regulations were eased.

Paliau was not spared severe attacks from Europeans. He was accused of setting up a totalitarian regime. In 1947 he was arrested, accused of terrorism and taken to Port Moresby.

After his return to Manus a new religion was developed by Paliau who spoke of the *nupela pasin* (the new fashion)—the word of God as proclaimed by Paliau. Missionaries were no longer considered necessary. The followers spoke about *bilip*—faith in a wonderful new world. Bilip became the password for the new religion. People attended meetings wearing hats which signified their membership. In 1949 Paliau was appointed luluai in Baluan, his home village. In Bunai village new dwellings were erected. Whole villages moved to the beach in order to be ready when ships with freight would arrive. This expression of a firm belief in cargo did not agree with Paliau's ideas. In an endless line, houses still stood along the coast as in a military camp at the time this report was written in 1966. Samol became the "high priest" of the movement's liturgy. People spoke about the brotherhood of all people. However, signs of decay became noticeable in 1950. The movement lacked spontaneity and its preachers complained about the people's indolence. The movement entered a critical phase as a result of the strong influence of the expectation of cargo, which Paliau was unable to counteract by his efforts to direct the people to more practical activities. Just as in 1947 the Guria Nois movement had made itself independent, a separation of a new cult from the Paliau movement began in 1950. This cult, later in 1953, became known as the *Spirits Cult* (cult no. 152). It was involved in anti-government propaganda. Apart from this separatist movement, the Paliau movement was weakened by the second arrest of Paliau in 1950. He was charged with having misused his authority as a luluai and sentenced to six months' hard labour. This did not detract from his popularity on Manus Island. He became chairman of the Baluan Native Village Council and in 1964 he entered parliament as the representative of the Admiralty Islands.

Having accepted the *nupela pasin* and professing *bilip*, the followers of Paliau had become apostates from the conventional Christian church. But they retained a church with priests and teachers which became known as the Baluan Church, which as a successor to the Paliau movements promoted Paliau's moral and social ideas. In 1966 ninety per cent of the population of Manus Island were non-Christians. Considering the absolute religious freedom in Australia, the development of a Baluan Church seemed a good solution of the movement's problems. The Baluan Church was independent of the Christian mission. It was non-Christian, but it was not a cult. Not unexpectedly a new crisis arose within the Baluan Church. It had not made any provision for the training of new preachers and teachers. The Baluan Church could not rely on Paliau because he was more and more concerned with social and political problems. But the new thinking and the *nupela pasin* have become permanent landmarks in the history of the Manus people. Members of the Baluan Church are characterized by their sense of self-possession and emancipation. In 1953 a United Nation mission visited

Baluan and praised the Baluan Church as an example of an "extremely orderly, progressive and flourishing society". The success of the Baluan Church, like that of any reform, depends upon the high potential of its goal. In Melanesia the prevalence of magic thinking still represented a threat to the Baluan Church. Perhaps the Christian mission has a chance to recover influence on Manus Island by offering help in training priests.

Support of thinking on practical lines was required because even practical enterprises of the Paliau movement or the Baluan Church were not immune against the influence of magical thinking. As an example, a leader of one of the many co-operatives on Manus Island is quoted. He said that the members of the co-operative had intended to pool their money in order to attract cargo into their villages. Yet they had learned that in every case goods had to be paid for in cash. They had, he continued, tried many different means to increase their possessions. For a time card games had been popular. Groups of players had been organized. He added that the main rule of the game had been that no money was to leave the circle of players. All "winnings", he concluded, had to remain within the organization and had to assist in increasing the basic capital.

Paliau, of course, and people near to him recognized the mythical basis of such arguments. They explained that the aims of co-operatives were to retain the cash earned by indigenous labour on the island and to prevent it from being returned to the Europeans. Even such rational thinking did not provide safety against the insidious power of magical thought, especially when as a result of co-operation money had been accumulated.

At one time the beliefs of the Manus people had been closely meshed with the fate of the ancestors. The religious co-ordination of the physical and the "metaphysical" spheres maintained society in a working balance. This equilibrium has grown very shaky today. Theodore Schwartz writes that the religious sanctions which were closely linked to clan and lineage interests and meted out by the familial ghosts have been replaced by Christianity, which as Manus natives experience it, relegates even the recently dead to a remote and impersonal heaven, leaving the discipline to God, who seems more concerned about adultery than such secular matters as public funds.[21]

Paliau's and his followers' effort to achieve an improvement of the economic situation is an attempt to recover integration between the secular and the religious in a changed situation.

JOHNSON CULT, 1964–

Cult no. 154
Scene of action: New Hanover (Lavongai)
Leaders: Anonymous freedom fighters
Character of movement: Politico–social: National, political striving for freedom.

The population of Lavongai of about 7,000 people has always had to think of itself as a minority in terms of its neighbours. Hence their efforts to stabilize their existence. They opposed the Europeans, who did not assist them in their endeavours. At first the officials were mostly unaware of this antagonism, and were astonished when in 1933 a delegation came to the mandatory Australian government and *petitioned for independence* (cult no. 137). Very quietly but most persistently, people had collected money until they had 5,000 shillings ($500), with which they wished to purchase their freedom. In return the Australians were to leave the island and give the people of Lavongai their independence. The transfer of the European-owned plantations was also to be included in this price.

The need for freedom appeared to be so fundamental that this sacrifice of money was worthwhile.

The mission was unsuccessful. But the idea did not originate in a naive fit of anger, but in a concern for their very existence. Through the years so much land had been bought from them that these people eventually felt like homeless strangers on their own island. In the succeeding thirty years this situation remained unchanged. The island is still called New Hanover, while the people still call it Lavongai. This insistence upon the name expresses the desire for self-realization.

The people finally saw another opportunity to present their own concern when, in 1964, the elections for the first Papua New Guinea House of Assembly took place. Somehow they had heard of the American president Lyndon B. Johnson and hoped to obtain a better government through him. The question was how to persuade Johnson to become a candidate for Lavongai, or better still, how could he be persuaded to by-pass the whole electoral procedure and come directly to the island. According to their means, limited insights and concepts the leading men saw a frank approach to Johnson, and a corresponding financial offer, as the only way. They began to boycott the election, to collect ten shillings ($1) from each of the movement's followers and to send the money to the USA. A large sack of shillings was delivered to the local priest of the Catholic mission, and he was asked to transmit the money so that President Johnson might be purchased, or at least his travelling costs be covered. News of this *Johnson Cult* (cult no. 154) caused a great deal of amazement. This was a curiosity, and its novelty caused many to miss the point of the whole problem. Long speeches and clever explanations were made to the leaders of the cult. The money was returned to them.[22] Since then collections of money have not been repeated. But it is doubtful whether the cult is at an end. On Lavongai, people can wait. They have already waited for thirty years.

9

Solomon Islands

PSEUDO–MILITARY MOVEMENT IN GOGOHEI, 1934

Cult no. 157
Scene of action: Buka; Gogohei
Leader: Sanop
**Character of movement: Magico–mechanistic: Expectation of wealth with a
    nationalistic accent**

Sanop came from Gogohei village on the island of Buka. He
was a *tultul* (the official representative of the administration in
the village). One day he began to experience dreams and visions,
as a result of which he predicted the arrival of a great cargo
ship. In February 1934 he announced that this ship would arrive
on Good Friday. He believed that the main cargo would be
weapons, which clearly indicated his hatred for Europeans.
Independence from the rule of the Australian government could
be realized by forcibly expelling the Europeans. The plan was
to fire at the police troops and establish authority by force if
the administration should interfere.

To begin with it was thought that the cargo would come from
Australia. Later Germany was thought to be the country of
origin. Large warehouses were constructed to store the expected
goods. The movement soon claimed 5,000 followers. All lived
in a state of anxious expectation. The men were drilled regularly
in *military exercises* (cult no. 157). They used sticks and
imitation arms carved from wood. Meetings took place in the
cemeteries. The realm of the ancestors would be contacted by
means of ten-metre high flagpoles. It is interesting to note that
the gift of wealth was promised only to the poor and needy.
Most people ceased to tend their gardens and simply used up
what supplies they had on hand. Large feasts were held. All
possessions were shared. They spent their savings. Everyone

wanted to qualify through generosity for a corresponding reward when the gifts of cargo appeared.

The practice of communal life, sharing and hoping was combined with unmistakably concrete, apocalyptic prophecies. A great darkness would spread over the land. An earthquake was predicted. Consequently people hastened to erect low houses on the ground. In the meantime, Good Friday 1934 came and went without any evidence of the fulfilment of the prophecies. There was disappointment, but the people's hopes were in no way dashed. Sanop, the leader, was arrested and taken to Sohano, the centre of the administration. The villagers returned to their daily round of duties.

POKOKOQORO CULT, 1939–1940

Cult no. 161
Scene of action: Choiseul (Nabusasa)
Leaders: Ex-constable Pokokoqoro and others
Character of movement: Magico-mechanistic: Expectation of wealth and "power magic"

Constable *Pokokoqoro* (cult no. 161) was dismissed from the police force for bad conduct in 1921. He participated in the famous Malaita Expedition of 1926, when traffic in illegal weapons led to the murder of Mr Bell and the subsequent massacre of over forty people. A further twenty were hanged. Pokokoqoro is said not to have conducted himself exactly humanely at that time. In the mid 1930s he started a movement by which wealth and the status of the people would be increased. He promised the arrival of a large steamship with all kinds of trade goods. From the faithful he exacted contributions of ten to thirty pounds ($20 to $60). Through these contributions he built up his image. He arranged feasts and sent gifts to the nearby mission teachers to make them sympathetic towards his plans. Clearings were made over the whole island and warehouses were erected for the expected goods.

When the steamer failed to arrive, Pokokoqoro moved to Varese in order to begin there anew. In the meantime the Methodist mission had left no doubt that it did not agree with these dreams, and this brought many of Pokokoqoro's credulous followers to their senses. However he succeeded in gathering around him twelve men who constituted a stormtroop which terrorized the inhabitants of the surrounding villages. They were six Roman Catholic and six Methodists who tried to realize the goal of their cargo ideology by force. Their leader supplied them with a magic article derived from an old magic prescription called Samuka, which was alleged to give each recipient the strength of ten men. Whoever remained faithful to the church was persecuted by this group.

This unique movement had an abrupt ending, through an equally unique action by several spirited mission assistants. A lame teacher plucked up enough courage to challenge those who had the "strength of ten" and organized a solid fight with them. The mission's "fighters for God" won and thoroughly discredited the braggarts. The victory was looked upon as a divine judgement and was honoured by a spontaneous religious service on the coast. The crowd rejoiced: "The Samuka has lost its power! Praise be to God!" Pokokoqoro was finished and he withdrew. Only a part of the collected monies could be repaid, but that was not the main concern of those who had been deceived by him. The decisive factor for them was that their faith in Christ had proved its strength and power. This experience lifted them almost to the heights of the prophet Elijah who on Mt. Carmel was victorious over the prophets of Baal (I Kings 18, 17–40).

BUKA WELFARE SOCIETY, 1953–

Cult no. 164
Scene of action: Hahalis, Buka
Leaders: John Teosin, Francis Hagai, also Sawa Korachi and others
Character of movement: Politico–social: Economic reform with magical and national undertones

On Buka, on the northern fringe of the Solomon Island group, the following saga is told:

In the beginning, a canoe came from the south. A god and his two wives were on this boat. The god chewed betel nuts. He threw the peels into the water. Thus small islands were made around the west coast of Buka. As long as the god himself steered the boat a straight and even coast rose in its wake. But the sun gradually climbed higher, it became warmer, and the god was tired. He asked his wives to take over from him. They did so, but could not agree on the course. While they argued with each other the canoe ran from one side to the other and thus made the numerous bays on the north coast of Buka. In this way the arrival of the big canoe made our land. The god who created our land and our people, however, left us again after he had done his work.

One day a man sat on a rocky cliff at the coast and fished. Then he saw something at a great distance on the water. It looked like an island. But it moved. He ran down the beach and called: "An island is coming towards us." Quickly the people assembled at the beach and watched a sailing boat approach and anchor before the cliff. The crew, the inhabitants of this new island, came ashore, and from that time onwards our island people ceased to have a quiet life. We lost our seclusion. Our world grew wider. We became a distant outstation of New Guinea. Now the Whites are living with us. They have a task. At this moment their work has not yet been accomplished. But soon it will be finished. Then the white man has to stop acting the master. Then he has either to become a simple human being or, like that creator god, he has to return to the south again when he has done his job.[23]

This story breathes a love of freedom. The drive for independence has crystallized in cultic actions of the present time. In 1946 a certain Sawa Korachi presented his fellowmen with a totally new religion. He called it Sori Lotu after the neo-Melanesian *sori* (sympathy, mercy, sadness, suffering, and longing) and *lotu* (prayer, meditation, worship and religion). This new religion was concerned with sun worship. Every morning and evening the faithful gathered on the beach and faced the sun in meditation.

Subsequently the movement took on more and more the character of a cargo expectation. It is told that on one occasion Sawa buried stones in the ground, from which gold should grow. He is also said to have suggested the abolition of marriage and the practice of free love. Sawa, as the grey eminence or the man in the background of the *Welfare Society* (cult no. 164) is difficult to characterize, but it is certain that it was he who always fanned the flame, nurtured the people's expectations, and provided the impulse of ideas. Later developments revolved around two young men, John Teosin and Francis Hagai, his younger brother-in-law by two years. Both were originally Catholic mission teachers . Both were strongly influenced by the old Sawa. Both loved their people and wanted only the best for them.

In 1952, after completion of his training, Francis Hagai had introduced a communal enterprise in the village. The money earned was not spent, but collected, saved and invested in a trading business. Soon others began to join this co-operative. However under John Teosin's leadership the movement took a new direction. In the early 1950s Teosin had been sent by his school-teacher to a technical school in Rabaul. The older men had repeatedly said that the secret of prosperity lay there. They had always stated that all earthly wealth was produced by the ancestors, but had been seized by the Europeans upon their arrival in Buka. Thus the distribution of wealth was a great injustice. On the eve of his departure, Teosin spent the night with his uncle, Sawa Korachi. He could not sleep because of his agitation. Suddenly he heard his uncle's voice:

"Tomorrow you go to Rabaul, John", the old man said. "There you must find the way, and come back and tell me. Here the white men live on the little island in the Passage, they are few, and it is easy for them to keep the secret; but in Rabaul there are many white men, they cannot all keep it."[24]

When Teosin was in Rabaul his heart beat high with excitement. All at once he saw before him cars, houses, machines. He had never seen anything like it before. He was convinced that here the secret could be learnt, but how? At the school party his thoughts went helter skelter. It was his first time in such wonderful surroundings. He listened when others conversed and asked the origin of many articles in the room. He noticed that the teacher often pointed to the floor, saying, "It all comes from the ground". Whether they were clay pots, metal objects or wood or bricks, John was impressed with the knowledge that they all came from the earth. In his excitement he drank too much and too hastily. Soon nothing mattered any more. He could not concentrate, but he was pleased now finally to know the secret of prosperity.

For all that, Teosin did not know what he should tell the people when he returned to Buka. They gave him a great welcome and a feast was arranged in his honour. People embraced him and rejoiced at his coming. In Hahalis village twelve elders were already assembled waiting for him in the meeting house. Silently they sat and his uncle Sawa was among them. Sawa looked around the circle. All were tense with the significance of the moment. Sawa arose and began to speak: "Go and tell all the people that our son has returned from Rabaul. Call together the whole population on the dance ground. There we shall speak to you for our son has come home and he has brought with him a message from the ancestors". John listened without saying anything. Sawa continued:

The men spoke about how the government had promised them roads and schools. Before they had believed these promises, but now they did not. In the past they had followed the white man's laws, now it would be different. Sawa stood up, and shouted to the watching crowd on the dance floor:

"We follow no more. Our ancestors make the cargo and send it to Buka. The white man steals it from our very shores. Our people work for the white man, work hard all day in the plantations, in the houses, and until our backs break with carrying the cargo from the ships. We work for nothing, hoping that the white man will tell us the secret of all this cargo. He makes us work harder and tells us nothing. We work no more.

"The white man is always telling us what to do, and he speaks to us like dogs, and we say, 'Yes masta, yes sir!' No more do we speak.

"We go to church every Sunday, we build the Father's house, and the Sister's house, and the hospital, and the school, and nothing but promises do we get in return. I tell you we worship our ancestors from now on. The white man's religion is part of the big lie they tell us to keep us from the cargo.

"Fear not, for John our son brings the secret with him from Rabaul and this time we will succeed. This time we will trick the white man. This time the cargo comes to us.[25]

This speech was followed by a deep silence. Then Sawa motioned Teosin to speak:

"It is true", he said. His voice sounded small and weak after the power of Sawa's speech.

It is true [he said again, much louder.] I have found the secret of the cargo, a white teacher at the High School at Rabaul told me; it comes from the ground. But to get it we must pray to our ancestors and follow their directions. Hear the words of our ancestors, and those to whom we speak; hear the words of the leaders of the people, for they are given power by our ancestors, and hear the wise old Sawa, for he is the great man of Hahalis.[26]

During the night there was much singing and dancing. The message spread like wildfire through the countryside. In Hahalis the system of communal enterprise was expanded. In 1957 shares were issued. In about 1959 a definite programme was started to "retrain" people in order to realize the great aim. The final result would be a definite welfare society. The programme was a peculiar mixture of sober planning and magical hopes. Sawa selected followers and appointed them as overseers. Plantation workers left their employment. Mission helpers discontinued their services and no one went to church any more. Each morning the people assembled for devotion on the beach. In Hahalis a small administrative office was erected.

In 1961 the movement became trying for the administration.

The membership rose to over 2000. Teosin allowed himself to be installed as "King John" and his wife as "Queen Elizabeth". His crown was made of cardboard and a large wooden chair was his throne. He had his own bodyguard; armed with clubs they guarded his "residence". There was a "police force" and a co-operative prison. When the administration sought to introduce everywhere a system of local government councils it met with open resistance. The population also refused to pay the annual head tax.

The local authorities felt unable to deal with this provocation and called for assistance from Rabaul. This meant an open conflict. The Welfare Society let it be known that they could get along quite well without the officers of the administration and that they were quite capable of governing themselves. As a result of this development, the government in Port Moresby lost all patience. On 6 February 1962, eighty–two police landed at Hahalis and demanded that John Teosin be handed over. The result was a great cry and uproar. Teosin advised that he would be ready to talk next day.

At the agreed time he put in his appearance with Hagai and Sawa and over 2000 men. This time they were armed. A last demand for a discussion with Teosin was unsuccessful and the troops marched to the coast. Here a large crowd of people had encamped. The administration officer addressed the crowd and said that he wished to avoid any trouble. But while he was speaking the crowd began to move against the police, using clubs, sticks and stones. Two warning shots were fired, but the battle continued. Many were injured, including twenty police. Only when the order was given to the police to be ready with their firearms was there a pause. The crowd drew back.

Subsequently an additional 400 police landed on Buka. The next day 166 men were arrested and taken away under heavy guard. Many were sentenced to imprisonment. Due to a fault in the procedure, however, most of them were soon released. They returned home proudly, feeling they had been victorious in the confrontation. Soon the Welfare Society was stronger than ever.

From then on all conflict with the law was avoided. The leaders received new names: president, secretary, manager, etc. The democratic facade made the movement presentable and immune to criticism. A proper co-operative centre was built near the village of Hahalis. It included a "bank" with "passbooks", a guest house, a playground and a "leader's house" equipped with refrigerator and radio. All this made a convincing impression.

A completely new tone was given to the co-operative by the club houses which began to appear in 1963. It was decided to assemble all single women in these club houses and to practice free love. Great emphasis was put on the full consent of the women who participated. It is astonishing how harmoniously this system functioned. The club houses became known as "baby farms" or "kindergartens". Sixty to eighty girls between the ages of fourteen and twenty lived together. Visitors paid no fees, but an "account" was kept which was then paid off with work assignments. Up to the present about thirty-five children have been born in the club houses. The young people were to have an opportunity there to know one another until they found partners with whom they then went off to build their own homes. The system may be regarded as a reaction against the traditional marriage arrangements made by the parents and the clan. Mutual attraction and love would be the basis for marrying.

Daily dance exercises of various kinds were a further special characteristic of these groups. The drummer beat the rhythm and called certain numbers in an indefinite sequence, whereupon a corresponding dance was performed with the accompaniment of a suitable song.

While Teosin became more and more of an ideologist, Hagai emphasized the practical side. Neither wished to have anything to do with the cargo cult.

At the present time the movement wrestles with organizational problems. In 1966 Francis Hagai attended a business school in Sydney. He was making good progress in Australia. However in Hahalis every truck was out of action at the roadside. The "trade store" was almost empty. A degree of uncertainty was evident. Even John Teosin seemed unable to give new impulses to the movement. On his return to Buka in 1967 Hagai took practical measures to rebuild the society. All is quiet at Hahalis. The future will show whether this is the end of the movement, or a pause before renewed activity.

KIETA MOVEMENT, 1960–

Cult no. 168
Scene of action: Kieta District, Bougainville
Leaders: Anton Kearei and other anonymous agitators
Character of movement: Magico–mechanistic: Expectation of wealth

In 1960 in Kieta all the crosses were removed from the cemeteries in order that the ancestors should not be annoyed by this new fashion when they brought their gifts. From definite sources they even knew that on a certain day in September they would receive the goods. At the same time there was a report about a man who had allowed himself to be buried in the village of Manob in order to be able to arise on the third day. However the "resurrection" failed. No one claimed to know any details. Administration officials maintained the man had died before the burial.

Great things were expected of *Anton Kearei* (cult no. 168) —the "big man of Sohano". For days people stood on the landing field to welcome him. They saw in this gifted, native administrative officer a precursor and representative of the ancestors. Anton Hinina Kearei, on the other hand, is far from being a mythical figure. He comes from Lonahan on Buka, is presently forty years of age, secretary of the district administration, is married and has two children. At one time he wanted to become a priest. Shortly before the conclusion of his studies in Rabaul-Vunapope he left the Catholic mission. Love affairs had a part in this break. However that may be, he now wished to follow a secular calling and expressed the opinion that priests had too little to do "with the world", where his conern lay. As a relative of John Teosin he was said to be one of the co-founders of the Buka Welfare Society. He withdrew when he saw that this undertaking was bound to meet opposition from the administration. From 1947 he was employed in Bougainville by the administration, which assisted him wherever possible. His people hope that one day he will come forward and tear away the veil surrounding the secret world of cargo.

10

New Hebrides

RONOVURO CULT, 1923

Cult no. 171
Scene of action: Espiritu Santo
Leaders: Ronovuro and others
Character of movement: Religio–spiritual: Eschatologism

Long before the existence of the Ronovuro cult there appeared a prophet who captivated the people. He was Ronovuro's uncle. A magician, he claimed to have a charm which, for a suitable compensation, would make a person immune against injury, and would protect against wounds by gunshot. He transmitted this secret gift shortly before his death to his newphew by breathing his last breath into his mouth. After that *Ronovuro* (cult no. 171) considered himself to be the magician's heir. At the same time he expanded this role by promising to raise the dead. (Originally the idea came from a man named Susu Moli who had prophesied that soon all the dead would return to life.) Ronovuro himself claimed to have risen from the dead, and promised the privilege of immortality to all who wished for it. At that time a saying was current: "The banana stalk is cut down, but from the roots new shoots appear". Naturally the prophet accepted compensation for his favours. The fees ranged from five to twenty shillings (50¢ to $2). Gradually other promises were added. The thoughts of the coastal people were occupied by the concept of a cargo-laden ship, which evolved from the older idea of a ship of the dead on which the ancestors would return. Watchers were posted along the coast and signal fires were lit whenever a ship passed on the horizon. A huge warehouse was erected on the coast. Ronovuro's emissaries went over the whole island of Espiritu Santo to win adherents. On one occasion Ronovuro had raised a "dead" cow, and also a "man who had fallen as if dead", but the population wanted to see cargo. When the cargo ship failed to appear the Europeans were blamed. The people had many strange associations of thought. For example if missionaries came to the island and died childless, they were blamed for the decline of the island's population.

In 1923 the situation became dangerous. Ronovuro had ordered the butchering of all pigs and the abolition of the social classes, the rank order according to which the individual was able to determine his place in society. Somewhat later he organized a large dance festival. He himself sat on a box containing money. This box stood on a raised platform in his house. At night he often received secret instructions. One of these directed him to kill a local settler, Clapcott, who was almost deaf. Then suddenly the prophet's wife died. The Europeans were held responsible. Vengeance drove them to murder and that was the end of the cult. Ronovuro and his two main associates were executed. Others were imprisoned. In the thinking of the people, however, Ronovuro has joined the ranks of the martyrs.

JOHN FRUM MOVEMENT, 1940–

Cult no. 173
Scene of action: Tanna
Leaders: Manehevi, Neloiag, Lokaeye and many others
Character of movement: Magico–mechanistic: Expectation of wealth and
   revivalism

The peculiarity of this movement is that it centres on *John Frum* (cult no. 173) who never existed. The John Frum myth manifested itself solely in individual cultists.

In 1940 Christians began silently withdrawing from their congregations. The puritanical style of living was found to be too monotonous. In ancient times the people had believed in the god Karaperamun. All life derived from him. From him they now expected new vitality. The old dances were revived. Kava drinking, forbidden by the mission, was practised in secret ceremonies each Saturday night. The new day of salvation was to come through John Frum, a supernatural being, in whom the god Karaperamun had revealed himself. The origin of the concept of John Frum is uncertain; perhaps it was derived from

John the Baptist. It seems evident that this is a parallel to the konors of the Mansren movement in West Irian Jaya.

One night a man stood up in the light of the fire at a kava-drinking ceremony and announced he was a manifestation of John Frum. He appeared as a spirit being, with bleached hair, wore a garment with glittering buttons and had a high-pitched, shrill voice. All who participated in the ceremony were later called Frum's messengers. It was, incidentally, the only occasion when John Frum allowed himself to be seen by spectators. Later his messages were made known only through middlemen whose credentials could not be checked. After some time a man named Manehevi, who was said to be the actor in the original manifestation, was handed over to the administration representative. The offical believed that in this way the John Frum myth would lose its force. Actually the cult lost nothing through Manehevi's arrest. They myth itself remained unassailable.

The following presents the purport of John Frum's message. After a natural catastrophe, Tanna Island would unite with the surrounding islands to form a powerful kingdom. The volcanic hills would collapse and fill the valleys. The land would become flat and fruitful. Men would retain their youth and no illness would harm them. Hard labour would no longer be necessary. John Frum, who would appear in human form, would give his followers everything their hearts desired. The Europeans would leave and freedom would reign. Frum would provide new money and distribute it to all according to their needs. The one condition was that the people should take up the old customs again and drive the Europeans away.

The arrival of John Frum would occur on a Friday, which would be observed as a holiday. Aeroplanes, which from 1941 could frequently be seen because of the war, were thought to be the first cargo carriers. An increasing sexual freedom accompanied this phase. In the background the old chieftain Sam Nako was agitating. He gave the instruction to tear down all church buildings, but the administration officer forestalled this action and arrested a number of the ringleaders. Among the twenty prisoners was Joe Nalpin, an ex-constable. During his nine months' imprisonment in Kila he claimed to be John Frum. After having dreamed of help from the "king of America" he told old Nako in a letter that Frum would send his son to America to fetch this king. In those days much was talked about Rusefel (Roosevelt); we may assume that Nalpin, as Frum, wanted to establish contact with the all-powerful ruler of the wealthy American war heroes.

At the same time the youth met in separate gatherings. In January 1942 it was suddenly revealed that John Frum had three sons: Isaac, Jacob and Lastuan ("last one"). Nalpin had already referred to one of them. The three of them had come by an invisible aircraft from America and landed at Tanna. There they appeared to a group of young people. They gave directions to a twelve-year-old girl in a secret language which the others could not understand. The girl, however, was able to translate the message. Immediately the whole group of young men and women dedicated themselves to the new gods. They ceased to work and moved into a common house. During the day they went bathing, at night they danced. Monday was a day of rest.

In October 1943 the authorities became alarmed by the existence of armed partisans. A man named Neloiag had proclaimed himself to be John Frum and also king of America and Tanna. He was surrounded by his own police force, through whom he compelled the people to work for him. He planned to construct an aerodrome. An American liberation army soon to be sent by his father would land there. Anyone who refused to work was threatened with destruction by aerial bombing. The administration stepped in again and arrested forty-six men. Neloiag was sentenced to two years' imprisonment. On Tanna, his wife was honoured as a queen until one day she followed a lover to Vila, where she too was taken into custody. The movement was, however, far from finished. Several more episodes followed.

According to the most recent reports, the movement has apparently deteriorated into numerous smaller splinter groups. Repeatedly, people maintained that they had received revelations from John Frum. They stated that the Europeans would not share in the reality and blessing of John Frum because they were unbelievers. It is obvious how misunderstandings arose and influenced the people. For instance, a picture of Santa Claus in a dark red suit was seen in an American illustrated magazine. From this it was assumed that the Europeans were responsible for Tanna's lack of such a dispenser of good things. Biblical promises too were often accepted without reflection or examination. One cultist had heard the Old Testament story of the serpent of brass. He thereupon fashioned a red cross and said: "Whoever looks on this cross and believes, will not be lost but will be clean. I will send him cargo, refrigerators and pocket knives, sewing machines and mosquito nets and everything he desires".

The Tannaese are convinced that many Europeans believe in John Frum but do not admit it. When a trader, for advertising purposes, renamed his goods John Frum soap, John Frum shoes, John Frum chewing gum etc., he was immediately sold out. But his action confirmed the opinion of the people that there must be some truth in Frum's promises.

Not much can be accomplished with rational arguments against the cult. During a conversation, a cult follower said:

> A white journalist pointed out to me that I had now waited twenty years for my cargo of dental supplies to arrive and they were still not in sight. I asked him how long he had waited for Jesus Christ to arrive and he replied that it must be nearly two thousand years; so I informed him that I was prepared to wait a further twenty years for John, but was he prepared to wait another two thousand years for Jesus? He said he would not be alive then—so I have far more chance of seeing my god than he has.[27]

The John Frum movement is like an iceberg; we always see only the tip of it. It operates in general terms of expectations out of whose mythical centre ever new actions can develop in an evolutionary process.

NAKED CULT, 1944–1951

Cult no. 176
Scene of action: West Espiritu Santo; Nakuvu on the Ora River
Leader: Tsek (also called Tieka) of Nakuvu
Character of movement: Religio–spiritual: Religious reform with revivalism and
     cargo tendencies

When a man named *Tsek* (cult no. 176) was about thirty-five years old, he became known as a preacher and teacher until his death from a painful illness about six years later. He had many followers and in 1945 he sent forth thirty emissaries to proclaim his teaching.

Tsek was a reformer of stature. He did not come before the public as a prophet to make blind promises. He critically examined the ancient culture in order to arrive at practical conclusions for a new order. It is another matter that his conclusions were unusual and problematic. The fact that his message was accepted so quickly becomes more striking when one considers that he used only the persuasive strength of his arguments. Never had he preached enmity against the Europeans as a matter of principle, yet he sensed any approach by them as interference. He did not take any particular interest in Europeans. They were of importance to him only in the transmission of goods, but he was wary of becoming too familiar with them.

Tsek's concepts were surely influenced by Christian teaching. He had worked near Europeans as a young man. There he learnt about new possibilities for living. He recognized his own culture as inferior and in need of reform. Thus the conviction grew that all that was old was bad and dirty, and a tendency to penetrate to a new purity was the answer. That this philosophy was combined with expectations of goods is part of the Melanesian pattern of thinking.

It is noteworthy that the movement did not hold large assemblies nor use mass-psychotic influence. In contrast to other movements, the Naked Cult had a philosophy of life. The central idea was to stop the island's population decline, check illness and return to the original and happy purity where no war, jealousy or shame existed.

Tsek's message has to be understood as a striving for a pristine condition. He stipulated:

1. Take off your loin-cloths. Women take off their leaf coverings, bead necklaces and armlets. All these things make you dirty.
2. Destroy all your property which you have taken from the white man—calico, money, implements; in addition, destroy all your own bush crafts such as basket-making and mat-making. It is best to be free from these.
3. Burn down all your present houses and build on the following new plan:
   i. Two big community houses to be erected in each village—one for the men to sleep in at night and another for the women to sleep in at night. No cohabitation of families at night.
   ii. Build a large kitchen with each community house. No cooking to be done in the community houses.
4. All food to be cooked in the morning. No night cooking.
5. Do not work for the white man.
6. Destroy all animals in your villages: dogs, cats, pigs etc.
7. It also appears that they were promised that soon America would come: they would receive everything good; they would never die; they would live forever.
8. A common language called "Mamara" (i.e. bright day) was adopted among all cult followers even though the villages represent widely separated language groups.
9. Many old taboos have been scrapped: the prohibition on marriage within the totem group; the segregation period after childbirth; the necessity for buying brides; and the burial custom

has been changed so that now the corpse is exposed on a wooden platform in the bush (as in parts of Malekula) instead of being buried in the floor of the deceased person's house (as is traditional in central Santo).[28]

The ultimate goal was a harmonious society. Since individual ownership of property often led to quarrels, a way toward communal living had to be found. Since jealousy often caused anger, marriage restrictions must be relaxed. Since feelings of guilt and shame inhibit people, these barriers must be removed. A keen logic is behind all these considerations. Even psychosomatic connections were surmised: all illnesses were traced to some kind of disharmony. The reformer, Tsek, recognized that some cosmic disproportion was contained in the private erotic practices as well as in the physical ailments of his fellow men. Here was a call for assistance. The fact that cargo means more than material possessions is hardly ever more clearly expressed than in the Naked Cult. What is only faintly perceived in all cargo movements is clearly outlined here. One must not be irritated by its extreme expressions.

At first Tsek ordered that all cult followers were to practise their sexual life openly "like dogs and fowls", that all women were to be available to all men, and that this was obligatory for all girls over eight or nine years of age. Toward the end of the movement however Tsek's demands were drastically curtailed. Even active members of the cult gradually chafed against a life lived by these precepts. It was rumoured that some men wanted revenge against the cult leader. They said:

> Jack Tsek has spoilt us; he has spoilt our heads; he has spoilt our lives. We know that these things we do now are not right. We don't want to do them any more.[29]

Finally some of the men left their homes to seek employment as labourers and the cult's influence declined appreciably.

As Tsek had promised a cure from all illnesses and eternal life, his death must certainly have caused doubts in the movement.

NAGRIAMEL MOVEMENT, 1966–

Cult no. 179
Scene of action: From Espiritu Santo, Nogugu and Vanafo to nearly all islands
  of the New Hebrides
Leader: Jimmy Stephens
Character of movement: Politico–social: Modern land reform with nationalistic
  and mythical tendency

A political movement has taken hold of the New Hebrides. Over 10,000' people are said to have contributed $50,000 to the movement, which aims to recover all land that previously had been obtained by the Europeans but is no longer cultivated.

The leader, Jimmy Stephens, is considered by many to be a prophet. His grandfather was an English sailor, who married a woman from Tonga. One of his sons married a woman from the Banks Islands, and Jimmy was born to this marriage in about 1924. He speaks English and neo-Melanesian. So far he has been a caretaker of a church and captain of a small schooner. He calls the reform movement *Nagriamel* (cult no. 179). This word is composed from two verbal roots, *nagria* and *mel*. They signify croton and cycad, two plants which are used ritually. Nagriamel is a symbol for restorative thinking.

The movement began in January 1966 when the chieftains of Santo intended to do something against the land rights of the Europeans. They started to establish a model settlement in Vanafo. It was soon considered to be an honour to have permission to help build up this farm, especially since Stephens presented land to each person. The leader's emissaries drove through the whole of Espiritu Santo and the surrounding islands to spread the Nagriamel "gospel". Today, taped speeches by Stephens are played everywhere. Money is collected and fed into the movement's coffers. Everywhere along the roads hoardings can be seen with the text: "Nagriamel Private Property—Please Keep Off", which indicates that the old property rights of the Europeans have lapsed at these places. The communal life is regulated by an almost military discipline. The cleanliness and the courtesy in Vanafo are remarkable. At certain times bells are rung to mark the time for bathing: at three o'clock for men, at five o'clock for women and children.

In October 1968 an important conference took place. A new flag was hoisted for the first time and Stephens received the title of Chief President Moses. The people regarded Stephens as a new Moses who, just as Moses had led the people of Israel out of servitude, should likewise take the people of the New Hebrides to the Land of Promise. Recently, in New Caledonia, Stephens obtained advice about cattle breeding and the use of timber. His own government offered to erect a school and a centre to care for the sick. Stephens declined both. He agreed only to the erection of a bush church by the Church of Christ mission.

This movement provides many possibilities. What will happen on these islands in the future will depend upon the attitude of Chief President Moses.

11

New Caledonia

COMMUNISTIC FREEDOM MOVEMENT, 1945–

Cult no. 182
Scene of action: Loyalty Island, Lifu
Leaders: Several anonymous leaders
Character of movement: Magico–mechanistic: Expectation of cargo and
    commitment to a political party

The presence of the American soldiers provided many stimuli
for the island population's fantasy. At Lifu the people believed
that America was the paradise of Genesis. They hoped a white
ship would arrive with cargo and the Europeans would acknowledge the islanders' dignity as human beings. Many of the ideals
of the followers of John Frum (cult no. 173) were transmitted
southwards to Lifu. The novelty of this movement is that in Lifu
a synthesis was achieved between the magical world of John
Frum and the politics of a communistic party. At first money
was collected. People of Lifu wanted to use their own ship to
trade with the capital, Noumea. Yet soon rumours were
circulating that this ship would come from France. The communist party of Paris would send a large cargo ship to all who
joined their party. These gifts would enable the Caledonian
communists to prove themselves equal to the Eruopeans and
eventually to gain the power which would help them to live their
lives harmoniously. In 1943 therefore, a communistic subsidiary
party (cult no. 182) was established in Lifu. One of its more
important actions was the construction of a dock for the cargo
ship. The movement very quickly spread through the neighbouring districts. At times the political message was completely
obscured by the expectation of goods. Finally the leaders had
to understand that their hope for cargo was a delusion, and the
political assertions came to the fore again. Freedom and
independence in the political sense now became the topic of

which they spoke. The desire for happiness is now linked with the striving for power. It is scarcely possible that their aims will change substantially. The people of the South Sea are still dreaming of a better world.

12

Fiji

LUVENIWAI OR WATER BABIES MOVEMENT, 1880–1920

Cult no. 184
Scene of action: Viti Levu; areas of Ra and Rewa
Leaders: Various anonymous young men and "sorcerers"
Character of movement: Religio–spiritual: Magical vitalism

Towards the end of the last century a secret society was formed by the younger generation of Fiji. At its centre were fairytale spirit beings called *Luveniwai* (cult no. 184), that is, children of the water. The spirit beings were elves, dwarfs and spirits which, according to ancient superstition, dwelled in the dense forests and waterfalls. Originally it was believed that premature babies of the families of chieftains returned into the realm of these small dwarfs. According to other versions, they were abandoned infants which had drifted away on the sea and had developed thus into "water babies". They could be malevolent, but mostly they were friendly spirits with supernatural powers. In the Luveniwai movement it was believed that every human being could have a powerful spirit of the forest as a guardian angel if he only took the required trouble. The members of the society usually met in remote forest glades, held kava-drinking ceremonies, sang and danced, oiled their bodies, adorned themselves with flowers and assumed new names. In a certain house they kept a consecrated coconut over which they meditated. Many girls belonged to these brotherhoods. They brought an erotic tone into the movement. It was believed that the spirits transmitted skills and taught new dances, revealed secret recipes, foretold the future, and bestowed manna.

Many missionaries took the Luveniwai movement, in its early days, for harmless play, and yet it was more than a "social game". The nightly gatherings often induced intense excitement.

Incessant dancing resulted in ecstasy. People started to tremble and had shivering fits. They lost the sense of pain and quite often they suffered injuries. During such rites people were killed in a condition of trance. Physical insensibility however was interpreted as invulnerability, and they sought it. Sometimes the water babies' power was by tricks. For example, followers of the cult would throw small sticks into a cooking vessel, and rotating the vessel several times they would produce a delicious meal of eels from it. It was also reported that the devotees had put a man into an earthenware vessel, which they let float on the river. People hoped they would strengthen the authority of their leader by spreading such fantastic stories.

Soon the government intervened. The gatherings were made illegal and criminal. The leaders were punished for laziness and unruliness. The punishment consisted of public flogging. It seems that the main problem lay in the refusal of the young people to work. Thus gardens and villages were neglected and food became scarce.

One of the earliest attempts to solve the problem of the movement may be called the cricket club action. A government official started the club with the intention of diverting the cultic interest to something neutral. This experiment was a little unusual, but by and large it was successful. Everywhere new cricket clubs were opened; guilds were formed, lists of attendance kept, codes and emblems evolved, secretaries elected, and a multitude of offices with high-sounding names were created, such as major general, lord high admiral, and secretary for foreign affairs. Soon the play became serious. The group elected its own governor, and a supreme court judge. This simulated British bureaucracy became an underground movement with nationalistic tendencies. The cricket clubs became the cells of a political movement, its members proving, albeit involuntarily, that this cult too was ideological in its conception. There was more to it than the friendly play of water and flower children. The water babies were also concerned for the discovery of a better world.

Like all the other cults, the cricket clubs came under official criticism. The leaders were put into the district gaols. Outwardly the activity gradually ceased.

APOLOSI MOVEMENT, 1914–1940

Cult no. 185
Scene of action: Viti Levu
Leader: Apolosi
Character of movement: Politico–social: Political Messianism with
   vitalistic–economical organization

The events surrounding the agitator *Apolosi* (cult no. 185) pervaded a whole generation. The leader had pretended to be the bearer of a divine revelation. His message of freedom from any kind of restriction was spread zealously. It was called "The New Testament of Welfare" or "Religion No. 8".[30] "Fiji for the Fijians" was the password. As a visible sign of their membership in the "new religion", members celebrated the Sabbath instead of the Sunday. On the Sabbath the great gatherings took place. The movement stretched across the whole island of Viti Levu and adopted an increasingly political character.

Under the lively leadership of Apolosi the anti–European feelings and the hatred against the Indians were methodically inflamed. The followers of the movement were promised freedom from all diseases. Apolosi was called King of Fiji and he claimed complete, ruling authority. According to rumours, he owned a case which the ancestral spirits had once brought in their canoe from paradise in prehistoric times. This wooden case allegedly invested him with supernatural powers and the ability to organize people and economy. He conceived himself to be the people's saviour, who recovered dignity and self-respect for his race. He also founded a commercial enterprise "Viti Kabani", that is Fiji Company, and hoped to usher in a period of fast growth towards wealth and happiness. Money poured in from all sides. But Apolosi quickly spent the money with his friends before it could be used for the proposed commercial enterprises. Also among the younger generation he organized the so-called Fiji Youth, an association of all youthful and politically progressive forces. Among the followers were also the *Leveni ruve* (the pigeon flock)—a number of attractive young girls who had to provide a suitable variety of entertainment for Apolosi, who normally was much occupied with economy and politics. The ex-governor of Fiji, Sir Harry Luke, concluded that here was a Rasputin of the Pacific, that Apolosi deluded people by intrigues, by seductive flatteries and excesses, and that he showed himself as a subversive genius without any scruples. The government soon charged Apolosi with promoting quasi-religious secret societies and with incest. Apolosi was sentenced three times to exile. Nevertheless his strong personality and his outstanding talent for organization meant that the movement's cargo ideas remained alive for many more years in spite of the suppression by the administration and in spite of the enmity of some tribal chieftains who feared for their own influence.

Efforts to influence the cultural development and to improve conditions of living were at the root of the movement. People hoped that Fiji would recover the status which, as a Pacific power, she enjoyed before the British colonial period. They attempted to achieve this status by a synthesis of the truths of the ancient culture with the facts established by the modern development. They sensed the revolutionary trend of the times and were unwilling to remain inactive.

In the long run the ancient tradition could not provide what they were seeking. Nor did conventional Christianity satisfy the demand for an integrated meaningfulness. There was more at stake than only some comfort and wealth. It was a concern for the value and the future of the people. These questions relate to the very centre of the battlefield of the worldwide religious wrestling. The cargo movements are more than an exotic curio. They deserve to be examined seriously. They mirror something of the secret of life, of the adventure of human research and of the hope which towers above time and eternity.

Part 2 of this book evaluates the cultic material and attempts an objective, critical examination.

Yali, the "Big Man" of the Rai Coast, Madang District, during an address at a local council by-election.

A father puts oil on his daughter's skin in preparation for the Padlma Cult festival in Alkena-Pawragl, Western Highlands of New Guinea.

The High Priest in Mendi buries skulls of the dead in the Highlands, New Guinea.

Stones for ancient fertility cults in the Highlands.

Two hundred skulls kept in Alkena for anointing during the Padlma cult.

Cult members carry sacrifical meat into the sacred forest of Alkena-Pawragl.

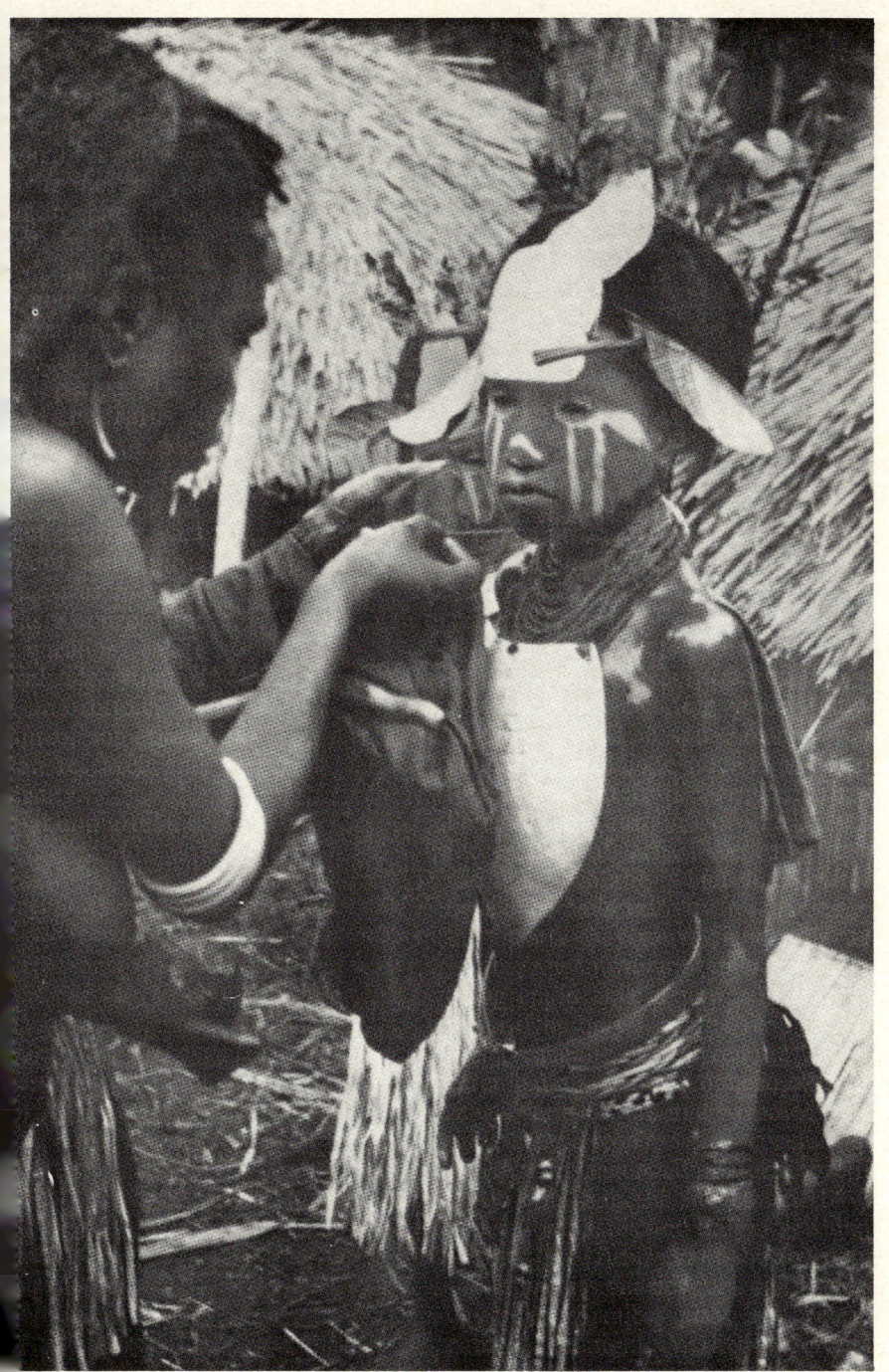

A mother paints her child for the ceremonial dance at Alkena.

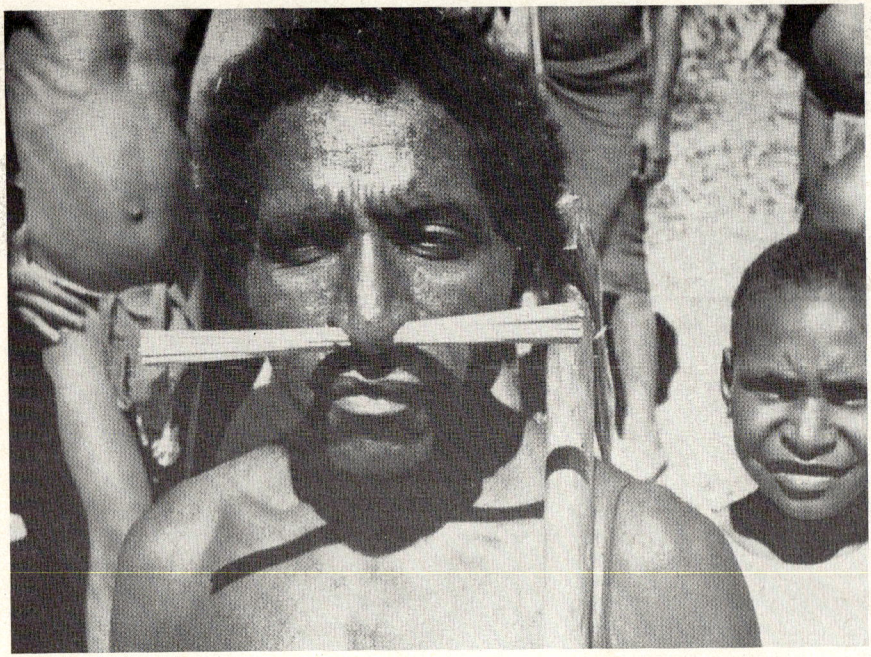

Gimi tribesman.

Cult forest near Awigusa on Mt Kenebi in the Highlands.

Collection point for "the suitcase movement" at Tirokave in the Highlands.

Clay pig idol, New Guinea.

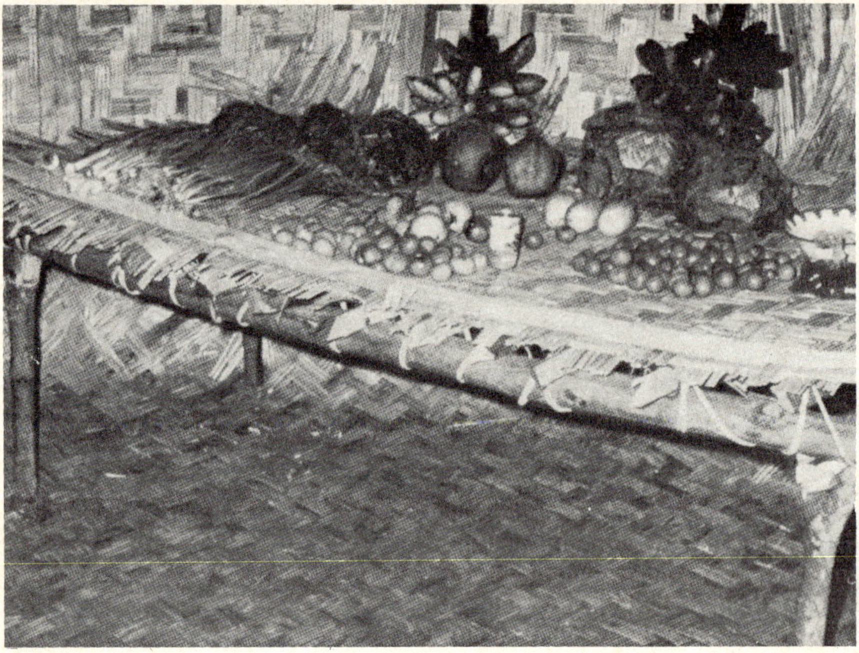

Cultic altar with sacrificial gifts, Asora Valley, Highlands in New Guinea.

A cult house is burnt by some evangelists.

PART 2

An Analysis of The Cults

1

Appreciation of Cargo Cults

EARLIER INTERPRETATIONS OF CARGO CULTS

1. Prominent Researchers

Faced with the variety of cargo cults we look for the meaning of these movements. What is really taking place in these cults? Research into cargo cults shows there are many different opinions. It is interesting that the results obtained by individual researchers often depend upon their basic concepts, areas of interest, and methods of research.

Earlier attempts at interpretation are not all of equal importance. In some cases only facts are recorded; in others, stress is only upon explanations. Personal experience is manifest in some publications; others convey knowledge acquired through reading. Although relatively well-informed about some events, we have only scanty knowledge of others.

Up to the second world war only short descriptions are extant. Gradually essays on interpretation are added by Bodrogi, Rousseau, Inglis, Bühler, Stanner and others.[31] New hypotheses are put forward in an attempt to fathom the thinking and behaviour of the Melanesian people. It is regrettable that some statements, however valuable they may be, are biased or wrongly interpret information. Belief in magic by a New Caledonian cannot be accepted and understood by Europeans. The converse is true for the indigenous Melanesian. Indeed, this is an essential premise for the origin of all cargo cults. Nevertheless, attempts at explanation are indispensable and important milestones on the way to a solution.

The cargo cults have not ceased in the Pacific area, although the interest of many Europeans has quite obviously declined. This does not mean that the problem of cargo cults has been solved, but rather it shows that we have reached a dead end with our interpretations. But if the previously animistic world is entering a decisive phase of cultural revaluation and—as Tippett claims—"is on the threshold to proceed from something old to something new",[32] if millions of human beings "are faced today with the decision whether they should exchange their traditional religion for the Islam, Christianity, Communism or a nativistic new-religion",[33] then the time has truly come for the churches to re-evaluate their role in order to avoid serious mistakes during this period of growing independence by the Melanesian people. Ten thousand baptized Christians have left the church in Melanesia during the past twenty years. The church should respond.

The wealth of evidence available on cargo cults is surprisingly large, but has remained largely hidden from the public. Approximately 150 authors with information on cargo cults have published nearly 400 contributions. A few definite types of opinion have crystallized from this multiplicity of voices. They may be divided into five categories (see Table 1).

Table 1

Year	A Social– political	B Christian– ethical	C Cultural– historical	D Economic	E Synoptic
1917	Chinnery, E.W.P. Haddon, A.C.				
1923	Williams, F.E.				
1928	Williams, F.E.				
1932	Firth, R.W.				
1934	Williams, F.E.		Lehmann, F.R.		
1935	Haddon, A.C.				
1936	O'Reilly, P.				
1937			Eckert, G.		
1939			Lehmann, F.R.		
1941		Höltker, G.	Eckert, G.		
1943		Inselmann, R	Linton, R.		
1945		Henkelmann, F.			
1946		Höltker, G.			
1947		Hannemann, E.F.			Stanner, W.E.
1949	Bruijn, T.V. de	Pilhofer, G.		Poirier, J.	
1950	O'Reilly, P. Allan, C.H. Belshaw, C.S.				
1951	Belshaw, C.S.			Poirier, J.	

Year	A Social–political	B Christian–ethical	C Cultural–historical	D Economic	E Synoptic
	Allan, C.H. Bruijn, T.V. de Rousseau, M. Firth, R.W.			Guiart, J. Bodrogi, T.	
1952	Belshaw, C.S. Berndt, R.M.		Kamma, F.C.	Guiart, J.	
1953	Lommel, A Belshaw, C.S.				Stanner, W.E.
1954	Belshaw, C.S. Berndt, R.M.		Lawrence, P. Burridge, K.O.L.		
1955	Firth, R.W.				
1956	Lanternari, V.		Kamma, F.C. Wallace, A.F.C.	Guiart, J.	
1957	Bühler, A.			Worsley, P.M. Guiart, J.	Inglis, J. Cohn, N.
1958	Hogbin, H.			Mair, L.P. Guiart, J.	Stanner, W.E.
1959		Laufer, L.	Wallace, A.F.C.	Mair, L.P. Guiart, J.	Inglis, J. Guariglia, G.
1960	Aberle, D.F.		Burridge, K.O.L. Shepperson, G. Eliade, M.		Köbben, A.J.F. Thrupp, S.L. Cohn, N.
1961				Jarvie, I.C. Mühlmann, P.E.	
1962	Aberle, D.F.	Margull, H.J.	Burridge, K.O.L. Schwartz, T.		
1963	Lanternari, V.	Lutzebetak, L.J.		Jarvie, I.C.	
1964		Wagner, H. Wagner, F. Kuder, J. Steinbauer, F.	Fischer, H.	Mühlmann, P.E.	Lawrence, P.
1965			Sterly, J.		
1966		Oosterwal, G.			
1967				Worsley, P.M.	Lawrence, P.
1968	Hogbin, H.	Wagner, H.			
1969	Brunton, R.		Saake, W. Christiansen, P.		
1970		Strauss, H. Hueter, D.			Steinbauer, F.

Main Theses of Earlier Researchers

All the theses of previous researches cannot be dealt with here, but a few are selected as examples to clarify some of the essential views represented by research. The selection of two representatives of each of the five main groups of interpretation is not an assessment of values. It is an attempt to give the historical development of the problem according to a few representatives. A bias can be found in the observation and judgment of, and the reaction to, the phenomenon of cargo cults. Thus one can allocate a definite position in life to the representatives of the individual types of opinion. The way in which they approached their evidence and the interest which guided them impressed their stamp upon their perception and their terminology.

Grossly simplifying, it can be ascertained that many government officals belonged to group A. Due to their office and commission they were especially interested in peace and order. Cargo cults were often a nuisance which had to be removed or suppressed.

Williams and Belshaw may be quoted as examples in group A. Both men acted very cautiously. Williams understood that the introduction of new morals and customs meant the loss of a traditionally integrated life. The resultant feeling of inferiority had to be balanced by a defensive reaction. Thus antagonism arose against Europeans who had to defend themselves as a consequence.

Belshaw recognized the affinity between many cargo cults. He searched for the releasing and irritating agencies and found that everywhere tensions existed between indigenes and Europeans. The Melanesians were discontented. They applied magic to achieve political goals. They lived "half way" from their own future and they had to be carefully guided in this process.

Group B lists mostly missionaries. They, too, very often noticed only a regrettable and wrong development which had to be overcome by church discipline. They started to voice their concern by writing much later than the representatives of the government. They had the great advantage that people trusted them like fathers and, for a long time, looked at them as allies. Yet gradually this trust weakened and gave way to hopeless disappointment. Those mission workers have continued to search for the religious momentum in the cargo cults.

Höltker discovered fanaticism for which there is scarcely any substantial evidence. Egoistic motives result in withdrawal from the demands of the Europeans. Strauss supplemented this opinion and pointed to the desire for a whole and integrated life. The ancient myths and understanding of the world are the seedbed. A solution for this spiritual confusion can only be obtained by a return to, and an inner renewal towards, a Christian view of man. Thus the loss of authority which had its origin in the contact of civilizations is transcended and converted to well-being.

The professional ethnologists are in group C, and always focused upon the changes of cultures. Sometimes they saw the ideal condition in the past which had been destroyed by a deleterious civilization. They finally took seriously what had been self-evident to the followers of the cults, and also recognized a meaningful and partly necessary process of development. Their attitude enabled them to begin a genuine dialogue with the people concerned and to start constructive help.

Amongst the historians of culture of this kind Lehmann, as early as 1934, pointed out the ancient and magic heritage. Basically the cults were not new to him, but only a modern revival of ancient prophetism. In 1969 Christiansen's argument was similar when he wrote of the structural contents of the Melanesian frame of culture. In periods of crisis man seeks answers from his own, mythical heritage in order to master the present. Inner conflicts are always decisive during transformations of culture. They are caught and digested by the cargo cults as necessary measures of protection.

Representatives of group D appeared only after the second world war. They continued the dialogue under the sign of economic development. The problem of social-political and interhuman relationships was their main concern. They all started with the experience of the war and were brimful of social ideas which occasionally were enunciated in a distinctly socialistic manner. Their arguments were determined by contrasts: poor and rich; colonial government and independence. Their attitude towards the cargo cults was preoccupied and sustained by the hope for a quick improvement of the situation. They saw as their goal an emancipated, secular-rational society which would overcome the cults.

Guiart and Worsley are two significant representatives of this rational–economic perspective. Guiart above all emphasized the erosion of the traditional societies by the European civilization. This causes the feeling of being exploited and provokes progressive ideas which result in the desire for self-liberation. The ritual is created to counterbalance the technology of the Europeans. Worsley adds to this by pointing to the ambivalence of all cults. Constrained by tradition, the cults remain passive and on a religious level. They become active through their simultaneous openness to foreign influences and grow into social movements. With time they drift into the secular space and become political entities.

Group E cannot be attached to a particular professional stratum. So far ethnologists interested in cultural history have provided a number of synoptic monographs. They want to condense the main points of earlier representations in order to prepare a synopsis. Of course they accept certain centres of gravity. But basically they intend to proceed as objectively as possible. Interest and terminology are different with all five types of interpretation. But all the representatives have in common the wish for peace and unity between the people.

Members of the synoptic group want to bridge and neutralize tensions. Stanner belongs to this group. He saw primarily a diffusional process of history in the movements. A Weltanschauung which proves a failure under new circumstances becomes meaningless. In the resulting crisis new concepts are found upon which a more viable Weltanschauung can be based. The phenomena are religious in so far as one hopes for a "new life". Lawrence pointed out the inevitability of misunderstandings. The materialistic, pragmatic, basic attitude of the Melanesians often prevents them from doing justice to the factual content of new thoughts which they absorb. European ways, Christianity and wealth appear to them identical. The new is simply built into an old frame of terms of reference. In principle, only that is sought which as secret knowledge seems to promise success. For Lawrence, therefore, an ordered system of education and a sound administrative policy to guarantee peace and economic progress are more necessary than anything else.

THE PURPOSE OF THIS INVESTIGATION

Several important points of view are represented by the attempts to explain cargo cults. Not all contradictions have been eliminated however. In this investigation a procedure is suggested which should help to overcome some difficulties.

A hundred characteristics which may be significant for the cargo cults have been classified and listed in Appendix 6. All cults which are shown in Appendix 3 according to the territories and periods of time where and when they have been active have been examined, and if a characteristic is pertinent for a particular cult it is noted. Such a statistical computation should lead to evaluation and improved understanding of the cults. But statistical assessment does not answer all questions. It must be remembered that the potential of a movement plays the most important role: for example Paliau has achieved much more as an individual with his enterprises than his five predecessors. The impressiveness and the spiritual impulses which emanate from a movement vary in strength. The same applies to its effects. Nor can it be automatically concluded that something did not take place because it is not mentioned. It should be assumed that much more happened than has been recorded.

One hundred and eighty-six cults have been examined. Eighteen thousand six hundred decisions are made for or against a positive mark. Chances for gross distortions should be only small. Only in 1 per cent of all possible statements was the answer qualified. This percentage varied with the twelve regions into which the cults are grouped. But it never reached 2 per cent and its lowest value is 0.12 per cent. In a few cases only (0.2 per cent of all cases) was the pertinency of a characteristic to a cult uncertain.

A simple computation will strengthen these assertions. Even with the fullest possible documentation only sixty out of a hundred characteristics can be pertinent to any one cult since the remaining forty are excluded due to mutual contradiction. It is found that in practice for very well recorded cults about forty characteristics can be attributed to one cult. The mean number of characteristics for one cult is found to be nineteen or close to half the amount for the best covered cults. Not only are the individual cults well characterized by a large number of details, but the distribution of characteristics upon the individual cults is such as to allow comparison between different cults.

Here a final judgement cannot be reached. Too much is still fluid. But time is ripe for a thorough stocktaking. The problem has been looked at as an exotic curiosity far too long and it has been treated accordingly. Either one saw expressions of a primitive culture, symptoms of defection from the Christian church, or the outgrowth of political-revolutionary action in these movements. In many cases one hoped to remove the arising difficulties by suppression. For a long time one saw only symptoms without recognizing the proper causes. Increasing misunderstandings, tensions and a growing loss of trust between the concerned parties were the result. Also, within the Christian missions, one tended largely to abolish the unpleasant problem by all too quick a condemnation because it disturbed the establishment of communities and did not fit into the planning for the development of the churches. Even today the majority of all those who are engaged in missionary work are convinced that the cargo cult ideology is something grievous which has to be fought. To begin with, the reaction is understandable. Nor is the reaction altogether alien to anyone who has been challenged by it in a real situation. The question, however, is whether it can be justified. The history of the cargo cult movements has sufficiently proven that condemnation alone does not suffice. We are concerned with elemental human emotions, thoughts and needs which cannot be quenched, however, by being prohibited. At the most one can produce a displacement which sooner or later becomes noticeable again in another situation. That does not help anyone.

Firstly insights into the inner events of these cults have to be dealt with, which requires a real interest and concern. Until now only a small circle of people recognized that decisive "switches" had to be made here. Occasionally one spoke of a "gnosis of the South Pacific". This is a good comparison. The church, however, must not remain silent when such a discussion arises, but must interest herself in the problem and proceed with understanding and expert knowledge. Expertise requires information. The present research supplies information.

Today approximately 3.3. million indigenous inhabitants live in the Melanesian area. Of these, 1.9 million are Christians.[34] At least 20 per cent of these people may have been involved in "cargo activities", according to the author's rough estimate. This does not mean that today all practise cultic rituals, but rather they are committed to "cargo-expectation" in a way which visibly determines their daily life. Approximately 380,000 Christians are influenced by the gospel as well as by cargo cult ideology. This nameless army challenges the church. Questions about adequate preaching have to be reexamined. Instruction at schools, conduct of divine services, the significance of church discipline, principles of evangelization and guidance of the communities require through deliberation. More than this, one must inquire into the basic tenor of the existence of missions. Of course, it is impossible here to produce a fundamental clarification of the universal, critical situation of theology and mission. Yet perhpas the concrete situation of a young church under attack may stimulate a few necessary thoughts.

Practical troubles certainly cannot be overcome with theo-

retical reflections alone. But the Melanesians will have to make
the necessary efforts themselves. Europeans, at the most, can
offer a solution by contributing an analysis of available material,
but the classfication and examination of it Melanesians are not
yet able to undertake. It is more important to make new
understanding possible through facts than to confirm conjectures, even if we risk having our previous opinions rejected.
Earlier analyses have been unsatisfactory in my opinion, since
they were based mostly upon fractional knowledge. An analysis
only seems promising using results jointly from different methods
and arguments. Therefore as broad a basis of examination as
possible shoud be applied when the cults are examined. Seeming-
ly alien and at first unproductive considerations have to be
included, which results in going outside the framework of a
single, scientific discipline. It is necessary to point out again and
again the concatenation of the ethnological context with the
history of religion and psychology. There are some central
questions which have to be viewed against a wide background.

The central themes of the cargo cults are determined by
evidence gained from descriptions of them, not by the assessment
of the individual observer. A few basic tendencies are always
repeated, which determine the centres of gravity for reflections.
It may be attractive to attend more carefully to some questions,
for example the parallelism with religious and political behaviour
in the Afro–American cultures or the connection with neu-
rological syndromes or intensive studies of the mythology of the
Pacific, but it is equally important to concentrate upon six types
of questions in order to reach a total understanding:
1. The tendencies of the movements
2. The leaders of the movements
3. The catalysts of the movements
4. The means of the movements
5. The aims of the movements
6. The results of the movements
We can proceed from these questions to those which follow
indirectly, for example the problem of a self-supporting structure
(coherence) of the cults or the problem of influences of external
forces (stimulation) in the history of a cult. The question of the
religious content and of the typical concept of salvation in the
Melanesian cults must be mentioned, and conclusions drawn for
missionary actions of the church. These movements stir up
questions of global interest. The theme of social justice is in
the background. The uneven distribution of power and happiness
and wealth on earth can be seen. A share in the blessings of

the modern world is desired. This desire is justified, but technical possibilities do not yet allow its fulfilment. Cultic actions offer an escape, dreams of a better world. The dream is ancient, worldwide, alien to none of us.

EVALUATING THE STATISTICS

1. General Remarks

The positive marks obtained for each of the hundred characteristics[35] are counted and the result is divided by 186 (the number of cults), and expressed as a percentage in Appendix 6. Thus a description of all Melanesian cargo cults is obtained as they are considered together as one phenomenon. This discussion will not deal in detail with any one cargo cult.[36] The important questions are: What is common to all cargo cults, and where are the signal deviations?

A glance at the indices 1 to 3 in Appendix 6 shows immediately and clearly the centre of emphasis. Cults aiming mainly at material wealth, and using magic practices to this end, outnumber all others. Figure 1 shows that about 64 per cent, or three-fifths, of all movements are magico–mechanistic. Eighteen per cent or one-fifth are idealistic, religious–spiritual, and the remaining 18 per cent are cultural, social–political. Considering the respective potentials, a ratio of 3:1:1 between three fundamental types of cults is obtained. It is thus established beyond doubt that materialistic expectations of goods are specific to the Melanesian expectations of salvation. There are still 36 per cent concerned with more than a simple hope for goods. This is cause for reflection.

A division by main geographical regions opens another interesting perspective. The pre-eminence of spiritual or political elements is dependent upon the surrounding ancient cultures. The following distribution can be shown:

Predominance of Magic Elements: East Irian Jaya, Papua, Madang, Morobe, New Guinea Highlands.

Predominance of Spiritual Elements: West Irian Jaya, New Hebrides, Fiji.

Predominance of Political Elements: Bismarck Archipelago, Solomon Islands, New Caledonia.

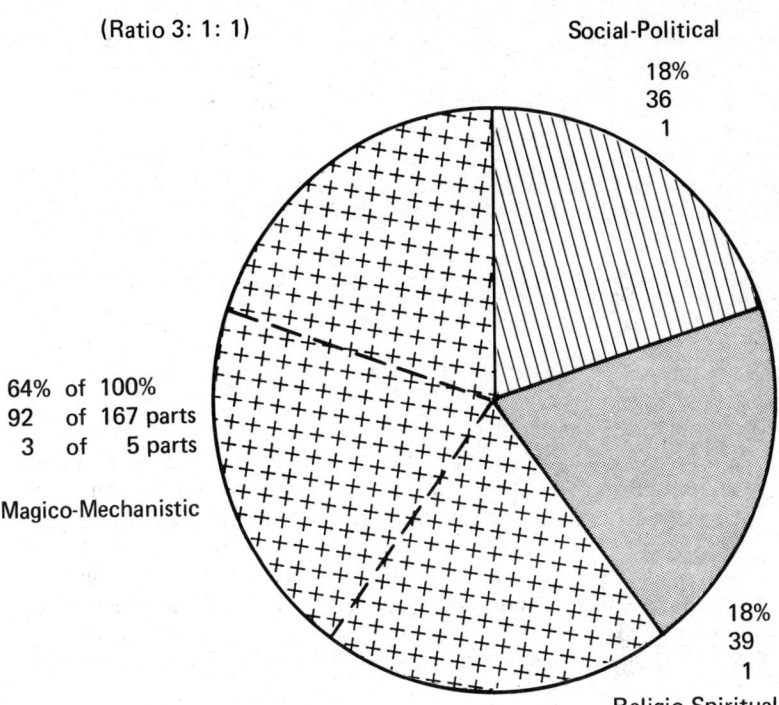

(Ratio 3: 1: 1)

Social-Political

18%
36
1

64% of 100%
92 of 167 parts
3 of 5 parts

Magico-Mechanistic

18%
39
1

Religio-Spiritual

Fig. 1. Distribution of three cultic fundamental types

In the Sepik River district, more than elsewhere, all the elements are active. This appears significant if three factors are considered which are all operative in this district, whereas in the rest of Melanesia one of these factors determines the cultic expression.

Firstly, there is a strong bond with the "primitive" level of culture of all inland dwellers, corresponding to the magical view and conception of the world. Therefore all mountain-dwellers of New Guinea tend towards the magical–naive type of cult.

Secondly there are people with a higher culture. The spiritual attitude of Melanesians is affected by the border contact with these people. In the east there is Polynesia; in the west, Indonesia. In both a more spiritual religiosity is prevalent. It is not surprising that the "fringe settlers" in West Irian Jaya and in Fiji are influenced and that their cultural expressions bear evidence of spiritual features.

Lastly, there exist those marine populations who have been isolated for a long time and whose awareness of their own identity is well developed. They always felt self-sufficient and valued their independence and freedom. We would indeed have to expect from them a political form of cultic activities. The best-defined social movements are in the Solomon Islands and the Bismarck Archipelago.

The first conclusions are that the more contacts there are with the spriitual forces of the world abroad, the stronger grows the social–religious component; and the more exposed people are the more political is their interest.

These assertions are checked with regard to the indices 4 to 12 in Appendix 6. The sum of all detailed characteristics should yield a similar picture if the aforesaid is correct. And that is the case. For this purpose we summarize all ideas according to their affinity by type, and measure them by their ratios. The magical elements are hope for goods, chiliasm and eschatologism. The spiritual elements are syncretism, Messianism, and vitalism. The political elements are nativism, revivalism, and economic reforms. Figure 2 again demonstrates the proportions 3:1:1 or 92:39:36 per cent—considering that overlapping occurs due to double characterization. The situation is the same indeed.

Figure 2 shows that apparently quite a number of cults do not aim exclusively at gaining material goods. It has always been known that such non-materialistic choice of goal existed, but it is surprising that the percentage is so great.

Help cannot be accomplished by material–technical assistance

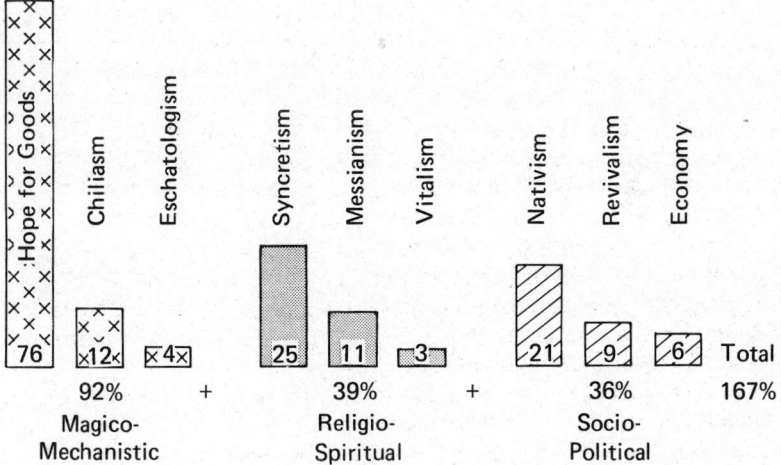

Fig. 2. Share of various fundamental types in the total of all cargo-cult movements (Owing to multiple tendencies the total rises to 167% from 100%. The recorded values relate to 167%)

and support alone if 36 per cent of all cargo cults do not strive merely for the consumption of goods, but for values which contribute to the humaneness of life. Rather one has to expect that a solution will only exist in both structural help and religious and philosphical help which can be accepted and maintained. The desire for freedom cannot be satisfied with a tractor; instead a religious message is needed which can provide a goal and, according to the circumstances, the basis for a political party.

Whether the cargo cults will change with time and vary in their aims is a different question. P. Worsley maintains there is a general trend for cults with primitive–magical beginnings to reach a social-revolutionary stage in the end. However an examination of frequencies of characteristics in one geographical region for cults of different historical periods, as indicated in Appendix 3, shows that this is correct only conditionally. Figure 3 indicates that during the period for which information is available a much smaller trend is apparent than had been assumed. The evolutionary aspect may pertain rather to the history of a single movement than to the overall course in a definite, geographical region where, on the contrary, a peculiar lack of change is observed. Most of the basic elements of cults are preserved for decades. Only in Papua, during the most recent phase, did movements become more political. Similar changes in trends can be observed in the Solomon Islands. But, strangely enough, in recent developments a move towards the magical pattern is obvious again. In the New Hebrides cults tend to change from a political direction to a religious one.

We may recognize from this:

1. Worsley's theories of an inevitable shift into a national–social direction cannot be applied when we look at the whole phenomenon. They are relevant for a few districts or for individual cults examined in isolation (for example the Welfare Society). They ignore, however, that many movements—within a certain period as well as within the history of their own development—strongly emphasized the political from the beginning, not just when they were pressed towards it by development; for example Paliau, Tommy Kabu, Atai, or Kauris' attempted riot.

2. The original culture is much more responsible for rates of change than any external influence. The ancient, spiritual heritage, including geographical position and pre-European contact with different Oceanic peoples, is of much more vital importance for the growth and transformation of cultic currents

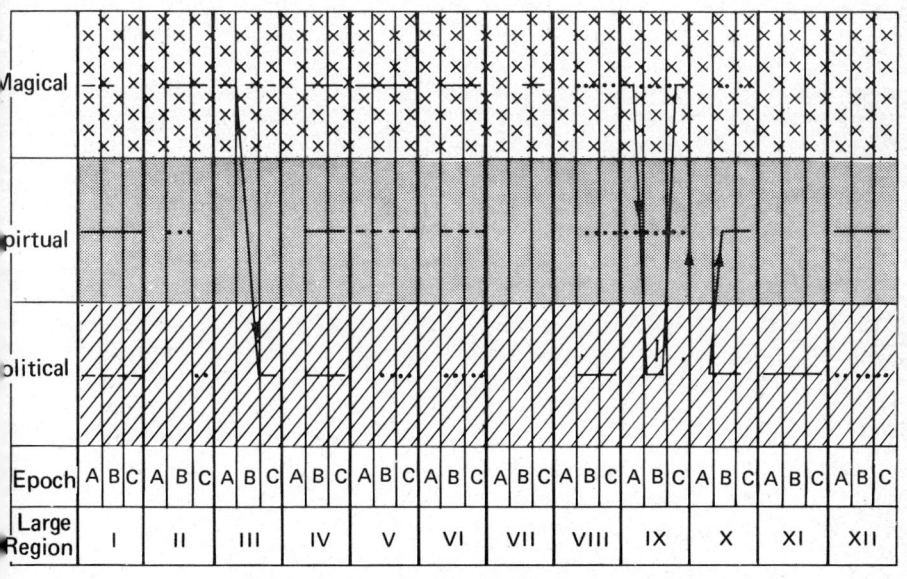

Fig. 3. Trends in the historical development

A: before 1914
B: 1918–39
C: 1945→
I to XII: Appendix 5

than the comparatively short-lived contact of civilizations during the last three generations. The influences of the modern period certainly leave visible traces. Indeed, techniques of cultic practice and forms of expression of the world of desires are strongly moulded by them. But the spiritual attitude behind them is not fundamentally changed at all; it is only adapted to the requirements of the time. Recognition of this forces one to consider the cultural relevance of the tradition much more seriously than before.

Figure 4 is derived from the statistical analysis. It demonstrates that about 17 per cent of all cargo cults have an aboriginal source. They grew out of the structures of the indigenous, mythical heritage of their culture as an always new and necessary actualization of the traditional myths, or as accidental metamorphoses or mutations of culture. The demand for cultic experiments existed in the traditional Weltanschauung. Events are often accelerated by contact with a foreign culture which is not necessary as a motive, but acts as a catalyst. Melanesian man has shown himself sufficiently creative without the stimulation of European civilization to give life to new images of culture.

H. Strauss gives an illustration of such continued innovations in the Highlands of New Guinea.[37] There a currency of shells has been known long before the Europeans came to the country. On long and arduous routes, these shells were taken into the inland from tribe to tribe by barter. In their ignorance the Highlands people believed that the shells grew on trees. It is therefore common usage even today to describe the shells as being "picked". In ancient times a shell cult similar to a cargo cult had developed in the Western Highlands to ensure a lasting supply of such shells. According to the laws of magic, shell spirits, which were believed to cause all new creations, were entreated and induced to provide their blessings. The men assembled in their cult houses, sang the shell's praise, and sacrificed to the spirits of the shell. The sorcerer priests called on the names of foreign tribes and of unknown places to attract more shells. They were convinced that these would soon find the way to their new owners. Quite a number of such "hidden cults" survive, such as the Padlma festivals of Alkena, which the author taped and filmed in 1963.

The ancient cultures of these people should be studied more intensively. The pre-European period should be credited with a good measure of spiritual productivity since, as proven, at least 17 per cent of all cargo cults grew from native traditions and

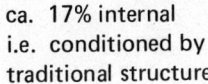

ca. 17% internal
i.e. conditioned by
traditional structure

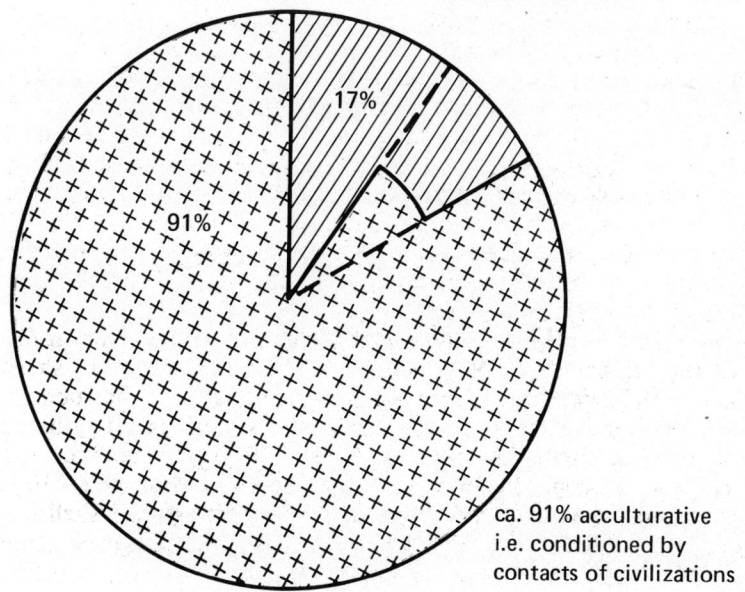

17%

91%

ca. 91% acculturative
i.e. conditioned by
contacts of civilizations

Note: There is superimposition
and overlapping
Borders are somewhat fluid.

Fig. 4. Share in per cent of internal and acculturative origin

by indigenous initiative. Obviously even new and quite decisive driving forces, which attempt to shape life and to cope with it, are anchored in the traditional way of thinking. The understanding of such mental processes is therefore an important condition for every kind of political, economic and religious activity in the Pacific area.

Percentages quoted under indices 15, 16 and 17 in Appendix 6 are used in Figure 5, which shows that 63 per cent of all the cults are extinct, and 38 per cent, although not actively practised, are endemic. It is quite possible that they will have vanished completely in time. But they may come to life again at any time and contribute to sensational journalism. However, 12 per cent are still active and attract a large following; they are the most interesting. We are only able to understand their potential if we consider that figure 5 encompasses a period of about 100 years, that is, four generations. Indeed, roughly a quarter of the last generation Melanesians since the second world war are followers of cults or sympathize with the ideology of cults. Exact figures are not available, but these figures are not too high. This is verified by their dispersion through nearly all Melanesia, even if there should be only an active minority in any locality. The church therefore cannot afford to ignore this phenomenon.

2. Leaders of Movements
(Indices 18 to 24 of Appendix 6)

It is true that the message of a cult is generally more important than the leader who proclaims it. But it is equally true for the cargo cults of the South Pacific that the leaders of the movements play a central role. This of course applies in principle to any leadership. Max Weber recognizes a fundamental law that, within a group of human beings, a few are always distinguished by greater individuation and therefore assume leadership. This greater individuation is often counted as a divine gift. For the Melanesian South Pacific, G. Eckert and J. Sterly have shown that prophets become especially active in periods of spiritual crises. The conservative element is dominant during periods of cultural stability, whereas the reformer has opportunities during periods of instability. No culture is a constant entity. It is always subject to influences and is always newly formed. Thus prophetic–religious forces should be especially suited for cultural mutations. They stand frequently in the focus

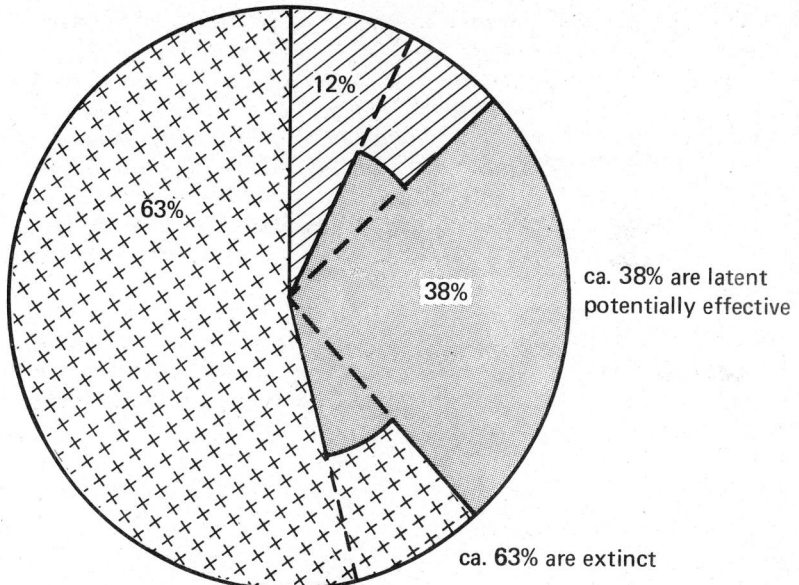

ca. 12% are still active today

12%

63%

38%

ca. 38% are latent
potentially effective

ca. 63% are extinct

Note: Superimpositions
cause overlapping from one
sector to another.
Borders remain fluid.

Fig. 5. Percentage of actual existence

of revolutionary endeavours. A prophet can nearly always be sure of success with the masses if his message "speaks to the condition of" the perplexed and if he succeeds in showing any proofs of his ability.

It is striking that frequently older men start a cult and guide its inner development. They refer to experiences of the past, have a strong interest in restoration, and they understand how to manipulate the feelings of their countrymen. For example, old Sawa of Hahalis acted as a "grey eminence" in the background of the Welfare Society. Youthful propagandists often swagger as spokesmen to the world around them. The real ideologists, however, sit in remote huts, chew betel nut or smoke herbs, and forge the spiritual weapons to fight a New Time which threatens the ancient concepts of the world.

Here we must distinguish different groups: (a) prophetic visionaries or Messiah figures, (b) leaders who prefer to play the role of organizers (Palle Christiansen has pointed this out very clearly)[38] and (c) the so-called psyche.

(a) Prophets always have the greatest influence in the initial period of a cult. They stand out by their greater spirituality and individuation. Sometimes they assume the role against their will. They act by charisma and "under order". They have an intermediate function and are of significance until their message —like a flame—has incited a sufficiently large multitude.

Occasionally a prophet develops into a real Saviour figure. Only in a very few cases was this transformation deliberately and consciously prepared by the prophetic founders of a cult. The followers force them into this new role of a Messiah. Only rarely the leader of the cult claims the title of Messiah from the beginning. Whenever this happens, as for example with Kelevi, it can be asked whether perhaps neurotic features played a part. Besides it must not be forgotten that the numbers acclaimed as saviours are small and represent only 4 per cent in Melanesia. This percentage is much less than with the comparable Negro-syncretisms in Africa and South America. Generally, those visionaries and bearers of salvation are completely honest people and nothing is further from their minds than fraud and deceit. Only very few can resist the temptation when the crowds glorify them as heroes. They let themselves be drawn into the current of expectations of supernatural salvation and accept the status of a divinely exalted hero.

Again we find here a confirmation of the intially stated hypothesis that the ratio of magical, religious and political basic types is 3:1:1. The true prophets and saviours, the interpreters who proclaim the religious-spiritual message represent the fifth to which vitalism, Messianism and syncretism belong.

(b) Organizers of cargo cults are much more numerous than prophets. They lead with an aim and maintain a system of a more or less tight structure. They are the technicians of piety or the officers of administration. They partly pursue their power-political goals unscrupulously. Schwartz compares them with the bailiffs of a *Mein Kampf* ideology,[39] but such harsh judgement is unfair. We can only understand them in their own situation. Then they appear rather as men on a frontier, placed between two different cultures, who are themselves not really happy in their situation. We may count among them also the various individual initiators of cults and, further, those forces who worked as a team to spread the idea of a cult. They all pull the strings and influence their environment with a goal in view. Together they account for three-fifths of all the personal leaders. That is parallel with the magic–mechanistic basic type of the cargo cults (Figure 6).

In this context a special feature must be considered. The female share in leadership is only 4 per cent, which is the result of the subordinate status of women. It is therefore even more remarkable that some women have obtained supremacy in the life of a cult. But some circumstances suggest that there are isolated eruptions and triumphal manifestations of the female element above the ancient antagonism of the sexes. According to repeatedly-told myths, women are said to have discovered and administered all religious secrets in ancient times. Only in the course of history have men succeeded in taking this knowledge away from women, which they had kept and preserved in secret societies ever since. Only the burgeoning of completely new cults seems to provide a release for women and girls. In the light of new morals which arose from the cargo cult development, women have gained greater liberties even where no true women's movement developed.

(c) Finally, the contribution of the so-called group psyche is important. It amounts to 26 percent—a fifth of the total division. It corresponds to the political section. By group psyche I mean a collective experience of a large proportion of the population which spreads atmospherically. In the case of cargo cults, this experience is directed towards the fulfilment of a satisfied life. The quick growth, the vigorous spreading and the surprising success of many cults are vouchsafed, since a large number of cultists apparently hope from the very outset to obtain satisfaction in life. Mass movements may be expected in Melanesia

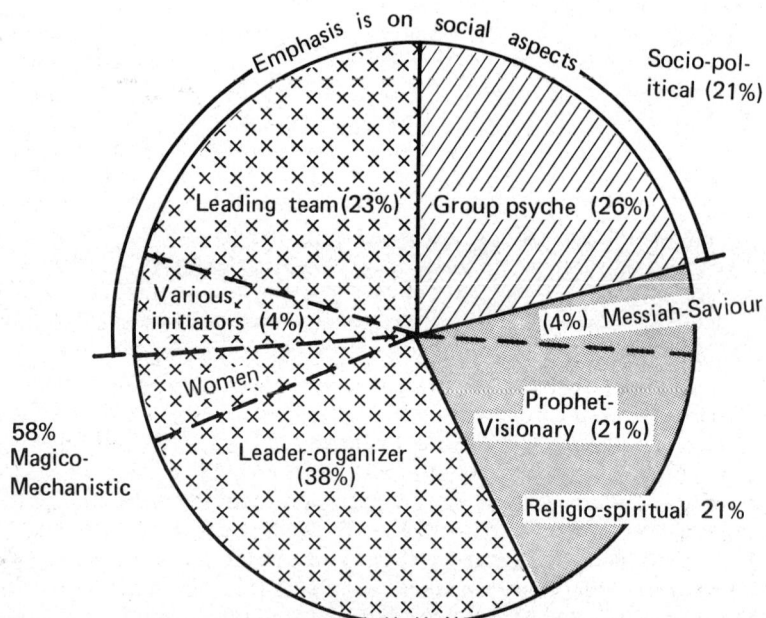

Note: The figures in brackets
mean percentages in the reference system of 186 cults.
By overlapping a total of 121% is obtained

Fig. 6. Distribution of leadership

whereas in Africa more often a large number of individual prophets call innumerable, smaller sects into life. The experience of the masses, the group psyche, still carries a movement even if individual prophets, Messiahs or leaders resign. This is the strength of the cargo cults, making it difficult to overcome them. It is possible to undo what depends on individuals, but one cannot destroy thoughts in the same way. A social current is rolling onwards which creates a political situation. The crowds are fascinated. They give weight and energy to the movement.

Today it is apparent that the tremendous consequences of the cults can only be understood in their social context. It is striking that an era of growing social awareness is worldwide. A worldwide increase of social–structural interests stands against a decline of a spiritual–prophetic attitude of faith. It is not surprising that this emphasis of the social factor often produces magical atrributes (cargo cults), is joined to a cult of a person (Maoism) or even appears in a spiritual garb (Macumba) and as rejuvenating religion (Soka Gakkai). In each case an inclination exists for a very earthbound happiness. This is made especially clear by the Neo-Buddhist sect, Soka Gakkai, which attracted many millions within a very short time. But all other efforts at reform and renaissance by the religions today point towards the same trend. We may indeed accept the social factor as the basic theme of international endeavours for justice, peace, freedom and happiness. Every idea of salvation therefore has to be in a reciprocal relationship with socially directed activities. For example, here we find parallels between European tendencies towards socialism and the cargo cult activities which are guided by the group psyche. Social movements intoxicate men in Asiatic cults and sects, as well as expectations of Utopias in Western society. In this way even the strangest South Pacific cultic phenomena follow the direction of a superimposed development of humanity.

It is a profession of faith that not only a process of apostasy lies behind this development, but also divine guidance. Perhaps we may trace in each individual case how far God's will effectively takes shape within the frame of this escalation of the human spirit and activities.

3. Causes and Catalysts of Movements

The true catalysts which are listed under the indices 25 to 36 in Appendix 6 must be distinguished from those factors which, as causes, remain in the background and which are denoted by the indices 37 to 45. The borderline between causes and catalysts is often vague. For example, a certain myth may be the reason for a pattern of thought in a cargo cult, and at the same time be the catalyst for an intense, cultic activity, especially if this myth suggests ritually conditioned repetition. It may be, on the contrary, that a myth provides only the base for a general way of thinking, while a concrete event—perhaps loss of liberty through arrest by a colonial officer—acts as a stimulus to form a cultic movement. There is a good reason therefore to keep causes and catalysts separate. We are always concerned with catalysts when an event becomes the threshold.

Causes	Catalysts
(a) Magic and mythos	(a) Contact of civilizations
(b) Materialistic thinking	(b) Metamorphoses of culture
(c) Eschatological concept of life	(c) Cargo cult propaganda
(d) Psychical structure and wealth of phantasy	(d) Visionary experiences
(e) Bioclimatic conditions	(e) The Christian message

Causes of Cargo Cults

(a) Without doubt magic thinking presented by index 39 is the most frequent cause of cults. This is decisive in 85 per cent of all cases. It is essential to consider imitative magic by which a desired effect is to be achieved in a way analogous to the results of a model operation simply by imitating this operation. One "plants" silver coins in the ground so that they may grow and "bear fruit", that is multiply. Or one pours water out of a bamboo tubing and recites "sacred verses" so that rain will be attracted and moisten the soil. Or by analogy with the army camps of soldiers, one establishes new villages on the beach to imitate the military life and simultaneously to gain the desired rations of the fighting troops.

The whole Melanesian concept of the world is very closely linked with this way of magic thinking. The cult of the ancestors which at least in a third of all cases plays a determining role, the mythology of the ancestors, and all misunderstandings of the modern world are part of it. Sometimes one speaks of a spiritual seedbed, meaning a magic–religious understanding of the world that believes and lives by a cosmic store of energy. This understanding is obtained in a way of thinking which is governed by a mythical causality. The logic of this thought is not governed by natural laws. Its rules are deeply religious and it reaches into the "superempirical" realm. All rational arguments against it remain irrelevant as long as the magic logic prevails. The cargo cults cannot be understood without this insight. Relevance of culture as it is shaped by mythos and magic is of fundamental significance for all movements in Melanesia. All explanations which place little importance on the relevance of the spiritual seedbed will automatically miss the centre of the cults. How the individual influences are distributed is of secondary importance in comparison. Whether the ancient cult of the ancestors is still alive and is realized in the cargo cult, or whether a myth is finally effective, or whether a Biblical story stimulates the fantasy may vary in each case. An understanding of the world largely evading rational logic is always at the bottom of it. It is therefore inevitable that religious and secular misunderstandings and difficulties arise when a cult collides with the modern world. In every case difficulties cause mistrust, and hostile fronts are established.

(b) The magic-mythical understanding of the world of Melanesia is earthbound. One is struck by the strongly materialistic quality. Certainly materialism means one thing to the European and something else to the mountain-dweller of New Guinea. In the West, mind and matter have grown asunder. The mind has assumed leadership, at least in theory. Melanesians think more of a totality. Matter is an integrating, respected and longed for constituent of a whole life. A religion seems useless to them if it neglects the material component. Every offer is tested for its material promise. It is inevitable that such materialistic expectations again and again manifest themselves in the cargo cults. On the other hand, we have to expect greater immunity where the material component is less significant. This, for example, is true for the Maoris. They have a share of the mentality of the Polynesians. The best of their ancient traditions have been preserved. Thus they have sustained a sense of their own value and mental balance. The Melanesians are different. For them the "worldly goods" have a value of a much higher order. They experience the meaning of life only in the web of mental and material dispensation of salvation. If at all, their hopes can be realized only on this plane. An intentional turn towards economic success is the natural consequence of such deliberations. This view is pursued rationally and secularly by 4 per cent (see index 45 in Appendix 6), which demonstrates that in modern times mythical and economic strivings may easily co-operate. The motivation, however, rests in the will to appropriate power, possessions and happiness.

(c) The native eschatology is also supported by this will. G. Vicedom pointed out several times that there is definitely an indigenous eschatology in the Southern Pacific which is not at all influenced by Christianity. We would go astray certainly if we considered the existence of an all-native eschatology in isolation. The computation of data only yields a modest proportion of 4 per cent as basically determined by eschatology (see index 4 in Appendix 6).

The recorded figure may be somewhat increased however by a sequence of emotions which are determined by eschatological expectations and which are universally dispersed. In addition it must be stressed that the Melanesians, although having conceived an eschatology, have not found any motivation or direction towards a final goal in life or history. One speaks of an end of the world and accepts the destruction of all that exists. But all this is viewed within the cycle of a cosmic regeneration. Thus the real seriousness of historical events is cancelled, the tension between the "now" and the "not yet" is neutralized and the Christian message is emasculated, the message which reasons from an absolute end and for that very reason calls for repentance and for a universal, new beginning. Basically this eschatology does not suffer change—neither of man nor of the environments—but searches for the very ancient expectations of salvation in the cycle of destruction and re-creation. As such it has a very formative character and provides the cargo cult ideology with great energy. One has to concern oneself with their eschatology and consider it in order to grasp the cargo cults at their roots.

(d) Mental attitudes which border on the unusual occur in about one-fifth of all listed cults. It is often difficult to decide whether we deal here "only" with an extraordinary talent of imagination or with a psychopathological disposition. Some cases certainly present a pathological condition. It has been clearly shown that illness provided the impulse for trance and revelation with some visionaries, for example Moro. On the other hand it is absolutely certain that many leaders of cults are not at all affected in this way. Finally, the awkward question arises: what should be counted as normal and how far is man dependent and determined on external forces? Accepting the European system of values and the psychosomatic constitution of the average European as the relevant standard, insanity and mental disturbances would often be found in the western Pacific. However, most happenings will appear to be normal as long as we refer to what has life-sustaining value in Melanesia, is adjusted to the environment in that area, and corresponds to standards which govern society. Nevertheless even within this setting, a number of unusual aspects of behaviour become apparent which can only be described as a result of excessive sensitivity or disturbance of co-ordination. It is not new that the religious life is symptomatic of such morbid conditions. Within this frame of reference roles are created with which we identify to some extent subconsciously. The roles belong to the world. Occasionally however they are parts of a supernatural realm, where every identification will lead to an assumption of religious functions. In what ways such roles originate in certain frames of reference and with particular human beings is largely obscure. It is probably that they are formed by earlier experiences. They are accepted as normal as long as they correspond to experiences of the majority. They will be deemed exalted or foolish if beyond this limit. In times of cultural subversion and of mental insecurity a need frequently arises for advice and direction. In the trend of such expectations, prophecies are voiced by men whose power derives from a perception exceeding the limits of what is normal. Such men are more easily susceptible to a spiritual reality. Such human beings are mostly endowed with a psyche of abnormal structure. They may be distinguished by a more sensitive receptivity for divine guidance, they may simply exhibit a better-defined imagination or be considered by morbid disposition as ecstatics and psychopaths. This element must always be considered as an essential reason for the cargo cults.

(e) Another source of cultic activities may have its origin in bio–climatic circumstances.

It may appear at first unlikely that the weather has an influence on the political or religious configuration of a community. But we cannot overlook the convincing results of medical investigations which show that climatic conditions are not unimportant with regard to human feeling, belief, and are of fundamental significance to social life. M. Curry[40] has co-operated with meteorologists, chemists and physicians to examine the influence of the weather on human beings—with some surprising results. Curry recognized that different types of human beings react in definite ways to climate and weather. He divides them into *W* and *K* types. Consequently, a greater or smaller propensity towards religious and cultic activities may exist. Conditioned by the trend of the weather, the non-voluntary responses of individuals and of whole societies are influenced. The origin of cargo cults and other movements could also be explained bio–climatically if we were able to show that a certain type of human being is predominant in Melanesia, and that there indeed a corresponding climate is prevalent. Such ideas have so far remained alien to our ways of thought. All pertinent statements are only conjectures. But it is suggested that K-types incline towards formation of religious sects.

All leaders of cults known to the author personally or by repute have a strong tendency towards the K-type. According to M. Curry, the K-type predominates in tropical regions near the Equator since the K-type is better adapted to the atmosphere there due to its comparatively lower ozone content.

The very high waves of cultic excitement in Melanesia may be explained with comparative ease if we correctly may assume that the K-type is predominant. In any case future investigations should consider this aspect.

Catalysts of Cargo Cults

(a) It is usually maintained that contact with civilization has been the decisive catalyst. Such contact certainly plays an important part, but it is not the only catalyst. The law of physics, pressure produces counterpressure, is also true of psychology and sociology. The cargo cults are so complicated, however, that this reasoning alone does not suffice. Without doubt, the arrival of Europeans has upset the Melanesian thinking and loosened the whole net of cultural interdependence. Once the tribes had been relatively self-supporting; now their authority was weakened. The coherence of life directed by the myths was broken, an imbalance existed. The sensation of being suppressed created social pressure which found vent in cultic activities. No further explanations are required to show that tensions were unavoidable in a situation where the superiority of the Europeans and their comparatively inexhaustible wealth were visible everywhere. It is not at all surprising that such a feeling of inferiority, accompanied by economic emergencies as a result of failing crops, catastrophes and disease led to envy and attempts at satisfaction by substituting Utopian expectations of happiness. Unfortunate symptoms of transition occur frequently in the course of acculturation. This change of culture must not be evaluated as if a period of stagnation were superceded by one of movement. Rather, every culture is moving continuously and thus energy is released continuously, by which it is reshaped. B. Malinowski preferred to speak of transculturation.

(b) F.E. Williams was the first to point out that the new ideas of the leading men in the cargo cults mostly originated in the indigenous culture, and had to be assessed as cultural mutations. Even without an impulse from outside, metamorphoses of culture are possible. Indeed, again and again tendency to change within a culture is seen, for example with the followers of the Taro cult or in the environment of Paliau and in the Highlands of New Guinea. "People can become bearers of a culture . . . only if being is conceived as movement in a historical process."[41] Wherever such being had continued for extended periods we may find symptoms of fatigue. These are checked by attempts at cultural regeneration. In a state of languor each culture has the tendency to rebuild itself by an internal rejuvenation—unless it is ready to surrender to final extinction. At the time of first contact with Europeans, many communities in New Guinea showed signs of a loss of resilience and of a decline of viability of their culture.

Transformation of culture offers the only way of escape. Occasionally we find such boost by regeneration, for example with the Muyu, with Filo or in Namatanai, also later in a religious character with Upikno. Such mutations may follow established patterns as social innovations of cults. The fertility theme is often decisive. They may also result in cargo cults in which "a forward escape" into the modern world takes place. In every case the Melanesian stands on very ancient ground. To his consciousness of self it is merely a variation of an ancient theme. Only thus does he understand novelties which are imported from outside. In the Mimika district (East Irian Jaya) after the Second World War a legend was told which clearly illustrates this.[42]

The present day is for the Melanesian a confirmation of his ancient belief. Everything appears to him as a return and an interpretation of what has been and of what he might have expected. For him this is not a misunderstanding of an alien culture, but he comprehends the new only so far as his own past becomes a future possibility through it. By the acceptance of such traditions new cultic activities are often released which should transmit salvation.

(c) Apart from external and internal forces, other conditions can encourage or catalyse new cults. Existing cargo cults radiate beyond the narrow, tribal confines into neighbouring areas. For example the idea of a "Black King" is found at the Sepik River and in the district of Madang. There are also cross links for Mambu, Tagarab and many others. Labour in compounds has contributed much to the spread of the wealth of ideas in cargo cults. New ideas were often transmitted by conscious propaganda to the most distant corners. "Rights to a cult" were purchased literally and thus they were exported outside the limited areas of their origin, for example with Letub and the Vailala Madness. Thus it becomes understandable that many practices are technically similar to each other as infiltration and overlapping have occurred. The share which this propaganda has in releasing new cults is about 11 per cent. It is not yet sensational, but it has to be registered (see index 34, Appendix 6).

(d) Experiences of visions and ecstatic apparitions are of greater importance than the previously mentioned catalysts. But it is an exaggeration to maintain that an experience in a dream always marks the beginning of a cargo cult. This would strongly support the preconceived idea of the religious character of all cargo cults, which is not true. In reality, visions and ecstasies are the beginning of about one-third, i.e. of that third which has a spiritual-religious character.

A few thoughts should be devoted to the psychology of perception, especially the religious experience. How does an experience happen? Probably, according to Sunden:

> . . . one or several of our senses are stimulated and the corresponding nervous processes are explained and supplemented in a manner which is conditioned by the stimulating situation . . . Further, a readiness of the organism which is influenced by the stimulus is required, and essentially determines what originates from the stimulating influence in the consciousness of the experiencing subject.[43]

Instead of speaking of readiness we may speak of the frame of reference.

> Religious experiences are inconceivable without a frame of religious reference, without religious tradition, without myth and without rites.[44]

Therefore the given, mythical way of the Melanesian decides the content of his religious experience. Within the frame of reference peculiar to him, a cultist consistently lives by the tacit acceptance of definite roles. Visions are symptoms of the process of acceptance. All visions, dreams and perceptions, and hallucinations are not only a theoretical reflection of symptoms at the fringe of life, but mostly concern the centre of existence. They can be perceptions for which we cannot discern stimulating sources outside the experiencing organism. They can also be caused by external stimulation of definite sense organs while the impulses conducted to the brain are fitted into a wrong pattern as a result of a certain frame of reference and of an unusually high readiness for the acceptance of roles.[45] Experimental neurobiology has taught us that such superimposition of stimuli can be directed to create hallucinations. Sometimes this may be the result of brain injuries. With regard to the content of religious perceptions, the rule is valid that they are the richer and happen more frequently the more intensively the religious life is lived during the waking state. A dearth of visionary experiences may easily be the result of a lack of religious activities. Anyone who is busy with other things for sixteen hours every day and has only five minutes for religion cannot be expected to have a very full religious development. Visionary prophets of cults frequently present a saturated religiosity.

Another factor is often completely overlooked: the influence of drugs. The statistical figures in Appendix 6 are lacking somewhat in this respect. They show only 1 per cent. That is probably too low. The literary evidence is apparently incomplete, due to the ignorance of the observers and interpreters as drugs and toxins play a great part in the life of the Melanesians. J. Sterly provides an interesting account of this.[46] The kava drink, which is prepared from the roots of a shrub, is frequently used in eastern Melanesia to induce conditions of trance. The root of the wild ginger, which is also called kava in New Guinea, has the same effect. The bark substance massoi and cinnamon are also used to increase readiness for experiences. Above all, people all over Melanesia practise the chewing of betel nut. Without doubt this has a pleasurable effect. It is sometimes used to procure abortion. Used in excess it has catalytic functon. A number of plants and toadstools may be added, but there is little knowledge of this. What in Mexico is known as peyote (the top of the bud of a cactus) and what is called mescalin in European literature has no pharmacological significance in Melanesia. It might well become relevant in a humane, biological sense. Aldous Huxley has experimented with mescalin. He found that the verbal and conceptual frame of reference is eliminated by mescalin and everything is experienced visually. Religious experience in India confirms this. However, Huxley found something much more interesting. The chemical structures of mescalin and human adrenalin are very similar to each other. Adrenochrom, an oxide of adrenalin, can produce the same symptoms as mescalin. Perhaps each of us walks about and produces a substance which in small doses may cause severe changes in consciousness.

Adrenalin is excreted through fear. After the first adrenalin shock, frequently adrenochrom is formed which raises the so-called opportune hallucinations. This could mean that man is equipped with a hallucinatory protective mechanism in times of emergencies and crises.[47] This opens far-reaching perspectives for cargo cults in Melanesia. However an exact examination is impossible. It is only certain that drugs are used in more than 1 per cent of the cases (see index 27 in Appendix 6).

Little can be said about the validity of the visions thus stimulated. One can ascertain their genuineness. Their truth, however, has an individual and a collective aspect and nearly always escapes our assessment. The criteria are linked too closely with one's own frame of reference. But visions have to be seriously considered because they all have important consequences through their reaction upon the community.

(e) The Christian missionary message is the last catalyst to which special attention must be drawn. At times this message can produce a sense of inferiority. Christian Keysser writes about how often the catechumens called themselves "the most wicked of all human beings". Even today one still hears in every second gathering of the congregation: We are "rabis tru", we have been the scum of wickedness, we have remained the stepchildren of the Lord. God has blessed everybody with his goods. We have no share in it. All know more than we do. Why are only we so backward? This question is made even more poignant by some Biblical parables: At the great supper only "the better people" were invited at first. Only when these had declined was an offer made to the "cripples and lame ones". It is always asked: Why do you, missionaries, only now come to us? Why has the Lord forgotten us until now?

In addition, the Christian teaching is misunderstood. The Christian moral laws were often understood in a legalistic way and, as such, they were preached. They appeared a presumption to the pagan, ethical thinking, which was determined by different standards according to which polygamy, for example, was assumed to be necessary. In spite of the unprecedented liberation from the taboos of burdensome, tribal law, the message of the missionaries often did not appear to give joy to the whole being, nor to redeem it. Too often people saw only a change of labels.

The old customs were cruel, but they were useful to release emotional tensions. After they had been abolished, life became ordered and decent, but frequently a little sterile and boring too. The loss of the earlier joy of living was only compensated to a small extent by the singing of Christian hymns. It always remained obvious to the people that they could never equal the white men and that they had nothing of their own to counterbalance this. In the long run this could only lead to an increasing loss of self-respect. Counter-reactions have been induced in the South Pacific by this diminishing sense of one's own value which, to a certain degree, is the unavoidable result of any call to repentance. The preaching of the Christian message is not without fault here, or without responsibility.

4. Means of Movements

The remainder of the statistic evaluation can be dealt with briefly. Once the origin of the cargo cults is recognized, only a technical procedure is needed to establish their associated features. It is obvious that the applied means have to be pertinent to the mental and material world of the Melanesian people. Thus here nearly all that has been said about causes and catalysts is valid. There is a profusion of events (indices 46 to 78 in Appendix 6) which will be treated as a whole. The ratio of the three types of fundamental domains is pertinent. According to our expectation it is approximately 3:1:1. Using individual figures the ratio 216:82:95 is obtained for the magic, religious and social tendency. This may be classified as follows:

(a) Those features which aim at "abandonment of the ancient, cultural heritage". Here, everything that concerns sacrifice and destruction is relevant. The existing is always renounced to gain something in the future, be it the destruction of artefacts, the slaughter of a pig, the sacrifice of a human life. The desire for a transformation of the world and for an improved situation of man is at the bottom of it. Ancient taboos have been abolished for this reason, existing customs invalidated and, in emergencies, the people constrained by acts of terror for the sake of their own happiness. If the Melanesian, locally-determined features of such procedures are disregarded, a universal, human behaviour which is known in all civilizations will be left. The universal attraction by a world-changing ideology has only been dressed here in a magic attire and realized in cults.

(b) The imitation of new forms: the Melanesians would like to assimilate the techniques of the European world to profit from it. The digging of pits, the erection of warehouses, the building of model villages or the attempt to raise the economic production are all means to lift the standard of living. The adjustment to military organization, or the acceptance of a foreign language and religion, points to the fundamental yearning to share in the wealth of a previously foreign world.

(c) Another group of incidents is based upon pyschosomatically stimulated action. For this purpose, panic and mass psychosis, intentional sexualization of the cultic life and actual ecstasies with shaking of limbs and glossolalia are used. These are difficult to interpret. Applying the usual concepts of ecstasy, trance and dream do not explain the basically existential event. Speaking with tongues, xenoglossia and polyglossia are widespread in Melanesia. The interpretation of this phenomenon remains difficult. A special condition of "obscureness" is peculiar to all remaining esoteric intuitions of the Melanesians and to their visionary experiences. A purely medical explanation is too shallow.[48]

The three-fifths of the phenomena which belong to the magic complex are presented by (a), (b) and (c). On the other hand we have in (d) the primarily spiritual and in (e) the primarily social features.

(d) The ritual exertion of influence upon the invisible world or the occult establishment of contact with the ancestors belong to the most important elements of cargo cult practice. It is believed that the source of all good things is in the realm of the dead. The people hope to uncover the mysterious secrecy of a supra-terrestial world by festive meals and dancing, by gatherings in cemeteries and by prophecies or spreading of legends. Propaganda for cults and the training of disciples who may pass as the successors of the once so powerful shamans supplement these efforts to obtain mental power.

These events have parallels throughout the world. The demand for a spiritual conformity is found not only in the growing South American Umbanda and the African independent churches, but also in a turning towards the spiritual realm in the non-Christian high religions. A sizeable proportion of mystery is brought into everyday life by feasts and dances, by parades and worship of the stars even in secularized surroundings. What is near at hand does not apparently suffice any longer. One demands the power which is fed from mysterious sources.

(e) Nearly 25 per cent (*see* index 87 in Appendix 6) of all cargo cults act upon a very practical political level. The world is to be improved by the application of political and social programmes. In many cases national union of all involved cultists is a means to happiness. Rigid organization, purposeful spreading of the cargo cult ideology and rejection of colonial systems of taxation simultaneously foment hatred against all Europeans. Many Europeans saw this hatred as the essential feature of the cults. Thus any understanding was blocked. The dislike of Europeans is only one symptom. The natural urge of all people to be masters of their own destiny is the true reason. Salvation is inconceivable without a certain measure of freedom and self-respect. Disregard of this produces rejection and contempt with ever new frustrations. The means of the cargo cults are much determined by the respective level of culture. But essentially they are common property of all those who feel neglected.

5. Goals of Movements

The feeling of being at a disadvantage is the link which holds together the followers of Yali as well as the supporters of Tommy Kabu, who died in 1969. Irrespective of any other conformity, all cargo cults have the theme of injustice. All are concerned with a better and more just distribution of happiness. The status quo is not accepted as destiny, but is a challenge for a militant will for change. Three categories can be distinguished among the concepts of aims (indices 79 to 92).

(a) The unfavourable economic situation determines the demand for the blessing of material goods which therefore occupies most of the field. Wherever one looks one sees the wealth of others and would like to have one's share. This is understandable, and any rash denial of these desires is hypocrisy. Very few of the representatives of the white race are prepared to permanently exchange their lot with the Melanesian. What is fair to one man should be for another with regard to his desires and hopes. We would require a wealth of dialectics if we wanted to dispose of the achievements of modern civilization as unimportant and not to see the value of such achievements for which all are entitled to yearn.

(b) It has been stressed more than once that a yearning for redemption in its broadest sense had been associated with material desires. We are concerned here equally with liberation from distress and anguish; suppression and hunger; and with a peaceful life without war and violence. All restorative goals are intrinsically only restatements of the mythical, whole, original condition. Men aspire to the whole original being whether they speak of the end of the world, of natural catastrophes, of the resurrection of the dead or eschatological deliverance. Liberation from the bond of present burdens is even the aim when economical independence and political freedom are invisaged. Even tendencies to establish a new morality strive to relax existing tensions. In a world with so much hatred and fighting, without any security and peace because of ever spreading and destructive aggression, the wish for a blissful and peaceful existence becomes so strong that it occasionally breaks the conventional, cultural forms and creates a vent for itself by new cultic movements. The longing for a diminishing pressure pervades the whole world.

(c) To be acknowledged is the aim. This is clearly manifested in the desire to have white skin or to live in a state of racial equality. But, in addition, attempts at national unity and a balance of cultures testify to this hope. The cargo cults are by no means structured as primitively as it might initially appear, and a theology which excludes these political expectations in order to retire to intra-ecclesiastical and historical dogmata does not do justice to its claim to render visible the rule of eternity.

In Melanesia one does not speak much of hypothetical motivation of actions. One acts and, by living, demonstrates the reasons for one's actions without words. It happens repeatedly that, during the course of events, the targets are changed or adapted to renewed requirements. The fundamental direction, however, is always preserved. In the course of the Paliau movement, goals have been altered several times. But always the triad of material wealth, spiritual liberation and social status has been continued.

6. Results of Movements

Have the movements been worthwhile in any way? The answer, on balance, is predominantly negative according to the indices 93 to 100, in Appendix 6 which show the story of permanent misery. Nevertheless it is surprising that the unfortunate results are limited to a total of 70 per cent (depression forty-two, impoverishment seven and increasing aggression twenty-one). One might have expected that the cults, without exception, ended in a fiasco. Apparently this is not the case. The failures are countered by 35 per cent positive results. The proportion of 8 per cent for psychic stabilization is not very high. One may probably count such a stabilization, if it occurs, as the maximum profit from a change of culture. The increase in self-respect to

15 per cent signifies a strengthening of the community, and substantially supplements the positive side. The remaining results are modest. Yet the cultic explanations of salvation in the crossfire of new and old philosophies have not remained completely in vain. They have created space for greater freedom and for a discovery of self-identity. Upon the bridge between two different worlds, human beings have gained experience and thus have been enriched in spite of losses.

Prophecies are not fulfilled in reality. Most involved explanations are advanced to support a continued belief in them. Each new argument is more general than the preceding ones so that finally they become unprovable and irrefutable. This is common to all sects and religious communities. One may confidently "hibernate" only when one has expressed oneself in sufficiently general and unassailable terms so that everyone can affirm the concept. It is this procedure which makes the cargo cults sinister. They cease to exist as cults, but continue underground. An external failure is no evidence for the strength of internal power of resistance, or the lack of it.

Worsley, Hobsbawm, Lanternari and Mühlmann believe in a slow change of all millennialism into secular movements. They want to understand this change typologically and not necessarily chronologically. But it is also possible to defend the opinion that a much stronger inertia is effective, and that the ideology of the cargo cult withdraws underground after obvious failures unless decisive changes affect the mentality of the people concerned. The cargo cult indeed provides effective values through experiences. The failure of one cultic activity does not automatically imply the end of cultic experiences. Only a new formation of the field of experience can prevent new cultic activities.

INTERIM BALANCE

Analysis and evaluation of the statistics have confirmed a few suppositions. It has also been made obvious that in some areas a rethinking is required. What is peculiar to these new insights? What is specific to this knowledge? Which are the surprising results of this analysis? To begin with, six propositions should be borne in mind:

1. A well-considered classification of the now-available statements about the cargo cults is important. These phenomena are meaningful attempts within a given frame to cope with life. They should not be derided. Compassionate understanding for the difficult situation of the human beings concerned must be stressed.

2. The cargo cults are strongly pertinent to tradition and the causal significance of the past. There is a marked orientation towards the native, cultural heritage, contradicting any theory of interpretation with a view only to the future.

3. By classification of characteristics three fundamental types can be distinguished: the magico-mechanistic, the religious-spiritual, and the social-political type. This characterization does not imply that a cult is restricted to a single type. Rather it indicates the prevailing direction of the cult. Yet in view of the essential similarity of the movements, a cargo cult which is a monolithic block does not exist. A multiplicity of appearances which, however, exhibit kinship in the common desire for a better life is our concern.

4. The distribution of the cults clarifies the influence of the cultural relevance of geographic position. The continuity of a cult's development in a particularly large area is the result.

5. It is interesting that, in the Melanesian movements, the prophetic element is weaker than the organizational. The people concerned are led by strong personalities and much more rarely by charismatics, as for example those in Africa who establish smaller splinter movements.

6. Occurrences are dealt with which have parallels in other parts of the world:
   (a) A growing demand for reformation of the world;
   (b) Removal of injustice and reduction of pressure;
   (c) Longing for the numinous;
   (d) Above all, the demand for a restructured society and community.

The followers of cargo cults are our contemporaries, in spite of the diverse articulation of the cultic landscape. They are contained by the same social trend.

2

Reflections on Ways of Understanding Cargo Cults

RELIGIOUS CONTENT OF CULTS

Index 2 in Appendix 6 records that approximately one fifth of cargo cults is characterized by a religious tendency. It also shows that another fifth is certainly not guided by religious motivation. What does this mean for the remaining cases? Do they too have a religious ground? And how true is it that social reforms have religious beginnings? This question opens a wide field. Religious self-knowledge differs in individual cargo cults. Enlightenment in the history of religion is equally variable and many sided.[49]

The wish to achieve a happy life and wealth is the common denominator for all cargo cults. Magic means to this end are suggested everywhere in the South Pacific.

In Melanesia, religion is the belief in a cosmic order. This order has an empirical and a supra-empirical realm. Both are concerned with living together in society. The external form is always a fixed ritual. The internal goal is success in the visible life. One is only content when success, security and continuity are vouchsafed for existence. The ancient religions of the Melanesians were fundamentally systems in which the wealthy and powerful ruled. Accordingly, in the whole of the Pacific area, it was usually accepted that what a missionary possessed was as important as what he said. Communal living provided primarily the frame of reference for Melanesian religion. But it is necessary to harmonize the empirical–social sphere with the supra-empirical–spiritual sphere in order to maintain the cosmic order. Both are closely knit in practice for this very reason. Every religion, at its core, is anchored in society.

This broad definition relieves us of the necessity to keep the religious and the social apart. The real border does not lie between the religious and the social, but the social-religious expectations and technocratic-secular behaviour. The opposites are also called religious and secular. This is relevant to the cargo cult as well as to the Christian faith. A field of tension exists between the two poles in both cases (*see* Figure 7). Ideological and social focal points exist in the two polarized spheres. Their relative importance has to be determined in each individual case.

The aspect of a cargo cult will be strongly spiritual as long as the force of an ancient religion is effective; but a trend towards secular self-sufficiency begins to prevail as soon as this nourishing soil loses its strength. The religious drive of many cults therefore depends on the kind of spirituality that existed before contact with Christianity. It is possible that the religious dimensions dwindle when secularization progresses, but it will never completely vanish as long as man seeks for the meaning of life. A certain polarization will always have to be reckoned with even if emphases are somewhat displaced. For only this tension between social behaviour and the "trans-social" doubt, and questioning of this behaviour guarantees the continued existence of the community. The original theme of the cargo cult remains possibly unchanged. In both spheres we are concerned with salvation whether it is religious or secular.

But what is salvation and how can it be made real? How can salvation be related to human welfare? And what in particular does Christian salvation signify for the Melanesian, whose earlier religions had been so strongly determined by the striving for success, and to whom every religion had been realized so far in the formation of his visible life?

Is not a conflict unavoidable if it becomes obvious that happiness and salvation are not identical for the Christian faith? The question of salvation takes us into the centre of our subject.

EXPECTATION OF SALVATION

Salvation means liberation from misery, poverty, oppression and lack of meaning in life both of individuals and groups. Christians search for the true significance of temporal wellbeing and eternal salvation. Many Christians are convinced that the liberation of oppressed human beings is the general theme of the Gospels. The interpretation of this may be subject to new deliberations in every generation, and in every situation. Only practical results will decide the merit of religious statements and their veracity. The salvation of the individual is related to the realization of salvation in society. Christians believe that the beginning of the saving process is not within the power of man, but depends on

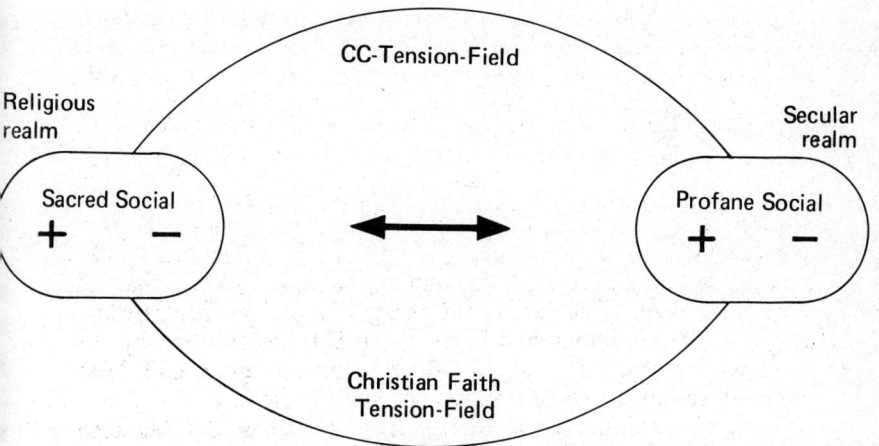

Fig. 7. Polarity of religious and secular forces

God, the central meaning, who gives direction. Missions must not disregard this centre. This has to be considered in conjunction with the needs of the Melanesians, who expect salvation to be realized as material goods on earth. Cargo cults strive to overcome the existing reality. They are unique and exist only in Melanesia, although a few have been transplanted from one district in Melanesia to another. But all spring from a similar heritage, and having their origin in the confrontation of the indigenous tradition with European civilization, manifest a variety of results.

INNER DRIVING FORCES OF CARGO CULTS

Problem of Understanding New Events

The sky is overcast. A plane takes off. It passes through clouds and mist until it reaches an altitude of 5,000 metres. The brilliant blue vault of the sky is above. The change of events can be explained realistically. But we frequently deceive ourselves. The passenger who did not watch the weather during the flight has three possible explanations: (a) The weather itself has changed. This corresponds to an evolutionary outlook. (b) The weather remained the same, but he himself changed his position. This is a result of a technical, rational attitude. (c) He can also, out of a naive sense of being alive, say the pilot has changed the weather in order to fly more easily. The fine weather had been the expression of the will and effort of the powerful pilot. There is a certain justification for this view since the pilot really has flown above the weather front. Yet this statement remains typical of the magical outlook on the world. In each of the three cases we are concerned with the understanding of the course of events. Each time preconceived ideas are brought to bear upon the problem.

A large part of the cargo cults' difficulties in coping with altered circumstances is the result of incorrect interpretation of facts. Understanding is a fundamental process which precedes all judgement and assessment. The phenomenon of understanding entails many steps. Human perception and comprehension are not as simple as registration of facts on film. A commentary and interpretation of the experience are always bound up in human comprehension. It would be naive realism to compare the activity of the brain with a photographic registration. Human perception only fixes partial aspects. Such abstracts are stored by memory and are supplemented by earlier experiences. Thus alone we can understand that perception or understanding is supplemented and interpreted.[50] This classification under an existing order is essential. In this process all irrelevant features are screened. The total reality is experienced only in parts. He who, for example, sees a colour or feels warmth rarely experiences the movement of electromagnetic waves or the rotation of molecules. This would presume the specially trained mind of the physicist and the use of appropriate equipment. Similar qualifications apply to religious experiences.

Religious tradition, and sometimes even ritual procedure, are required to enable us to recognize God's work in daily life. Reality is not limited to the foreground. It has several dimensions. To comprehend it we have to rely upon supplementation and interpretation of that which is experienced. It is self-evident that mistakes can occur. The chance of correct understanding is coupled with the possibility of misunderstanding. The list of characteristics in Appendix 6 shows that such mistakes account for roughly one-fifth of all cases and can be proven as such. But the understanding always depends upon the previous frames of reference, upon the attitude and the readiness to interpret the new through the old.

An example may clarify this: A teacher in Melanesia talks of the vocation of Peter as a "fisher of men". He explains this phrase. He describes how the fishermen catch fish and says that Peter should likewise gather men and lead them to God. Testing the class by questions he immediately receives the answer: "A fisher of men is a man who distributes fish amongst men". One can wonder at this nonsensical answer, but it is easily explained. According to the law of association of stimuli, the known and important word, fish, became the trigger. There was inner readiness for it. Further associations started from there and any further information remained concealed. The word fish became the subject, the next well-known word, man, consequently became the object. The result is inevitable: fish are brought to the men. Of course the original statement is distorted, but this often happens with Melanesians.

Van der Leeuw uses the word *epoché* in his explanations of the process of understanding.[51] By this he means the involvement of an event in its environment. Without the background of the contemporary history nothing can be grasped properly. It is an essential characteristic of the process of understanding that it presents a phenomenon only as something transparent.[52]

The result is that one and the same event is often understood
and judged differently. Continual openness and amendment are
necessary because the process of understanding may be likened
to an interplay between known and unknown entities, and
because the known ones always admit to an association with
similar entities. The foundation of all understanding is laid by
experience. Such experience, however, is already coupled with
an interpretation of what has been experienced. Several simultaneous experiences react upon the mind which has to digest them.
We are concerned with variable entities. They change as soon
as one touches them. This means that only when working with
them can one understand and develop such understanding. Mao
Tse Tung applied this to politics in Red China and he said: "If
you want knowledge, you must take part in the practice of
changing reality. If you want to know the taste of a pear, you
must change the pear by eating it yourself."[53] He alone who
plans change will have an opportunity for real understanding.
In Melanesia changing the picture of the world and the
Weltanschauung by continued efforts to learn will be unavoidable. But this requires some appropriate training which has
to be planned to broaden experiences.

In pedagogics, one speaks of islands of understanding which
are enlarged by systematic additions until bridges can be made
between individual islands. In the end, several islands will be
linked so closely together that they represent a new unit of
knowledge. In the beginning foreign elements are used only by
following the rules of earlier experience. What cannot be fitted
in is repelled. Only that which finds an island of understanding
of an equal structure is absorbed. The more such islands are
available, the more new elements can be joined to them. It
should therefore be the aim to spread the net of understanding.
Such considerations have to be applied by the missionary.

Relationships of Dependence

A number of contingencies complicate the problem of cargo
cults. On the one hand there are the forces of ancient culture
which react with each other, and on the other, the influences
of modern civilization, which mould life and hopes. External and
effective forces are:
1. The cultural fluctuations in the pre-European time
2. The contacts of civilizations since the beginning of the
   colonial period
3. The Christian Gospel with its content of demands and
   promises

4. The structural consequences of the process of formal Christianizing

Then there are the internal, driving forces:

1. The geographic-climatic conditions
2. The old economic system
3. The political power structures of the different tribes
4. Social orders and lists of values coupled with them
5. The traditional picture of the world which is mediated by religion and manifest in myth.

Nearly all of these forces may be correlated with others. This yields an extremely confusing pattern of interdependence which no longer allows simple conclusions (*see* Appendix 1).

The mythology, as the collective vessel and starting point for the tradition, must be treated separately. A myth often became the seed for crystallizing a cult. It is certain that at all times mythology exerted decisive influence on the content and form of cargo cult ideology. The mythical is still governing the mind of many Melanesians and influencing their understanding of the world. Therefore the birth of new cults is not surprising. Such new beginnings are a consequence of mythical thinking. The more alive the tradition of a mythos, the more easily cultic practices crystallize around it. Conversely, the practices become ever more intelligible the move clearly a particular myth can be discerned in the background, i.e. in the context of the total number of myths which play an important part beside the formal coherence of a story and its unity.

In principle, all myths pursue similar ends. It is their task to answer enigmas of life and to show paths for coping with life. They are aetiologies which explain the happenings in the environment. They also offer a proof for the identity of man; that is, they tell him who he is and what his purpose in life is. And finally they provide the standards of behaviour for the social field of a particular group. Nearly without exception, they are concerned with origin, destiny and conduct. Conceptions of hierarchies of gods are largely alien to the Melanesians. For that reason their mythology is even more earthbound. Certain types and themes always reappear. The flood, the cycle of birth and death, the exertions to influence fertility, the remembrance of an offended innovator of culture, and above all, the dark and mysterious departure of a prehistoric saviour whose return is expected in periods of emergency. The individual sagas often contain wishful thinking which compensates for a disagreeable present. What is true for the function of the ritual is equally valid for the mythos which alone had made the ritual possible.

Both should counterbalance the helplessness of the individual in life's crises. The mythos helps to manage life. Thus it is the foundation of all religions.

Some aspects which, of course, do not have equally strong bearing upon all myths are of special significance for cargo cult ideology. This is shown in the following:

1. The division of humanity. This is pertinent to the difference between races.
2. The two hostile brothers. This relates to the reasons for colonial oppression and the lack of many goods.
3. The lost paradise. It is an attempt to find reasons for the present isolation and emergency.
4. The arrival of a final time. This betrays the wish for world change.
5. The delivery or recovery of the goods of salvation, whatever they may be. This shows the elemental demand to overcome all emergencies.

The traditional wealth of myths is unexpectedly projected into the present time and interpreted from this vantage point. This entails the loss of a real understanding of the world.

Secularization as a Means to Understanding the World

The cargo ideology has its roots in a magic-mythical explanation of the world. The extreme opposite is a purely secular interpretation of the world as it has evolved in the process of secularization. One has to talk of this counter-position if one wants to outline the chances of overcoming the cargo cults. The assessment of secularization in the Christian camp, however, is not at all uniformly achieved. Terms must be defined.

The following must be kept in mind:

(a) Secularization signifies the transfer of political responsibility from the hands of the church dignitaries to the civil realm. It is an historic process.

(b) "Secularism" is the name of an ideology, a modern and complete *Weltanschauung* which is most effective as a kind of new religion.[54] It is based on the opinion that man is fully autonomous, that the world is subject to human reason ·alone and its realm of responsibility, and that any salvation depends upon man's consent. Here any divine reference has been abolished and in the sense of all "isms" a new and absolutely obligatory system has been established. H. Zahrnt agrees with Gogarten that we may speak of a "degeneration of secularization". This secularization is our real concern here.

(c) The growth of secularization had its beginnings in the Christian faith. It is the evolution which led from a mythical imprisonment of the mind to the freedom of thought and action. "God delivers us from the hands of the gods . . . God has removed the gods from the world", C.F. von Weizäcker writes concisely. It is correct that this removal of gods from the world has an ambivalent character at all times. It remains tied to its Biblical roots and has its origin in them, which must not be overlooked even if the banishment of gods may be used as an independent concept thus losing its Christian meaning and asserting itself as its own message of salvation as part of a different, non-Christian ideology. Nevertheless, its origin in Biblical ideas must not be overlooked. According to the creative and cultural mandate of Genesis I, 28, man has obtained a new relationship with the world. He has become independent with regard to it. Thus the doors were finally thrown open to all modern technology and science. The consequence of the removal of gods from the world in a sense also became the humanity of man. Only where the world becomes the object can man work upon it. Thus history is made possible. Man is able to be himself and to recognize the difference between created nature and creative technology only by his liberation from the mythic, cosmic limitations, the liberation from religious powers. This evolution by no means cancels the bond between God and man. Yet this often did happen as the result of false development. The Christian preaching is not quite blameless in this respect.

Early Christians did not consider biblical thoughts such as those expressed in Genesis I.28: "multiply, and replenish the earth, and subdue it . . . ", they were preoccupied with eschatology. But Christian teaching has changed. We discover the beginning of the epoch-making delivery of the world from magic and belief in magic. H. Cox, somewhat too pointedly yet correctly, calls the record of the creation a kind of "atheistic propaganda". There is no room left to make nature divine. Pre-secular man lives in a realm which is full of ghosts and demons, of fatal powers and anxiety. Magic thought accepts the world as a partner. Using its secret forces adroitly, one can protect oneself against other powers. Sorcery is the means to conquer the world. Sorcery is the tool of pre-secular man. All is alive to him. All religions at a higher or at a lower level participate in the magic unity of this view of the world.

In secular thought, however, the world becomes the object. Natural forces which had been described and related to cosmology by myths are deprived of their power to hold man as if under a spell. The world begins to become subject to the creative power of man. It must be emphasized that, in spite of the deliverance from the fetters of a personal dependence upon nature, man can very well remain oriented toward Christ. It is surely significant that the introduction of modern techniques alone does not suffice to solve the growing problems of the so-called developing countries. As long as the thinking is pre-secular, that is, determined by magic or myth, the modern equipment of Western technology will only be fitted into the given structure of the ancient *Weltanschauung* and accepted as a modern magic. This is very obvious with the cargo cults. A more real view can take its place when a readiness for an intellectual conversion is present. This often presumes a degradation of the traditional religion—and also of an uncritical, Christian religiosity. That is the price for the new knowledge of the world, which affects everybody. The advantage of a new understanding always signifies the loss of an idea to which one had become accustomed. The Christian missions have undermined the premises of magic thinking in Melanesia to a considerable extent. Thus many religious hindrances against factual understanding of the world have vanished. Yet many barriers still exist. This is partially due to the power of persistence of the tradition, but may also be a consequence of the fact that the Gospel had not been preached radically enough at times and that the sermons themselves had not been free from a pre-secular comprehension. The secularization was too new a concept and had not yet been established as a necessity. It is not surprising that a defence against this process of secularization was often attempted.

We can only agree with H. Zahrnt:

> If the process of secularization in modern times, directly or indirectly, has its roots in the Christian faith, it is meaningless to call for the "pure gospel" to ward off its consequences. Thus one would only summon the power which had set this process in motion . . . In fact one does not mean the gospel at all but the law: One would love to give the world a . . . religious constitution and thus repeat even if subconsciously the ancient mythical world in a Christian fashion.[55]

The liberating message of the worldliness of the world will be owed to man as long as Christian missions, out of an inner conviction, favour a pre-secular concept. Equally, the road will be barred to independent, creative, human action which is oriented towards Christ, as long as the cargo cults remain unassailable and unavoidable. We ought to provide a testimony for a secular foundation of our relationship with God so that the Melanesians can discern that the gospel gives evidence for secular thought, for secular life before God, and for a secular, that is, not only ideal religious purpose of being.

The decision as to whether Christians want to affirm secularization has been made, and indeed they are now in this process which has liberated both destructive and creative possibilities. It is up to us to "use it in freedom and with courage".[56] Cargo cults exist in Melanesia only because secularization has not yet gained decisive influence. The absence of cargo cults among the Maoris of neighbouring New Zealand is certainly partially due to the fact that people have been living there in a relatively secular area for some time. The process of secularization demythologizes cosmology and thus it liberates life from rigid laws which are based upon speculation and metaphysics derived from myths. That is worth welcoming. This liberation has not necessarily made people free everywhere. A vacuum has arisen for many which was filled by "new gods". Interest, therefore, has to remain centred much more firmly in Christ, "the great secular man".[57] This becomes more important the more the previous religious obligations lose their strength so that deliverance from metaphysics does not result in a total isolation and in a mortal severance from the life-giving power of the creator. Only thus a meaningful way forwards can be shown to the followers of the cargo movements. They cannot avoid secularization either. The question is whether they will use the opportunities which are made available. At the same time, this is also a task for the church mission. The church should endeavour to make people aware of eternity in their daily experience.

APPEAL TO THE CHRISTIAN CHURCH

The Work and the Missions

The different Christian churches and their missions are faced with the ecumenical challenge to co-operate. This is an internal problem. It is complicated by the different cultural background of the missionaries. The tasks they have to perform have organizational, practical, educational and theological aspects. In 1965 the Melanesian Council of Churches was founded. But organizational solutions provide only an instrument for the real job, the creation of an independent, indigenous, Christian church.

The Mission and Belief in Progress

In discussing a theological and fundamental attitude, the difference between progress and the belief in progress has to be distinguished. What is progress? Are automobiles part of it, saving endless and arduous walking? Is it relevant that one can take a cool fruit drink out of the refrigerator in the heat of the tropics? Or is it an essential feature that one is able to alleviate the pain of a seriously ill person with medicines? If the latter belongs to progress—and that cannot be denied—who would be against it? We all live by this progress and we are not living too badly either. The word "progress" corresponds to the Biblical "growth" and "increase". The Biblical term refers of course to the advance of the gifts of God. But we do not take that to be only the gift of a spiritual faith which puts asunder a spiritual and bodily being of man. It always concerns the whole man in whom God lets knowledge, grace and faith grow. Therefore it is said in Colossians II.19. "the whole body . . . can reach its full growth in God." Or Ephesians II.21. "all grow into one holy temple".

Electric light and antiseptic bandaids are fruits of human progress which has been initiated and catalyzed by the message of the Bible, even if the Church did not always force it ahead. Certainly we should be grateful for progress. It is not a blind cultural optimism if we make such a statement to begin with. A devaluation of progress is not yet a sign of a special piety.

It is surely equally certain that all progress has two faces and can become the object of idolatry. Whatever progress takes place serves at its best a temporal, limited welfare in a transitory world; that is its contribution to the historical evolution of mankind. This is its great significance. If we expect more from it we may flounder in our *Weltanschauung* as in the currents of a fast river. The development itself does not cause us to pause, but rather the conception of the goal which is often coupled with a naive belief in progress. We forget that history can proceed in leaps if we think that that which is coming is always automatically better. Emil Brunner and Paul Tillich, at the end of the First World War, articulated this insight on behalf of many. Following their historical optimism, they were made aware of a negative experience with regard to progress, and they subsequently spoke of the crisis which always lies hidden in history. Our situation is strange insofar as we have to be careful in two respects when we are concerned with progress: in an ecclesiastic–pessimistic and in a secular–optimistic regard. The church often underestimates the possibilities of progress. We like to speak thus of the curse of technology and of an ideology which tempts us by its blandishments. On the other hand, in a secular sphere many talk with great naivety of the blessings of progress.

Such an optimistic attitude, of course, meets the hopes of the followers of cargo cults. It promises the happiness for which one is longing. Therefore assistance in development will often be accepted as practical help, which becomes the work of the missions. Service or practical charity seems to overtake the mission. That of course is nothing new. Towards the end of the nineteenth century, missionaries of the London Missionary Society got ready for their departure to the South Seas. At their farewell service, they were told that their highest aim was to make fertile fields on these islands, fine dwellings, schools and churches, and to raise all the people to a higher level of Christian civilization.[58] The Europeans have long been aware of their vocation, and have been anxious to meet the challenge of organizing new community life. We understand therefore why the seventh thesis of the Frankfurt Declaration with regard to the crisis of the foundation of the missions cautions us against "identification of progress, development and social change with the messianic salvation". In fact, it is as H. Bürkle writes: "There is an immediate impact of technical achievements and progress of civilization upon Africans and Asians which bewilders these people by utopian horizons of expectations."[59] All unreflecting belief in progress may lead to fateful activity just because the expectations are utopian or essentially unrealizable. In the course of secular development belief in progress is closely linked with salvation. But technical assistance and machines alone cannot satisfy all psychological needs. Salvation encompasses a spiritual element. Salvation is not fulfilled by progress, but it includes progress and it works in harmony with human possibilities. Belief in progress is a challenge to the Christian mission. It draws the mission's attention again to the dimensions of its own task and at the same time compels it to be unremittingly concerned with the concrete needs of the world. Thus we are obliged to study history and the history of salvation.

The concept of a world which has its roots in the life of a peasant society is vanishing in Melanesia. Technological ideas have become predominant, taken its place, and they create a new vitality. This change is evidence of the transience of the world. The synthesis of diverging tendencies depends upon successful attempts to gain a better understanding of the nature of things. Fruitless controversies between believers in reason and progress and those who seek support in tradition and piety will become meaningless as soon as progress is no longer restricted to technology alone, but stimulates a growing understanding of intellectual and spiritual processes. Then progress becomes genuine progress. Then the mission will have its proper importance as a critical court which testifies to the work of God and thus prepares the ground to deal objectively with the world.

The Mission and Education

Tractors do not heal the world, but today a whole world cannot be conceived without tractors. In order to understand the world in which we live we have to know it. Knowledge of reality is obtained by a process of civilization and education. Using Heidegger's concept we may say that culture is an existential of man. Life is lived while it is recreated. Thus life is guided at the same time. Can we influence the cargo cult ideology by culture and education, and can we thus prevent a wrong development? If culture and education are means to guide individual and social development then they should also be helpful in influencing thinking in the cargo cult movements. Sometimes this is denied. One argues that our rational–causal thinking cannot overcome magical thinking, since a religious background cannot be overcome by knowledge and reason. One is astonished by the incredible stories which were spread by a visitor to Germany after his return to his island country in 1968, and one likes to remember that undersecretary of the Treasury in New Guinea government who had seen a mint in Australia and had arrived at the conclusion: "All we need is such a machine with which we can make our own money. Then we can easily overcome all the other difficulties." Such arguments do not prove much. At the most they are a sign that education is lacking. At one time all education helped the survival of the tribe and the preservation of its viability. It was never designed for a single individual, but always referred to the well-being and health of the community. The European educational system, however, was always mistaken in assuming that something substantial had been accomplished when a man had gained self-knowledge. Thus only a kind of half-education was provided which neglected the most important thing, that is direction towards a whole, integrated society. Misunderstandings are most frequent and serious where very little genuine education is evident.

Basically, the work of the mission could not make amends for this failure since the Christian schools were mainly used as instruments for the spreading of the Gospel. This was often inevitable, but at the same time it made it impossible to provide a factual and thorough explanation of the world. Today we understand that a well-meant training and teaching of the catechism alone is insufficient to answer, for example, questions concerning space travel. Letters from readers to the editors of church magazines make it only too clear that, even after eighty years, the foundation for an understanding of the modern world is frighteningly meagre. Without timetables and physics one cannot find one's place today. Not too much, but too little education has been provided, to date [1970] only 0.2 per cent of all students having reached an "acceptable level in the secondary schools". It is striking that this thin layer is indeed immune to cargo cults. Insight into reality protects them from Utopias. Not more than a few exotic impressions should be expected from visits abroad by Melanesians. They return like a European from a photo-safari in Africa: stuffed with pictures and yet lacking any comprehension of the background of such a strange world.

There is a need for well-planned, thorough and ruthlessly objective, educational efforts which try to awaken a sense of self-criticism. These attempts will remain quite problematic for the time being. The widening horizon will create more tangible desires and needs. The rate of change will be accelerated. Racial questions will gain more prominence. But there will also be barriers against Utopias which had been fostered by cults. Education is not a universal remedy. It cannot realize the salvation of God any more than secularism can. But while saving from false expectations it can lead people to practical tasks. It can make significant enquiries into confusing details of religious experiences, and thus it can avoid follies and lead towards responsible actions. What happens in the cargo cults is no mystery. It remains comprehensible in spite of confusion. One can therefore help with knowledge. Knowledge is the fruit of education. And education is accomplished by the pursuit of concrete educational tasks. Pedagogical research has established a few maxims for this purpose, which can be applied to the cargo cult situation.[60] Accordingly, the tasks of Christian education are:

1. The development of a sense of history
2. The acquisition of the ability to interpret common experiences
3. The transition from magic concepts to a life by faith
4. Avoidance of moralizing. Growth towards the recognition of the forgiveness of sins

5. The development of a Biblical view of God which replaces images determined by tradition.

Success of such an educational programme removes support from the cargo cult ideology. These educational tasks will open doors. Education is not the only means in the struggle for the better understanding of the world, but it will always be an important instrument. This work will have to rely on hope and it will never be finished.

Hope—the Motor in Living Our Lives

Hope points towards the purpose of life and to eternity. It affects the present while building a bridge to that which is beyond time. It orders the quality of our life and determines the future. If we talk of hope or future we always think of more than the sum of individual expectations. That our life is measured by our hope can be shown parabolically in Maxim Gorki's story "Night Asylum".

A life without any hope is hard to endure. Much has been written about this during the last few years. It cannot be dealt with here in depth, but a few thoughts suggest a synthesis between the main opinions. In the present argument we are concerned with two completely divergent approaches.

One of them presumes that hope fundamentally determines the structure of a man's existence. The second describes hope as the intuition into the possibilities of the evolutionarily conditioned future. In Figure 8 I call the first attempt the approach of the humanities and the second that of the natural sciences. The central question with each problem involving hope is the enquiry after the source of energy by which hope is maintained. Only if we know the driving "motor" can we understand the concept of a goal. It is obvious that the cargo cults are also permeated by hope. Yet what is the foundation of this hope? How does it correspond to thought concerning hope outside Melanesia? How do we interpret it?

With reference to the two Western hypotheses:

(a) In the first cycle the motor is seen as the *conditio humana*. We begin with the discrepancy between the joyful feeling of the world as being free and the burdening feeling of the world as being strange. We recognize ourselves as beings who live between opportunity and danger. This experience of "having no world" leads to loss of direction. Man is really the only living being suited for every kind of environment and therefore for none in particular. He is adaptable and able to develop. But that makes

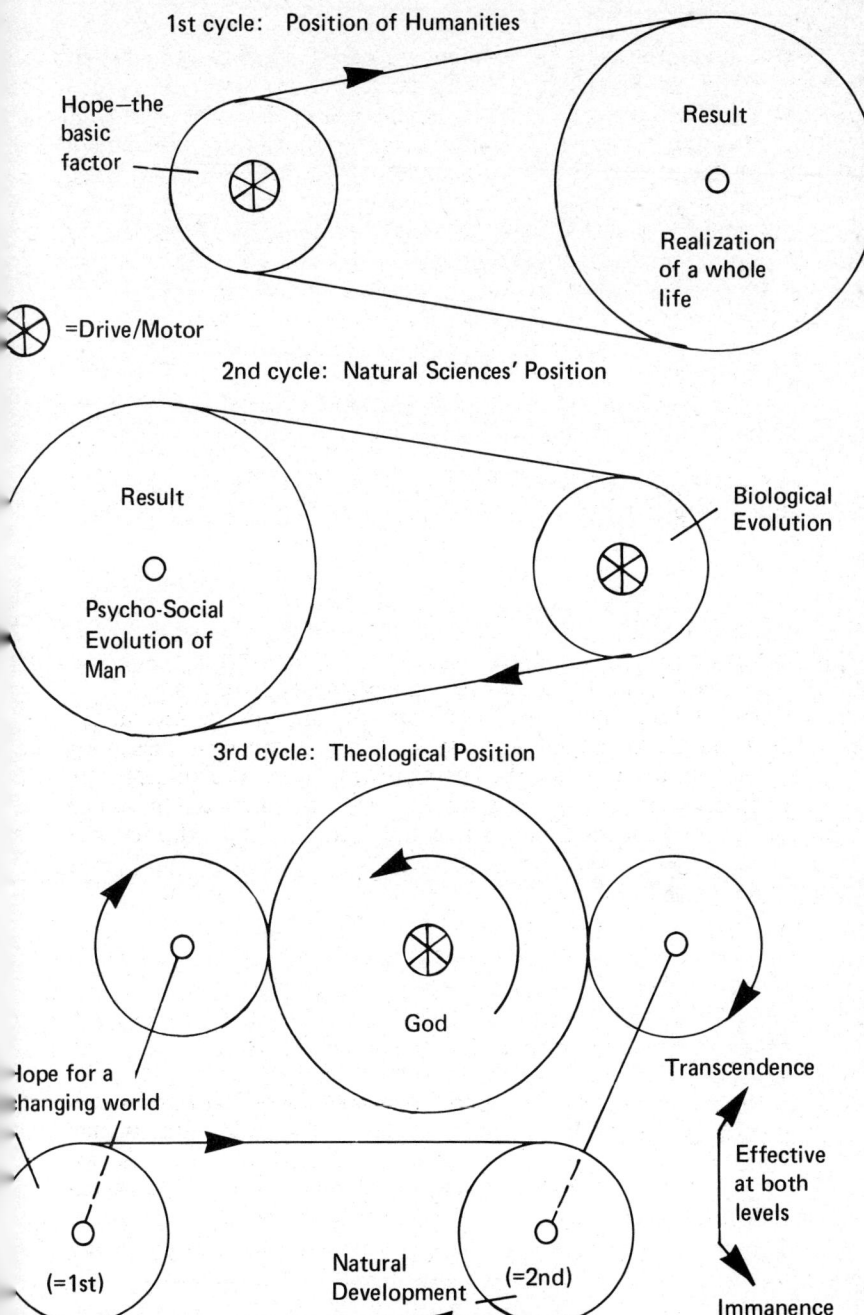

Fig. 8. Three fundamental cycles of thought nurtured by hope

him "homeless" as well and compels him perpetually to reshape his world. In the end, all that becomes part of religion or culture is the result of such striving for a home. The demand for it or the imagination with which he supplements the fragmentary world drives man to hope. The hope for the ability to make perfect what is imperfect now provides him with a life which is directed towards a goal. Even if there were nothing real to hope for, he would remain in principle open to what is ahead of him. He requires hope to be able to live and to stand up to life's threats. Man himself is hope. He lives, always taking into account the not-yet-available. This defines the motor which drives the hope for a concrete reshaping of the future. The aim is to bridge anxiety and longing. Salvation is seen as the result of the realization of self-identity and of the continued renewal of life. A happier future will release ever new opportunities for expanding the self which again will instigate hope and supply fresh impulses to it.[61]

(b) The theory of evolution is made the unifying principle. The force of biological evolution is the higher one and it ranges above hope. Hope becomes only a by-product of the evolutionary process. In it man is promoted into the spiritual centre. Tensions can be overcome when we accept what is biologically legitimate and consciously influence it. Man becomes determinable because he can be manipulated. This attempt suggests that biological evolution is the driving force of hope. It can be said that man has hope in so far as he knows the evolutionary processes and understands them to be the force which gives him direction. He has only to translate these judgements into a universal pattern of thought in order to produce subsequently a psycho-social improvement of man. Once that level has been reached evolution can be increasingly boosted by didactic methods, by genetic interference and eugenic programmes. Hope becomes buoyant since even if the goal has been marked in the far distance it has been placed visible before the eyes. As Julian Huxley points out, it is the strongly effective, ideal world in which all wishes of the society can be fulfilled. This vision refers to the perfect man, the "new Prometheus". It is almost a variety of the paradisaic future which one expects in the cargo cults.[62]

(c) In the cargo cults of the South Seas one knows, in principle, the same two patterns of hope. It is their very problem that on one side a conscious will is active to shape the environments, while on the other perpetual doubt and anxiety and the potential meaninglessness of all enterprise cripple the strength. Their expectations oscillate between fear and hope.

Their reflections on hope naturally are not quite so intellectually articulated. Nevertheless the first cycle is mirrored in their all-powerful wishful thinking while the second conception becomes manifest in the magic practices and manipulations of the Melanesians. The first is the essential destiny of the human being, the intrinsic inevitability to question, to search and to hope. The second is his attempt to shape and alter the world according to his will by staking all means available to him.

(d) How can these diverging concepts be reconciled? Both patterns relate to a part of reality and have a certain justification. This is true too with regard to the cargo cults. Both suffer, however, from their inability to do justice to each other, because each presumes the exclusiveness of its own motive. It can be assumed that both are correct, but at the same time that it is impossible to place the driving force for hope on either side. The motor has to be outside both systems, that is we cannot but consider transcendence. Obviously, biological evolution as well as the basic, intellectual determination of man is guided by a superimposed "steering mechanism".[63] It is a confession of faith that we are here concerned with God of the Bible. His will makes human action possible. His planning stimulates the inner hope. On the plane of immanence both patterns are of equal value and interwoven. All hope has its origin in God who provides the means to live and who determines the needs of mankind. This is made manifest in the unfolding of historical events and in the dimension of divine revelation. Guidance is always behind it whether it is visible or not, since the driving force emanates from the centre of the transcendence.

This knowledge has eminent significance for the reality of the cargo cults. It does away with the compulsion to create salvation oneself and reveals at the same time the freedom to participate in the realization of a whole world. It makes room for responsible shaping of the world and prevents us from becoming a prey to blind mechanisms of salvation. It allows the world to be improved with all available strength and quickens awareness of the impossibility of creating paradise on earth.

The ideology of cargo cults can be overcome only by a hope which is greater than it and which transcends it. This wider hope takes shape in the Christian faith. Due to the limitations of human thought all endeavours to achieve salvation will remain inconsistent with human life as long as only human expectations and technical problems concerning the transformation of the world dominate and guide human activities. The eye is then directed at the novum of salvation in the New Creation of God alone, when it becomes known that the driving force comes from outside. The new variety of salvation, its being of a new kind, has been shown to us by Christ. It gives liberty from a utopian, mechanistic narrowness of expectation of salvation. This will be especially true for the cargo cults. The historical action of Christ, on the other hand, opens the way for a broadening of the human, creative powers and directs it towards salvation.

Earthly salvation will probably remain only a shadow of eternal salvation. It is therefore more than temporal welfare, but also less than the last fulfilment. By our very hope we participate in the salvation of God.

Summary and Conclusions

The knowledge gained from the presented material may be reviewed in three steps and formulated by the following statements. First the essence of the cargo cults is examined (1 to 8), and then the problems which they raise (9 to 11) and finally we seek the direction in which overcoming the cults appears to be possible (12 to 16).

1. The cargo cult does not exist. There are only cargo cults in a multiplicity of diverging phenomena. In a wide spread of variations, we find various movements about which generalizations cannot be made.
2. Cargo ideology as a background is more important and significant than individual, cultic actions. It determines thinking, feeling and action of the people concerned, even when they keep apart consciously from a specific cult.
3. There is concern for gain of material goods, but also for happiness in the widest sense. This implies an integrated order of the world, giving sense to being and the conquest of all oppressions of the body, the intellect, society, and religion. Cargo is the symbol for the expectation of salvation and it has to be treated seriously for that reason.
4. We are dealing with the Melanesian form of a worldwide development which aims at the enhancement of life. The peculiar aspect of the cargo cults is their turning to the past to find support for their ideas. An unhappy synthesis between magic-mythical thinking and elements of modern civilization is the result which leads towards Utopias.
5. The cargo cults are socio-religious phenomena which sometimes show a trend towards secular-technocratical stages in the end. The extent of such development varies from case to case. The particular cultic past always determines the

expectations and the religious content. In the past, however, there was no separation of social from religious life. They are determining elements of an unceasing cultural movement and thus they are only indirectly dependent upon the invasion of foreign cultures.

6. Under given circumstances, their formation seems unavoidable since the will for change in times of crises has to find a form of expression in order to be able to articulate itself. Cults are acted out in a necessary, transitional period of cultural development and they require as wide a field of experimentation as possible to mature their processes of learning.

7. Their positive function is the subdual of a threatening feeling of inferiority, which shows itself:

   (a) by increasing self-identification in face of foreign influences;

   (b) by strengthening self-respect and establishing physical equilibrium;

   (c) by preserving national traditions;

   (d) by creating a training field for a modern style of life;

   (e) by an attempt to unite different national groups and by increasing political awareness;

   (f) by efforts to interest foreigners in their emergency;

   (g) by forcing government and churches to provide concrete assistance, for example building of roads, economic assistance, in the field of education; or by a useful proclamation of religious salvation.

The practice of hope is of special value. Hope releases energies to cope with life and a satisfaction is achieved which is subjective, but which fills the spiritual needs. The cargo cult diminishes frustration through the constant regeneration of hope even if this hope gradually grows weaker.[64]

8. The cargo cult ideology is also hostile to progress and destructive since it is oriented backwards and, due to its domination by magic-mythical, obsessive concepts, it is not free for an objective concept of the world. Thus it stands in its own way and hinders the recognition of reality.

9. The potential to grow in knowledge and to mature depends upon the freedom to change the traditional ways of thinking. A cult may just become extinct. A genuine education, however, is required to replace or transcend it by a new force from within the cult. A mere increase of factual knowledge does not suffice. Yet it is uncertain whether such a development will take place within a broad section of the population in the near future.

10. The answer to the enquiry after truth has to suit the enquirer's power of comprehension. As long as we look at the world as divided into matter and spirit we shall see the cargo cults only as unsuccessful attempts to find meaning. Stressing the wholeness of life we shall recognize cargo cults as legitimate endeavours to improve life. From this point of view they are justified and consistent with their purpose. Frequently however dubious and untrue elements are added when they are active.

11. The influence of Christianity is often manifest. Yet on the whole its force does not make a deep impression or really penetrate. Many cargo cults are rather pre-Christian than post-Christian phenomena. The encounter with Christ as the renewer of human thinking lies still largely in the future. Here is the great opportunity for the mission. There, too, is the opportunity for the people.

12. A battle has to be fought to remove the mental isolation and to find access to the Biblical offer of salvation.

13. Success cannot be achieved by punitive measures, shutting one's eyes in condescension, or moral proscription, but only by readiness to understand and by serious consideration of the interests of all. This presupposes looking ahead and learning from one another in order to gain a wider horizon.

14. There is no escape from the stagnation of cultic thought without the readiness for a new orientation. Working as deputies or assistants of Europeans is not sufficient. It is necessary that Melanesians consciously develop an indigenous, Christian theology. Not much of that can be noticed so far.

15. The required reversal of polarization in thinking should be expressed in three directions:
    (a) in an active approach to life in the sense of a Biblical–secular progression;
    (b) in asking the question, "What is God's will?" while stifling the question, "What is useful for me?"
    (c) in a preparedness to suffer in the service to one's neighbour.

16. The Biblical proclamation has to outline a factual, eschatological concept which presents a comprehensible offer of salvation encompassing social welfare.

3

Practical Conclusions

Record of What Has Been Done So Far

It is regrettable that the author is not in a position to present accounts of great success. Embarrassment is rather the hallmark of all pertinent discussions. Certainly much has been tried, but nobody has the temerity here to speak really of achievements.

Even today the church practises ecclesiastical, disciplinary measures; for example celebration of baptism is deferred and communion services are withheld to make room for pastoral talks. But because of unfavourable personal relationships and the alienation of many people from the churches, only a few expect much from such practice and their number diminishes. More and more the present educational programmes appear to be unsatisfactory. They provide a formal knowledge and they only rarely achieve an intellectual mastering of the real problems of a *Weltanschauung*. What has been accomplished so far by *Action for Development* is of great value. Technical help is accepted, but it is seen only as the result of a power-charged ideology. Namasu (Native Marketing and Supply) has gained a good reputation in New Guinea.[65] Its purpose is to help in a practical way by stimulation of economic activity. It has widespread success. But even here it seems inevitable that again and again magic miscomprehensions creep in. Technical, agricultural and business colleges lay the foundation for the knowledge of rational contexts. Agencies of church and government act with keen interest and achieve much good. The results, however, often remain somewhat elusive. One instance only is reported of a modest attempt in a limited field to create insight into the production process of breeding sheep and the manufacture of woollen wares by the inhabitants of Tarabo and Goroka. Nothing of worldwide significance happens here. But there is the justified hope that many such enterprises may slowly alter the horizon of expectations.

Within the church, in 1964, Lutherans of the Finschhafen

area worked out a confessional formula which was intended as a help for the pastoral services.[66]

The declaration contains valuable beginnings for an indigenous theology. But on the other hand, it is still too narrow and includes some material which is not correct. For example not every dream is "a deception by Satan" as is said there. Also there are goods which come from the inside of a mountain. The present working of the copper mines on Bougainville or the recovery of gold in Wau simply disprove the fourth thesis. Yet these are all milestones on the road into the future. But there is much room left for the development of an indigenous theology in Melanesia.

PROGRAMME FOR FUTURE WORK

The Call for Solidarity

Mrs R. Finney, an American anthropologist, has carried out an interesting investigation into the attitude of New Guinean youth towards Europeans. In four centres she asked students of secondary schools to make pictures presenting a New Guinean and European in a working situation or at leisure. Also a short written explanation of the pictures was requested. The evaluation showed that co-operation of the races was of central importance in 64 per cent and that the Europeans played the leading role. It was surprising that the students from areas which are economically better situated emphasized the positive co-operation more frequently than those from poorer districts, who selected a theme of conflict. The essays yielded the same ratio. It was the common opinion of all that the Europeans were there to help the indigenes. There is disappointment if that does not happen; if it is true, one bestows unlimited sympathy upon the Europeans. All who participated in the test complained mainly about the Europeans' attitude of superiority, which was always noticeable. They deplored the lack of solidarity and the absence of a genuine partnership.

It is actually very difficult to advance from mere words to an authentic realization of solidarity. The Europeans have a greater technical knowledge, a very definite way of living adjusted to hygiene and efficiency and they possess more money and goods than the average indigine. All that raises them above the standard of their surroundings. Without intention they drift inescapably into a mentality of superiority. Philip Potter, director of the division for world mission and evangelization of the World Council of Churches therefore rightly says:

> There is a demoniacal influence which besets a powerful, rich and missionary institute which takes an interest in poorer people. How can a true exchange exist between poor and rich? Partnership was a word which we used in the past and which today we dare not speak aloud since we know how it appeared in practice.

One should not forget here that indigence and poverty are not necessarily always material, but are the results of being less qualified and of suffering from a lack of self-esteem. How far this condition developed during the last generations is not known. Potter once stated that it did not exist to such an extent during the eighteenth century. He illustrated this by adding that the first two Moravian missionaries on the Virgin Islands (West Indian Islands of Central America) offered themselves as slaves in order to be close to the slave workers.[67] This attitude appears to have vanished today in spite of all readiness for sacrifices in the mission. In 1910 the Indian Azariah said at a world missionary conference in Edinburgh: "You staked very much when you brought the Gospel. You have given your bodies that they might be burnt for us. But you have withheld your friendship from us. Give us friends!"

That is the problem. One can preach the Gospel to the whole world and yet one has not done anything significant. All troubles are in vain unless the gospel teaching is seen to be practised in one's own life. However difficult it is, since it means a violation of our own way of living, it is urgently required that attempts to proclaim the truth by practising it are risked again and again. We shall not be able fully to understand cargo cults until we experience their challenge as a personal grievance. Nor will our counsel be accepted until we *do* understand. It may happen one day that the missionaries' presence in New Guinea will be resented and friendship will be denied them. That will be the sign that we have lost our opportunity. In this situation we have to remain humble and patient. Normally today we still expect that Christians and Melanesians will find their common aim. A whole series of adjustments are required for this purpose. One has to learn how to comprehend their thinking. One has to consider their culture and their religion. One has to be familiar with the working of their minds, with the atmosphere of their devotions and prayers and, above all, one has to participate in their daily and personal lives. This too presumes a conscious and thorough readiness for friendship and love.[68] This is much more than a jovial patronage. It combines tact and understanding with a real humility which is able to receive and to learn. Indeed it is more important to listen than to give. Potter occasionally maintained that the mission often failed because it had passed by the proper problems of social justice and thus had not gained the hearing of the people. To gain such hearing is only possible by being aware of the problems of one's fellowmen. Sensing the need happens only in identification. Its meaning is that it opens the eyes for what really is, and it smoothes the path towards appropriate actions.

Solidarity or identification cannot exist without loving involvement; no pertinent preaching of the gospel can be accomplished without mutual identification; no encouraging future without such pertinence.

Relevance of Preaching the Gospel

Every preaching becomes relevant only if it implies the interplay of the participating powers. It is never relevant with regard to the content matter alone. The matter which concerns us is man's salvation. The presentation of salvation and its reception take place by action and reaction. The three decisive terms of reference are:

(a) The message, i.e. the preached gospel;
(b) The mediator of the message, i.e. the preacher or missionary;
(c) The one who confronts the mediator, the addressee, to whom the Gospel is presented.

(a) It has been taken for granted that the mission of the church had a *message* for the non-Christian world. The testimony of Christ, who offers redemption from guilt and the possibility of salvation for eternity, is the constituent element of all its work. The mission cannot remain satisfied with the reflection that its message is self-evident. It has its life by seeking its authority in an event outside its own control and by communication of the news of this event to others. The existence of this message is the fundamental condition for the work of the mission.

(b) A *mediator* is required to confront people with this message. It is his task to solicit interest and to call for a decision. It is the preacher's duty, as far as such autonomous views become apparent in syncretistic cults, to lead the people so inclined into the field of the forces of a Christo–centric belief. The message, in the beginning, is new with regard to the frame of experiences of the recipient. Therefore the mediator has to demonstrate it. Thus only will it become attractive. Of course, such a manifestation within the situation of a mission can be effected only by the mediator himself, since for the time being he alone knows the purport of the message. It must be affirmed that fundamentally the whole church is subject to this challenge and that an individual acts as a vicar only. Though the bearer of the message, he nevertheless has a part in the role of listener and thus equally is a recipient. As a representative of the church he has to live what he preaches. That is part of his proclamation. In this way he exerts great influence—not only on those who hear him but also on the fate of the message itself.

(c) Much depends upon the *addressee*. At first it is not very likely that he will understand the message correctly. He selects and extracts and hears and comprehends only what suits his own pattern of thinking and acting. The danger of an adulteration of the message arises easily. Later it is difficult to rectify mistakes which have led into wrong directions. Linguistic facilities alone, or their limitations alter the original content of a statement to some extent.[69] The preceding range of knowledge, the given horizon of expectations and the dependence upon the environment influence and colour understanding of the Gospel. Content as well as form and method are affected by this understanding and a perfectly new Gospel may be the result. The formation of sects will be unavoidable until the Gospel can be correctly interpreted.

Relevance presumes that the three terms of reference or entities—Message (M), Preacher or Mediator (P) and Addressee (A)—are made fertile by a correct mutual relationship. In Figure 9, four models correspond to certain stages of development during the course of a mission.

Three conclusions may be drawn from the models:

1. Mediator and recipient are united by a common fate. Both depend upon a successful meeting. Progression in the wrong direction or a disruption of the relationship always implicates both sides. A mission may speak of success only when the partner freely co-operates while accepting the gospel, when he has digested it by his own efforts and when he has passed it on by his own initiative.

2. At first glance it may be surprising that the message itself is subject to influences. We are accustomed to believe that the proclamation of the Biblical texts is unchangeable. At the most we admit a changeability of the picture of the world. But the difficulty of answering exactly what finally belongs to our picture of the world, especially when we are concerned with members of a culture very different from our own makes it necessary to consider a changeability of the proclaimed message. At all times

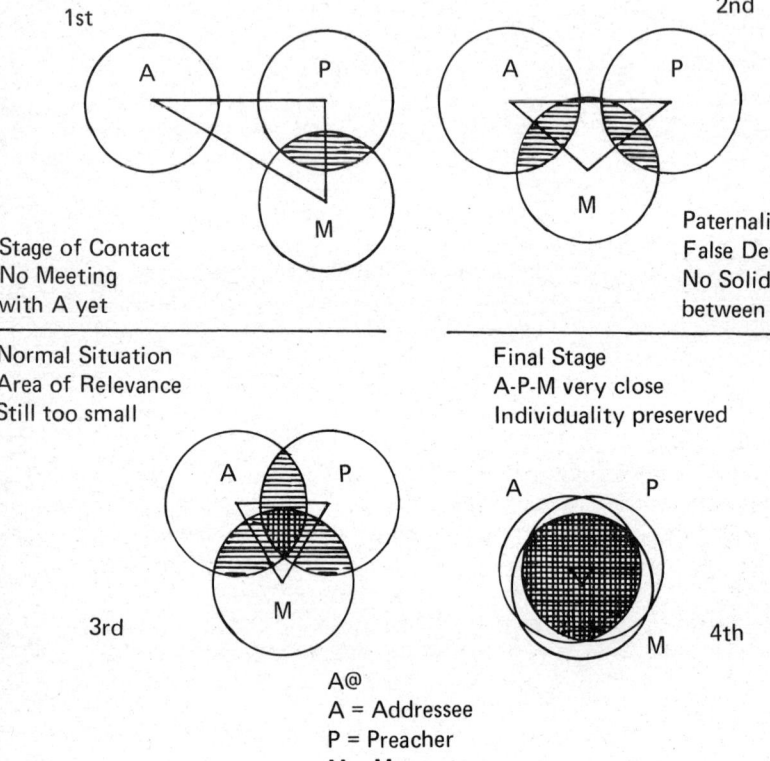

1st

A   P

M

Stage of Contact
No Meeting
with A yet

2nd

A   P

M

Paternalistic
False Development
No Solidarity
between A and P

Normal Situation
Area of Relevance
Still too small

Final Stage
A-P-M very close
Individuality preserved

A   P

M

3rd

A   P

M   4th

A@
A = Addressee
P = Preacher
M = Message

Fig. 9. Models for relevant evangelizing

religious statements were declared to be obligatory at least with regard to the religion as long as they corresponded to the prevailing picture of the world. A deviation from them implied self-exclusion from the religious association concerned. Only after a sufficiently significant advance of public thinking one dared to assign the once binding theses of faith and morals to a changeable picture of the world and to restrict their binding force.[70] Similarly, the meeting of the Gospel with different addressees resulted repeatedly in the change of dynamics of the Gospel.[71]

3. The most striking teaching of Figure 9 can be expressed in the following sentence: The more distant the centres of interests are from each other, the less relevant the preaching becomes; or the closer the foci of the two interrelated systems of expectations move to each other, the more relevant the mission grows. Of course one may fear that this implies indirectly the request for an assimilation of Christianity. A decisive loss of substance could be the consequence. Assimilation does not necessarily signify a loss of value; it can even be a gain. One may expect collisions, for example, between the law of blood feuds and the love of one's neighbour. But here especially an investigation of the interests of the other is necessary. The more we study the ancient tribal cultures the better we understand the relative necessity of a vendetta in such an entanglement. On the other hand, an intensive occupation with the Sermon on the Mount cannot fail to make the head hunter aware of the significance of the love of one's neighbour. To consider seriously the interest of a fellow being makes an approach to him possible. That produces trust which will let new knowledge grow.

Mutual trust has so often suffered in the cargo cults. Encouragement is needed to bury the past and to permit new beginnings so that we can establish a way of living together in freedom and trust.

Encouragement as the Operative Principle of Freedom

Encouragement is a concept taken from pedagogics. We may accept it since to surmount the cargo cults is like wrestling for the human being as in pedagogics. We know how negative the development of a youth may become if he is discouraged. Repressive forces cripple his energy and turn him into a drop-out. On the other hand, positive education and a benevolent interest help to unfold forces that had been unthought of. All education is really concerned with "the unfolding of the ability to cope with hindrances and difficulties".[72] Courage is an important means of obtaining this ability. One has to be encouraged to take courage. We surrender to anxiety if we see only difficulties and no way out of them. Fear of a threat against the possibilities of life has indeed always tended to develop psychic disturbances. Fear and courage are the two poles around which, since ancient times, thinking in Melanesia revolved. H. Henz is right to look for example at the magic of a hunting spell as a religious form of encouragement.[73] In the face of a threatened existence and of the struggle for life in nature and society, the aggregation of a group to perform ritual magic conveys great strength. The feeling of communion provides courage and strength. Therefore the formation of groups is also very important for the cargo cults. Fear easily upsets self-esteem, which is frequently expressed as a feeling of inferiority. This has to be compensated. In Melanesia this compensation can be most easily realized in cultic actions. The result—since we are here concerned only with an apparent compensation— will soon be a failure of real effectiveness and that again will cause an increase of fear and a decline of self-esteem.

An escape from this vicious circle can be provided only by goal-oriented encouragement, which considers the human being seriously, acknowledges his needs and helps him towards a true experience of his own value. This of course is not an easy venture. It is a dynamic process, which follows a course conforming to special laws. According to F. Birnbaum, the curative encouragement always takes place in five steps.[74] He speaks at first of the step of making contact during which sympathy and acknowledgement of difficulties are to be accomplished. In the next step, bridges have to be made to achieve a psychic release. Man needs to be aware that he is able to do things and that it is never too late for a new beginning. The spiral of a previous discouragement has to be dampened far enough to make a new direction of development possible. Thirdly, false hopes are to be uncovered. That is the recognition of one's own wrong attitude towards life and of the secret pattern of life, which is sometimes also called "Dressat" (an internalized, subconscious and stereotyped pattern of responses, as in horses trained by dressage or perhaps with men dressed in formal apparel). Without this understanding one cannot advance. It is the recognition that one is responsible for one's own actions. Fourthly, it is followed by a new set of tasks which can be fulfilled. The ability to cope with larger tasks grows through this experience of improvement. The origin of all encouragement rests in the appreciation of the performance. And fifth and finally, the process has to be crowned by the so-called weaning. One is dismissed and continues to live by one's own responsibility. Performance has led to freedom. By encouragement one is freed from early fears and wrong attitudes to reality.

Figure 10 should illustrate the spiral of cultic destiny and the release from it through the process of encouragement.

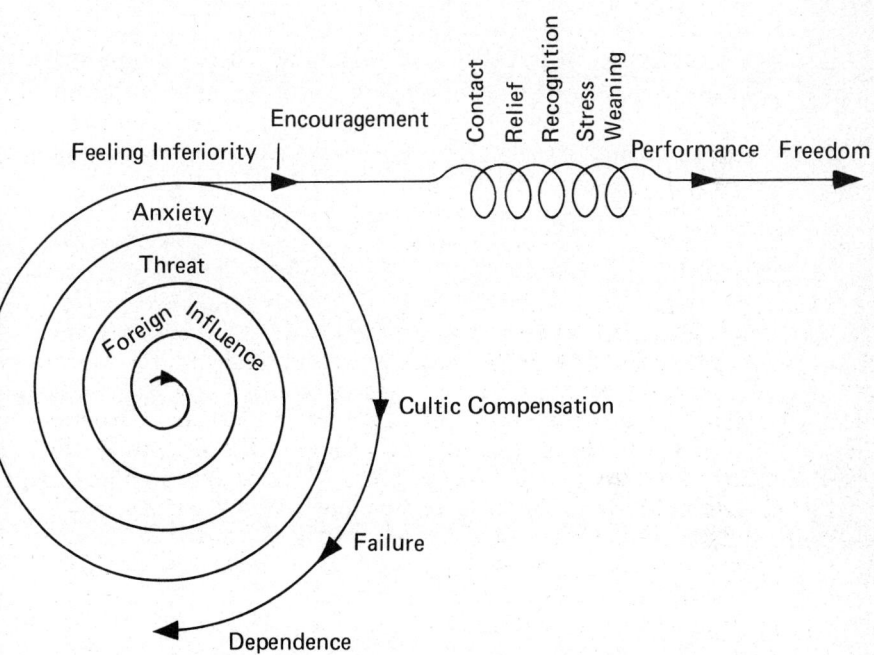

Fig. 10. Anxiety–spiral. Its conquest by encouragement

Paliau at a council meeting on Manus, Admiralty Islands.

Reverend Dietsch with a Baluan preacher on Manus, Admiralty Islands.

Peri children on Manus, Admiralty Islands.

The village Peri on Manus, centre of the Baluan church.

A junior leader of the Welfare Society on Buka, Solomon Islands, is the drummer at the evening dance of the village commune.

Wallpainting in a Lutheran church in New Guinea, "Christ, the Judge of the World".

The "Gate of Heaven", wallpainting in a Lutheran church, New Guinea.

APPENDICES

Appendix 1

Diagram of Interdependence

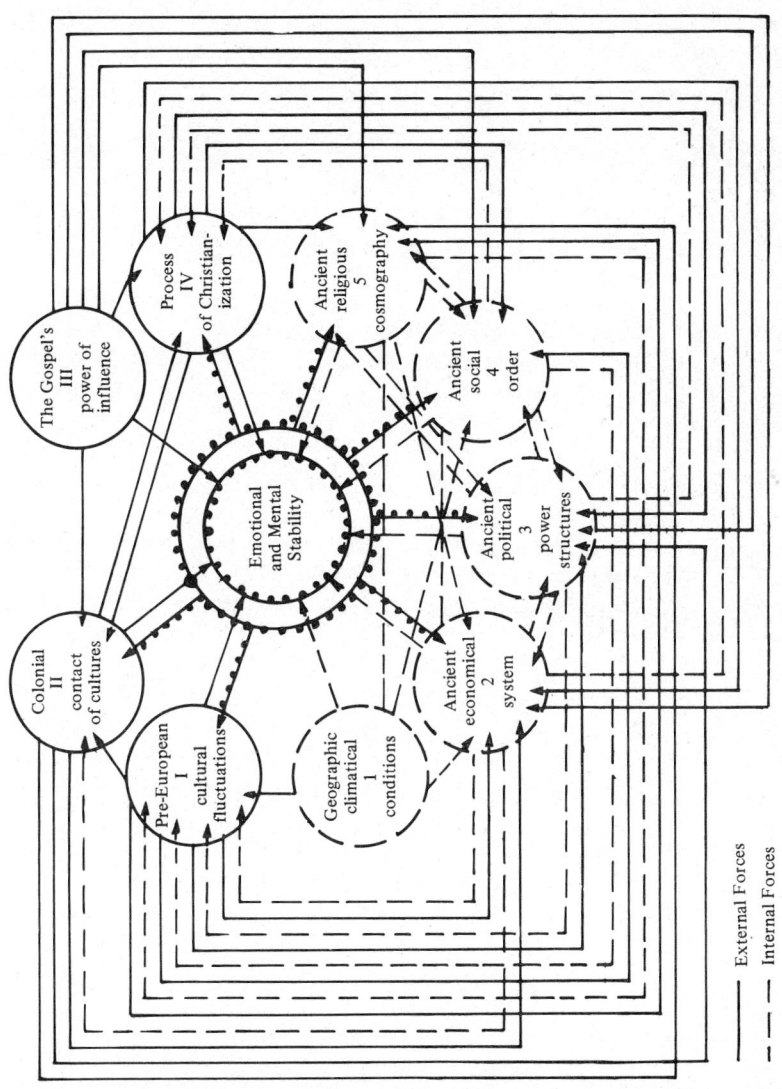

The Gospel's III power of influence

Process IV of Christianization

Ancient religious 5 cosmography

Ancient social 4 order

Ancient political 3 power structures

Emotional and Mental Stability

Ancient economical 2 system

Colonial II contact of cultures

Pre-European I cultural fluctuations

Geographic climatical 1 conditions

External Forces ———
Internal Forces - - -

Appendix 2

Some Myths as Instances of Cargo Ideology

Here are a few narratives from a rich fount of material, affording an insight into the magical thoughts of the Melanesian population. The myths are classified according to five cycles of themes:

1. Division of Mankind

(From R. Poignant, *Ozeanische Mythologie*, London, pp. 81–108.)

Myth 1: The woman from Tangu. With the people of Tangu in the north of New Guinea, lived a woman who had to maintain herself without the help of a husband. One day her child was left alone in the house. A stranger came, killed the girl and buried her body. But the woman had a dream which revealed the site of the grave to her. She found the body, put it into her string bag and wandered from village to village until she found a suitable location to bury it properly, as well as a man, the younger of two brothers, whom she married. She had two sons from her new husband. Now and then she visited the grave of her daughter. When she once parted some palm fronds she saw salt water flow out of the grave and fish swimming in it. The woman took some water and one small fish as food for the family. The results were miraculous. During the night, one of her sons grew to manhood. Her husband's elder brother looked with envy at this son. The woman showed him the grave so that the same miracle might happen to his son. Yet instead of taking a small fish, the foolish man grabbed a big one which was as long as an eel. Then the earth trembled, there was a roaring and water poured out. The ocean was made and the sea separated the two brothers. After some time they could communicate again as they let leaves drift across the sea on which they wrote their messages. Thus it became manifest that the younger brother could invent and build wonderful things, like boats with steam engines, umbrellas, rifles, and tinned food, while the elder brother could only copy them. Therefore some people have black skin and eat the roots of yams.

The misuse of a gift is seen here as the reason for the division. The Massim in south-east New Guinea on the other hand speak of disobedience and fraud. This variant is as follows:

Myth 2: The cleavage of the tree. The members of two clans cut down a tree. The sea then poured out from it. While one group rested from work and danced the other stole all "goods" and sailed away in one half of the tree trunk. Afterwards the two clans developed quite differently from each other. Later the clan returned and surprised those who had stayed at home with sundry new, cultural goods.

The people who returned were recognized as the Europeans. Thus it was explained why the Europeans had everything while they themselves were poor. This is a reflection upon the historical date of arrival of the Europeans. Their existence is fitted into 'the frame of ancient tradition.

The theme of a world divided by a flood recurs everywhere. The Tanna on the New Hebrides tell it thus:

Myth 3: The snake water. Once upon a time there was a snake father who kept the mother of his son as a prisoner. The woman poisoned him eventually. Then a river of fresh water sprung from his grave and the first coconut palm sprouted from his eyes. The woman bathed her son in this water, rubbed his body with oil and gave him nuts to eat so that he might grow fine and round and big. But one day she discovered that he did not obey her and had told the secret to the other children. She became angry, destroyed the enclosing wall and freed the sea. People were carried off to other islands. Coconuts too floated elsewhere to bear fruits there. In this way bush men and saltwater men were separated. This explains the difference between human beings.

2. Two Hostile Brothers

(From R. Poignant, *Ozeanische Mythologie*, p. 95.)

Myth 4: The miracle hill of Mekeo. The Mekeos in Papua say that one brother ate fruit while the other consumed only meat. The poor brother secretly followed the other to discover how he got the meat. One day he found that the brother who ate meat entered a hill. This hill opened in a mysterious way and closed again behind him. Soon after he reappeared with a wallaby and two bush hens. After his brother had gone, the poor man also tried his luck. But he was too slow and stupid. He did not close the door properly and all the animals escaped. This caused a quarrel and the two brothers parted in discord. They are also separated from their wives. The intelligence of one is confronted with the foolishness of the other. The creative action of one is frustrated by the lack of attention of the other.

On the Bismarck Archipelago a similar story is told:

Myth 5: To Kabinana and To Karvuvu. The two heroes, To Kabinana and To Karvuvu were born in a miraculous way. Later they slew a man-eater and made a peaceful life possible on earth. Later however

Karvuvu, being simple-minded, was left far behind by the ingenious Kabinana. They made women for themselves out of coconuts. To Karvuvu threw his nuts so clumsily on the ground, that is, with the eyes downwards, that they landed wrongly and botched women with flat noses were created. Everywhere he did the wrong thing. Once he made the shark help him catch fish, yet ever since sharks swallow both fish and men. Sometimes he would watch his mother to see how she stripped her old skin and changed herself into youthful beauty. Since he did not know her when she was young again, he screamed and wanted to see her in her old form. Then the mother put her old, wrinkly skin on again. From that time, human beings grow old and have to die. They have lost the ability "to strip their old skin". Gradually the brothers became jealous of each other and there was rivalry between them. Finally the one even planned the murder of the other.

At times this theme is applied to a wider group, a whole clan or a host of brothers. On the New Hebrides the youngest and most inventive brother is opposed by a whole clique:

Myth 6: Quat and his eleven brothers. The eleven brothers Tangaro lived with the youngest brother Quat on the Banks Islands. They created the land by fishing it out of the sea. They liberated the water from its enclosure, they killed the man-eater and they made man. But Quat stood out from the others by his clever tricks. He was born when his mother burst like a stone and released him. He himself created the women as one makes ceremonial hats, out of straw and sticks of the sago-palm, and of its petals. Another time he carved men out of wood. Then he danced and beat the drum and thus woke them to life. His antagonist, Marawa, did the same. When the figures stirred, however, he laid them into sand and buried them; after seven days he took them out again. They had decayed. Since that time all men have to die. Later Quat made a boat out of timber, drilled a channel to the sea, loaded the boat with many good things and sailed away.

It is interesting that at the arrival of the first European Quat and his many brothers were remembered immediately.

3. Lost Paradise

(From R. Jockel, *Goetter und Daemonen, Mythen der Voelker*, p. 187)

Myth 7: Why we have to die. An old, good woman had died and had been buried. But she dug herself out of the grave. By chance a child passed by and she said to it: "Fetch me some fire that I can warm myself". But the child refused. It did not obey the good old woman who in vain tried to persuade it. Thus the old woman died again. If that child had obeyed her we would not need to die a final death. We would be buried but we could reawaken ourselves to life and warm ourselves near the fire. Because of that disobedience we do not wake up again and die once and for ever.

Myth 8: The cut rope. The Ayom pygmies tell how once Tumbrenjak descended to earth in order to hunt and to fish. When he wanted to return he discovered that the rope by which he had come down had been cut to pieces. He called out loudly and his wife looked down and also called out. Then he began to build a house. His wife threw down fire for him and several kinds of fruit and many vegetables, including four cucumbers. When the man went into the bush with these cucumbers they were turned into four women. On his return to the house all work had been done. He heard the laughter of his wives, and his children became the ancestors of the different tribes of the Ayom. The return into the real home country, however, remained barred. Only the memory of the empire of peace was preserved.

The Keraki in Papua also tell this myth:

Myth 9: The clouds of Kambel. Kambel sprung from the sky and was an aerial being. Once he heard unintelligible words from the inside of a palm. He was curious and cut it down. Thus human beings became free. When evening came a shiny little thing arose from the tree, slipped from his hold and escaped into the sky. It was his son, the moon. Then Kambel sent out small lizards to fetch fire. They brought it and Kambel roasted the pith of the palm and flung it into the sky. Thus he created the clouds. However these made themselves independent and, without anyone being able to say how it happened, they pushed the sky higher and higher. In this way the inhabitants of the earth were separated from the country of their origin. Kambel himself left the earth after incest had taken place between his son the moon, and his mother. But he slew his son. Subsequently his dog reproached him. But Kambel fastened the tongue of his dog with the feather of a cassowary so that the dog could not report this deed to the mother of that son. Since that time not only men but also dogs are exposed to the anger of Kambel. They can no longer talk but only howl.

4. The Coming of the Last Times

(From a private collection of myths of New Guinea)

Myth 10: The last days. (Noted in May 1963 in Nuyaguna near Tarabo.) When the last days are coming, our ancestors will visit us and bring us rich gifts. In ancient times the earth was barren and empty. But then the water came and flooded the earth. At that time a great darkness covered the earth. The clouds burst and everywhere huge swamps were formed. The fruits of the garden rotted and perished. Life seemed to be nearly extinct. Then the old people assembled in their houses and took counsel together. They stoked up the fire so that it burnt brightly. Then they gave torches to the young people and sent them out. With their torches the young ones compelled the sun to appear again. They walked around the village and the gardens with their burning bamboo canes. The land became solid again like stone.

The sweet potatoes grew firm and palatable. Life flourished again. Such things happened when life was in danger. Yet the ancestors knew what to do and rescued life. When their hour comes they will return and help the living ones. We have to prepare for their arrival. Loin cloths for men and women have to be made. And everyone should slaughter a black pig which has red bristles. One should paint oneself with the blood of that pig. Those who would not do that should die. Be it man or woman or child, all should die at the coming of the ancestors unless they had eaten of that pig. The ancestors will come from the surroundings of Kainantu. They will assist us and care for us. They have great power and they have not forgotten us.

The first Europeans came into the country from Kainantu in 1950. This description originated in South Fore and had been known in about 1900.

5. Acquisition of Material Goods of Salvation

(From a private collection of myths.)

Myth 11: The forest man from Mount Michael. Behind the mountains of the southern spurs of Mount Michael a strange forest man is living. He has long black hair like the Chinese and thin fingers which can grasp through the finest slots and cracks. He also has the ability to render himself invisible. He dwells in a rock house under the ground. There he hoards great treasures. In his subterranean warehouse he has nearly everything that is for sale in the large cities and their retail stores. Sometimes one sees him slipping through the villages at night. Those who do him little favours will one day be laden with gifts. He invites the villagers to his home occasionally and shows them his riches. The doors of his house have no locks. He speaks secret words and forthwith all doors open themselves before him. Nothing can be seen from outside. He tells his secrets only to those whom he trusts. Once he was suspected of theft. The government officer sent policemen for him. Yet each time they came very close to him he sank into the ground and vanished without a trace. He is in league with the ancestors. He does not depend upon the Europeans. Sickness has no power over him. He has no personal needs; he does not eat nor drink; he has no wife. All his possessions are destined for the population of Papua. Some of us have seen him already. Many know the way to his house as well. But only few have entered it. No door can be seen from the outside. It is like any other rock.

This information stems from men travelling with me from the village Iwaki in the surroundings of South Fore and it was recorded in November 1962. It shows how ancient and modern elements are fused into the content of the legend. The following three myths are also from my collection:

Myth 12: The lake of Numparu. (This tale is based on fact. When it was noted in Tarabo–Awigusa on 26 March 1965, four widows whose husbands were drowned in a pond about 1935 were still alive there.) There was continuous warring and tribal feuds when the Europeans had not yet come further into our country than Kainantu (in about 1931) in the north-east. One day we heard that men had come from the coast into our neighbourhood. We were told they had many shells, and knives and axes made out of steel. Some of our leaders set out to visit the new arrivals. They also acquired by bargaining a few of these implements, and cloth. Everything was admired when they returned. Suddenly one of the older men remembered that in earlier times such a village had also existed near us in which all these things had been available in abundance. In ancient times our ancestors had lived in this village; but one day it had vanished and in its place a small lake had been formed which was at a distance of about two hours from the village. This pond is the bay of a river which separates two ranges of mountains in that area. The old man thought that it should be still possible to find many excellent things at the bottom of the pond.

We listened and decided to make a trial. Four young men who had married only recently were selected. They would dive into the pond and lift the treasures. The whole village assembled at the banks and watched what would take place. The four men jumped into the water at the same time. The river makes a bend at the spot and thus produces a slight whirlpool. Therefore none of the men succeeded in rising to the surface again. The whirlpool lasted a while; then the bodies emerged again. The women started to wail loudly and mourn. A few older people suggested trying to dive again immediately. But nobody cared for that. So they returned home. Perhaps one day our children will succeed in lifting those treasures.

Myth 13: The country of the snake. (Noted in Keti near Tarabo in summer, 1963.) One day two sisters went into the forest to collect firewood. In the deep jungle they lost their way. Suddenly they heard the call of a strange bird. They looked around and noticed a bird which they had never seen before. The bird came down from a very, very old tree and hopped in front of the girls. They followed him and arrived eventually at another old and rotting tree. At its foot there was a snake. The snake said to them: "I shall show you the path to your village if one of you agrees to marry me." The sisters were at their wits' end and acquiesced. They decided that the elder of the two should marry the snake. She took the snake, put it into her string bag and carried it around with her. Soon night came. They built an emergency shelter and waited for the morning. When the girls awoke, the snake had vanished. They found in its place a new-born child which perpetually cried.

The elder sister went for a walk with her child and suddenly came again to the tree under which she had met the snake. This time the tree opened at its roots when it heard the cries of the infant. The sister passed under the hanging down lianas and inside the tree she came to steps which led downwards. There another door was opened. She saw a wide and bright room before her. The snake welcomed both.

Everywhere valuables and trinkets hung. The girl marvelled at the room and asked to whom all this belonged. The snake answered: "All this belongs to me. Men were masters of these things when they were not yet as numerous as they are now and when they were living in small groups in the jungle. At that time pigs too were much bigger and the fruits of the fields were also better than they are now. Now I guard the heritage since they left this country, moved into the grassy areas and make continuously war upon one another." Thus speaking, the snake led the girl into another room where she found even more beautiful things and marvellous wares in vast quantities. The snake continued: "If you stay with me, all these things belong to you. If men would return to their ancient rites and customs then the way would be also open to them to come here. For the time being my offer is open to you alone."

The girl thought for a long time. However she wanted to return to the village. She received sugarcane and bananas for the road. In the village all tasted of the gifts of the snake and they longed to be in the paradisiacal place in the jungle. Yet they could no longer find their way to it. So it happened that our life is poorer today. But perhaps one day someone will find the right way to the snake country. Then there will be an end to all troubles. We shall wait for that. The story has to be handed down from one generation to the next so that nobody forgets it. For the ancestors have not forgotten us either.

Myth 14: Padlma. (Noted on 16 August 1963 in Alkena–Pawragl. There a feast of the spirits took place in honour of an ancestor. The author has a film and tape-recording of this feast.)

Padlma had blessed the fruits of the fields and he had granted growth. Then he had moved on to settle the country. He had two wives —a black one and one with a light skin. One day they sat in his hut and rested; then Padlma created the fire and taught his wives how to cook. Soon after that the light-skinned woman went outside and rose into the sky. Then the earth became wet. Thus she created the rain. After the country had been settled Padlma returned to the realm of the spirits. He left his black wife on the earth. She became the mother of Papua. His light-coloured wife, however, went to the West to teach other human beings there. What people in the West created can finally be thus traced back to Padlma. All goods of the earth are given by him. We have to honour him.

Appendix 3

Geographic-Historic Synopsis

Cargo Cults in Melanesia

The following does not list all cults, but the majority known up until
1970. The first column gives the time that a cult was active; the second
column indicates whether the cult is reported in the text; the third
column names the cult and the scene or district of action; the fourth
column cross-references the cult to the text and Appendix 6 (the
numbers used are those F. Steinbauer used in his thesis which deals
with all cults); the final column indicates the tendency of a cult or
movement by designating "m–m" for magico–mechanical, "r–s" for
religio–spiritual, and "p–s" for politico–social.

Years Active	Recorded in Book	Cult Name and Scene of Action	Cult No.	Character of Cult
West Irian Jaya				
1857–1901	+	Mansren–Koreri Movement (1st Phase): Geelvink Bay, Biak	1–8	m–m
1909–17		Mansren–Koreri Movement (2nd Phase): Numfoor	9	m–m
1928–37		Mansren–Koreri Movement (3rd Phase): Biak, Numfoor, Japen, Waigeo, Reni	10–13	r–s
1939–42	+	Koreri Movement of the Angganita: Biak, Supiori, Rani, Insubabi Islands, Sowek Village	14	r–s
1942–47	+	Mansren Revolts of the Stefanus: Geelvink Bay, Manswam on Biak, Japen, Numfoor	15–16	p–s
East Irian Jaya				
1925–35		"De witte mens" 1925,	17	r–s
		Pamai Movement 1928–29,	18	r–s
		Damo Movement 1935:	19	r–s
		Sentani Lake, south of Sukarnopura (Hollandia)		
1940–44	+	Simson's Cemetery Cult: Tanah Merah Sukarnopura to Tanah Merah	20	m–m
1945–52		Nimboran Movement,	21	m–m
		Spirit Movement;	22	m–m
		Sentani Lake		

Years Active	Recorded in Book	Cult Name and Scene of Action	Cult No.	Character of Cult
1942–55	+	Muyu Unity Movement; Irian South Coast, Merauke, Muyu tribal area	23	p–s
1952–54		Situgumina Movement: Wissel Lake, Migani tribal area	24	m–m
1910–30		Mansren–Moszkowski Movement,	25	m–m
1956–62		Martewar Movement,	26	m–m
		Warria Cargo Cults: Mamberamo River, Kaowerabedj, Airmati	27	m–m

Papua

Years Active	Recorded in Book	Cult Name and Scene of Action	Cult No.	Character of Cult
c. 1893		Tokeriu Movement: Milne Bay, Gabugabuna	28	m–m
1913–15		"German Wislin" Movement: Torres Strait, Sabai Island	29	m–m
1912–14–20	+	Baigona Cult: Mt. Victory (Keroro), Massim, North Gira, Kumusi River	30	m–m
1914–19–28		Taro Cults (Kavakeva),	31	m–m
		Diroga Cult, Ereri Cult, Hohora Cult: Buna Bay, Gira River	32–34	m–m
1914–		Kekesi Manau Cult: Lower Mambare River	35	m–m
1919–31	+	Vailala Madness: Gulf of Papua, Vailala	36	m–m
1930–37		The Pig Killing: Central District, Kairuku near Mekeo	37	m–m
1934		Sosom Movement: West Papua	38	m–m
1930–47		Assisi Cult: Assisi near Popondetta	39	m–m
1940–41–47	+	Filo Cult: Mekeo, Inawaia	40	m–m
1942		Kumusi Murders: Gulf District, Buna and Gona, Orokaiva	41	p–s
1945–47	+	Tommy Kabu Society Movement: Purari Delta	42	p–s
1948–50		Goilala Gogodara Batawi Movements: Central District, Lakekamu, Golilala	43–45	m–m

Sepik District

Years Active	Recorded in Book	Cult Name and Scene of Action	Cult No.	Character of Cult
c. 1930		God Father Movement: Sepik Delta, Suain	46	r–s
c. 1931	+	Four Prophets Movement and Walman Movement: Aitape to Wewak, Sumpu, Wau	47–48	m–m
1932		Revival Movement (Procession of Statues): Moagendo near Angoram	49	r–s
1935	+	Mountain King Movement (Black King): Wewak, Ulingan, Alexishafen (See Cult no. 61)	50	r–s
1943		Aitape Revolution: Aitape (previously Berlinhafen)	51	m–m
1943–45		Keram King Movement (Native King): Keram River towards Ramu–Banara	52	p–s

Years Active	Recorded in Book	Cult Name and Scene of Action	Cult No.	Character of Cult
1961–		Expectation of Salvation on the Sepik and Korowori: Upper Sepik and Korowori	53	m–m
1971	+	Cement Marker Cult: Mt. Turu, Yangoru	53(a)	m–m
Madang District				
1871–1900		Pre-Christian Cargo Hopes (Maclay): Sarang to Saidor	54	m–m
1900–14	+	Madang Revolt,	55	p–s
	+	Kilibob-Manup Expectation,	56	r–s
	+	Man from Heaven Movement: Sek to Bongu	57	r–s
1914–33		God and Christ Movement or Pseudo-Biblical Story of Salvation: Sek to Bongu	58	r–s
c. 1933–35		The Coming of Jesus	59	m–m
	+	As–Bilong–Kago Movement: Bogadjim-Buged/Bongu	60	m–m
1934–35		The Black King (Mountain King Movement):Madang towards Sepik (See Cult No. 50)	61	r–s
1936		Return of Christ Movement: Rai Coast, south of Madang	62	r–s
1937		Yerumot Movement: Kambot area at the Yuat	63	r–s
1937–39	+	Mambu Movement: Bogia–Banara, Madang Hinterland	64	r–s
1939–42		Kauris Revolt,	65	m–m
		Letub Cult: Sek, Nobonob, Amele, Muguru, Kauris, Kamba	66	m–m
1940–43		Kukuaik Movements: Karkar Island, Mom, Mater	67–69	m–m
1942–44		Tagarab Cult: Madang South, Yabob inland	70	m–m
1944		Bagasin Revolt: North Bagasin, Sekwari	71	p–s
*c.*1946	+	Pre-Yali Cults: Madang, Bagasin, Garia, Rai Coast	72–78	m–m
1945–55	+	Yali Movement: Rai Coast, Bagasin area	79	m–m
1948–52		Tangu Manam Movements (Post Mambu) Hypnosis Cult,	80	m–m
		Sexual Cult,	81	m–m
		Manam Expectation: Bogia Manara, Tangu, Manam Island, Baliau	82	m–m
1950–	+	Post-Yali Movements: Rai Coast, Sarang to Saidor, Ramu Valley	83–95	m–m

Years Active	Recorded in Book	Cult Name and Scene of Action	Cult No.	Character of Cult
Morobe District				
1921–22		Timo Movement: Huon Peninsula, Sio–Maladum, Mula	96	m–m
1922–38	+	Money Magic: Finschhafen to Sattelberg	97	m–m
1927–34		Eemasang Renewal Movement: Finschhafen to Sattelberg	98	r–s
1932–33		Was Spook (End of the World Movement): Markham Valley, Azera area, Pokwap	99	m–m
1933		Boana Ecstasy (Enthusiast Movement)	100	m–m
		Zaribera Prophecy: Rawlinson Mountains, Kalangandoang	101	m–m
1933–36	+	Marafi Satan's Cult: Markham Valley near Bunki	102	m–m
1933–38	+	Upikno Cult: Kalasa, Finschhafen, Gitua	103	r–s
1935–36		End of the World–Sosom Beast of Burden (donkey) Movement: Boana, Elap–Solop area	104–6	m–m
1945		Sipura Kiap's Imitation: Upper Markham River, Ngarawapum Villages	107	m–m
1946–	+	Yali-Mangzo-Waizodang Movements: Huon Peninsula	108–13	m–m
1958–	+	Neo-Mangzo Cults (Pseudo-Pentecostal Movement): Huon Peninsula; Kalasa to Finschhafen	114–19	r–s
New Guinea Highlands				
1943–45		Arrival of Jesu Expectation: Eastern Highlands, Markham Border	120	m–m
c. 1945	+	Ghost Wind Movement: Eastern Highlands; Kainantu South	121	m–m
c. 1945		Hine Movement: Western Highlands, Wabag, Mt. Hagen	122	m–m
c. 1946		"Large Pigs" Expectation: Western Highlands, Wabag, Mt. Hagen	123	m–m
1947–		Siane Dene Cult: Central Highlands, between Goroka and Waghi Valley	124	m–m
1951–	+	Sporadic Cargo Cults: Eastern Highlands, south of Goroka/Kainantu	125–34	m–m
Bismarck Archipelago				
1929–30		"Golden Age" of the Baining Population: New Britain, Rabaul, Malaguna	135	m–m
1929–37		Rabaul Strikes: New Britain, Rabaul and Kokoro	136	p–s
1933	+	Independence Movement: New Hanover (Lavongai)	137	p–s
1938–39		Namatanai Marriage Rights Movement: New Ireland, Namatanai	138	p–s

Years Active	Recorded in Book	Cult Name and Scene of Action	Cult No.	Character of Cult
1941		Dog Movement: New Britain, Kokoro, Duke of York Is.	139	p–s
1940–42	+	Batari Movement: New Britain, Galilo near Talasea	140–43	m–m
c. 1945		Ninigo Movement: Ninigo Islands, north-west of Manus	144	m–m
1945–54	+	Paliau Movement (and precursors): Admiralty Islands, Manus, Baluan	145–50	p–s
c. 1947		Guria Nois Movement: Admiralty Islands, Rambutjo, Pak, Baluan	151	m–m
1953–54		Spirits Cult: Admiralty Islands	152	m–m
1955		Baining Revolt: New Britain, Rabaul, Alaisum Village	153	m–m
1964–	+	Johnson Cult: New Hanover (Lavongai)	154	p–s

Solomon Islands

Years Active	Recorded in Book	Cult Name and Scene of Action	Cult No.	Character of Cult
c. 1913		Lontis Movement: North Buka, Lontis	155	m–m
c. 1932		Buka Enthusiast Movement: Buka, Lemanmanu, Malasang	156	m–m
1934	+	Pseudo Military Movement: Buka, Gogohei	157	m–m
1935		Renewal Movement in Selao: Buka, Selao	158	m–m
1935–39–45		Bougainville Cargo Cult: Bougainville	159	m–m
c. 1935		The Chair Independence Movement or "Pre-marching Rule" Movement: Malaita	160	p–s
c. 1936–40	+	Pokokoqoro Cult: Choiseul (Nabusasa)	161	m–m
1943–50		"Masinga–Lo" Movement (Marching Rule): Malaita, Santa Ysabel, San Christoval	162	p–s
1953–57–		Moro Movement: Guadalcanal	163	p–s
1953–	+	Welfare Society: Hahalis, Buka, Hanahan	164	p–s
c. 1953		A Cargo Prototype of Tikopia: Tikopia Island	165	m–m
1959–62–		Eto Movement: New Georgia	166	r–s
1960–	+	Kieta Movements: Kearei Volcano Factory and Siar/Selao human sacrifices: Kieta District, Bougainville	167–70	m–m

New Hebrides

Years Active	Recorded in Book	Cult Name and Scene of Action	Cult No.	Character of Cult
1923	+	Ronovuro Cult: South Espiritu Santo	171	r–s
1937		Avuavu Prophecy: South Espiritu Santo	172	r–s
1940–58–	+	John Frum Movement: Tanna	173	m–m
1941–51–		Malekula Co-operative Movement: Malekula	174	m–m
1944–46		Atori Movement: South Espiritu Santo, Viase	175	m–m
1944–51	+	Naked Cult (Mamara Movement): West Espiritu Santo, Nakavu on the Oro River	176	r–s

Years Active	Recorded in Book	Cult Name and Scene of Action	Cult No.	Character of Cult
1945–47		Bule Movement: Pentecost Island, Melsisi	177	m–m
c. 1950		Ambrym Freedom Movement: Ambrym with Uro, Paama	178	m–m
1966–	+	Nagriamel Movement: Espiritu Santo and other Islands	179	p–s
New Caledonia				
1878		Atai Revolt: New Caledonia	180	p–s
1941		Pwagac Affair: North New Caledonia	181	r–s
1945	+	Communistic Freedom Movement: Loyalty Island, Lifu	182	m–m
Fiji Islands				
1873–1920		Tuka Movement: Viti Levu, Muaira District	183	r–s
1880–1920	+	Luveniwai or Water Babies Movement: Viti Levu, areas of Ra and Rewa	184	r–s
1914–40	+	Apolosi Movement (3 phases): Viti Levu	185	p–s
1942–47		Kelevi's Restoration Movement: Kandavu, Nakausele	186	r–s

Appendix 4

Anthropological Glossary

acculturation (acculturative): the process of becoming adapted to new cultural patterns; melting different cultures together.

ambilateral: referring to both or more sides or aspects of an event.

animism (animistic): The attribution of a living soul to inanimate objects and natural phenomena; the belief in the existence of spirits and demons in natural phenomena

anthropomorphism: the attributing of human characteristics to gods, objects or animals etc

anthropophagism (s. cannibalism): the habit of eating human meat

apollonian way of life: orderly, co-operative, modest, sound, commonsensical

bio–climatology: the branch of science which deals with climate and climatic conditions in relation to human life and its socio–psychological effects

carbon–14 dating(=C¹⁴): dating of prehistoric relics of former living things by measurement of radioactivity (half-life period—5770 years)

cargo-expectation: the hope for imminent delivery of material goods by supernatural powers to the living population

chiliasm (s. millenarism): the doctrine or ideology that Christ will reign in bodily presence on earth for a thousand years, connected with the expectation of a happy life under materialistic aspects

cognation (cognate): related by same ancestors or through same origin; derived from a common original form

cult: a system of religious rituals, devoted to special persons or aims and organized as group of followers

deism: the belief that God created the world but thereafter assumed no control over it; consequently the rejection of revelation and God's authority

denomination: here a religious group of same doctrine or custom

dionysian way of life: aggressive, emotionally exuberant, individualistic

divination: the act or process of becoming the bearer of a prophetic and supernatural power by occult means

eclecticism (eclectic): the method of picking out parts of existing doctrines or systems in order to present a new arrangement of thoughts

enculturation: the influx period of a foreign culture to an already existing cultural framework

endogamy (endogamous): the custom of marrying only within one's tribe or social group

epileptoid: like epilepsy, but not really the same

eschatology (eschatological): the branch and doctrine of theology dealing with the last things, for example death, resurrection, judgement, immortality etc.

eschatologism: the ideological expectation of this world's imminent end and the consequent renewal of all human affairs in a better one.

ethnology (ethnological): the branch of anthropology that deals comparatively with the cultures of various peoples

etymology: the origin and development of words, tracing them back as far as possible

exogamy (exogamous): the custom of marrying only outside one's own tribe or social group

glossolaly (glossal): speaking in "other tongues"; expression of excitement in an emotionally uncontrolled babbling (= incoherent sounds)

gnosis: a certain form of religious knowledge, such as was claimed to have been mystically acquired by gnostics in early Christian sects

heteromorphism (heteromorphic): the condition of being different from standard type and having another shape or form than the normal development presents

homeomorphism (homeomorphic): a close similarity to an otherwise different form or composition

hybridization (hybridism, hybrid): producing anything of a different origin into a crossbred new species, or mixing varieties and forming a new shape out of old elements

imitative magic: magical imitation; a certain magic or a ritualized spell aiming for desired values by copying similar procedures of a related field of experience; the belief that similar activities lead to similar results

immanency (immanent): thinking and operating entirely within the framework of a certain system or the scope of objectives, disregarding external occurrences

initiation: the social or religious practice of leading boys and/or girls from childhood to adulthood, stating their sexual and socio–religious maturity by certain rites, for example circumcision or cultic blessings

internal: here: without direct influences from foreign cultural forces; originated by own or inner nature of a thing *magic:* the pretended art of producing effects or controlling events by charms, spells and rituals, supposed to govern certain natural or supernatural forces; also sorcery and witchcraft

mana: the impersonal and supernatural force to which some people attribute magical powers

matrilineal: of descent or derivation through the mother instead of the father; emphasis on the mother as head of the family

Messiah (messianic): the promised and expected deliverer of the Jews; in Christianity applied to Jesus Christ (= messiah)

messianism (messianistic): expectation of salvation by a messiah mostly thought to be a supernatural deliverer or liberator

millenarism (millennium): period of thousand years in which Christ will reign on earth; the resulting ideology of such a period of great happiness, peace and prosperity, an imagined golden age

moiety: either of two halves in the subdivision of some tribes

monogamy (monogamous): the practice of being married to only one person at one time

monotheism (monotheistic): the belief that there is only one God

moralism: belief in or practice of a system of ethics apart from religion, usually emphasizing the prohibiting character of moral rules

morphology (morphological): any scientific study of forms and structures in a certain organism

movement: a series of organized activities by people working towards some social, political, religious, economic etc. goals

mutation: the sudden variation and change of a form, nature or quality in a living organism or cultural pattern

mysticism (mystic): Any belief that seeks eternal knowledge, spiritual truth and communion with God through contemplation, methodological meditation or intuition and love

mythology: (mythological): a. the prescientific world view and world interpretation; b. the belief of people in tales and legends dealing with spirits and gods; c. the anthropological concern with those tales, legends and myths

nagalism: the belief that man can change and act in the shape of an animal and vice versa

nativism (nativistic): here: the attempt of the renewal of a culture or nation by segregating from foreign elements and enforcing race-consciousness, nationalism and tribal unity

neolithic: of the latter part of the stone age, when man developed polished stone tools and raised domestic animals etc.

nomadism: the state of living without a permanent home, moving constantly in search of food, pasture etc.

paleolithic: the earlier part of the stone age, when man started using stone tools

pantheism (pantheistic): the belief that God is not a personality but the summa of all laws, forces and powers in the universe; since God is in everything, every kind of gods can be worshipped

patrilineal: of descent or derivation through the father, neglecting the mother's contribution

phantasy: fantasy: the imaginative, unreal and mental configuration of ideas, hopes, wishes and desires, often in visionary form or as day-dream

phenomenology (phenomenological): the science dealing with any fact, circumstance, experience, appearance or feature (= phenomenon) that can be described and is often of unusual or extraordinary kind

phratry: any similar units as clan which make up a tribe

phylum: any of the broad, basic divisions of linguistic families

polyandry: the practice of having more than one husband at one time

polygamy: (polygamous): the practice of having more than one wife or husband or mate at the same time in plural marriage

polygyny: the practice of having more than one wife or concubine at one time

polytheism (polytheistic): the belief in many gods and their worship

prophetism: the phenomenon of prophets rising in a society, predicting future events and guiding people toward certain socio–religious goals

psychopathology (psychopathological): the science dealing with diseases and abnormalities of the mind

psychosis (psychotic): the more severe mental disorder which causes a serious change in personality by functional disturbances (for example the schizophrenic or manic-depressive type) or organic insanity (as general nervous diseases, brain tumor, alcoholism etc.)

psychosomatic: to describe the relation and interference between some physical and emotional occurrences or processes in an individual

relativism: the theory which maintains that the basis of all judgement is relative, differing according to events, persons, circumstances etc.

revitalization (revitalized): the attempt of restoring new life into a culture during its period of declination

revivalism: the tendency or desire to revive former ways, customs or institutions in order to get salvation for such a renewed culture

ritual: a set form or system of rites or formal procedures to be observed to gain religious values

salvation: its expectation: the hope for an improved life, excluding hardship and passion, aiming for freedom, happiness and satisfaction

schizophrenia (schizophrenic): a mental disorder characterized by withdrawal, hallucinations and delusions of persecution

secularism: the depravation and deformation of secularity in a semi-religious system which rejects any form of normal religious faith and worship besides its own doctrines and practices; the ideology of a world interpretation which makes everything subject to our human intellect

secularity: the quality of being secular, that is belonging to this world and age; the liberation from a mythological world view; the process of becoming intellectually mature

secularization: the conversion from religious to civil ownership or use; the historical process of handing over secular affairs to secular agencies

semantics (semantic): the branch of linguistics concerned with the method, nature, structure, meaning and development of words and speech forms

shamanism: the religious belief that the actions of gods and spirits can be only influenced by special mediative men, the priest-like, so-called shamans

stimulation (stimulus): something that rouses or incites to action

symbiosis (symbiotic): the living together of two dissimilar organisms in close association and giving advantage to both sides

syncretism (syncretistic): the combination or reconciliation of differing beliefs in religion or philosophy, resp. the attempt of merging disparate ideas into such a new framework of harmonized understanding

taboo: the (sacred) prohibition put upon people, things or acts, which makes them untouchable or unmentionable

totem, totemism: an animal or natural object considered as being related by blood to a given family, clan or tribe and taken as its symbol to distinguish them

transculturation: the process of shifting over from a previous stage of culture to a new level of cultural activities

transcendence (transcendent): surpassing the ordinary human understanding beyond the limits of our possible manipulation; the sphere of divinity, distinguished from immanent activities but reaching into all the secular affairs

tribe: a group of persons, families or clans, descended from a common ancestor and forming with all their dependants a community, possessing common leadership, religious ideas, habits and occupation

typology (typological): the study of types and symbols and their meaning or representation

vitalism (vitalistic): here: the expectation of an imminent salvation under predominantly spiritual aspects; a life which is caused and sustained by a vital principle, distinct from bare physical or chemical forces

world interpretation: the philosophical explanation of the meaning of certain occurrences in nature, history etc.

world view: the cosmological reflexion about the technical structure of the world

Appendix 5

Map of Distribution and Characterization of Cargo Cults

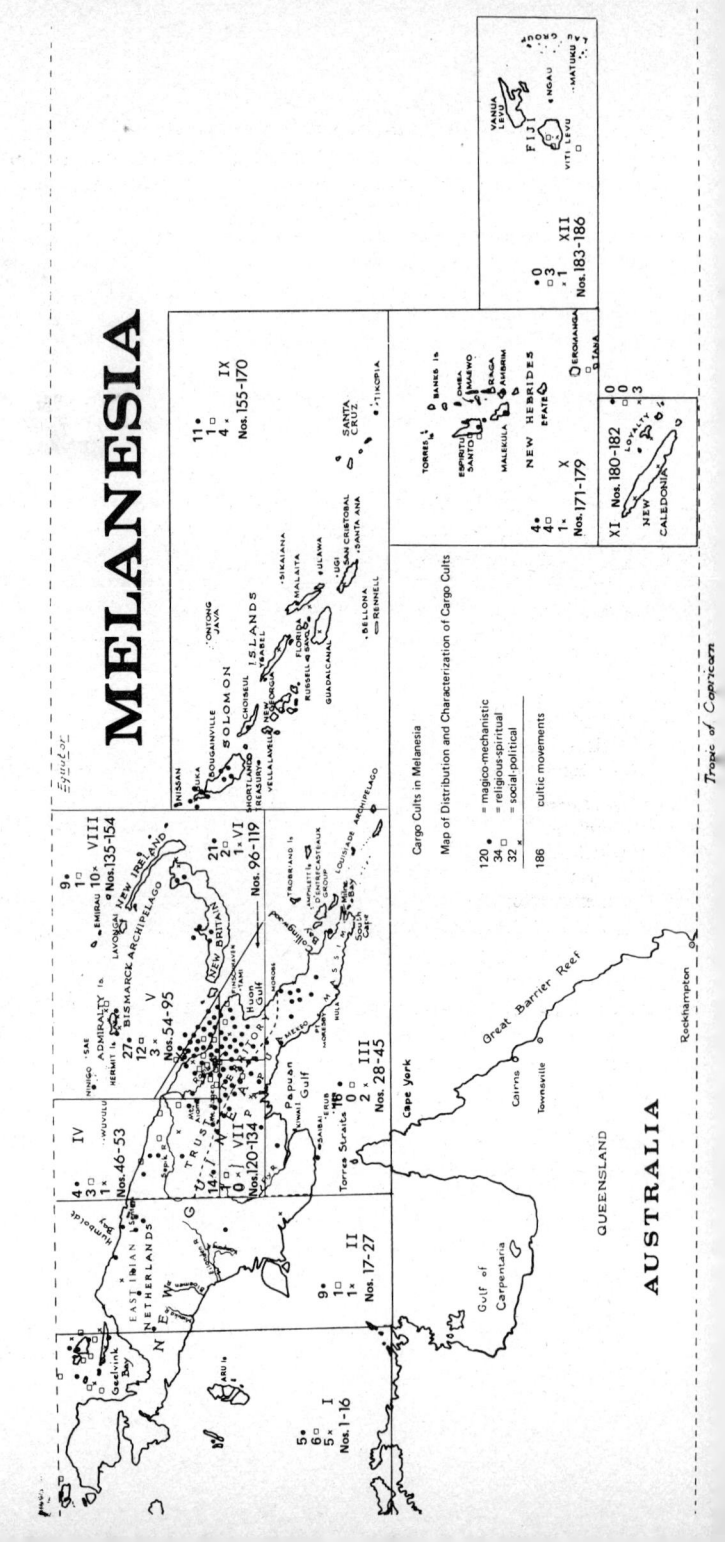

MELANESIA

Cargo Cults in Melanesia

Map of Distribution and Characterization of Cargo Cults

120 • = magico-mechanistic
34 □ = religious-spiritual
32 × = social-political

186 cultic movements

Appendix 6

Evaluation of Statistics

	Pertinency or average frequency Per cent	Index No.
Basic Tendencies:		
Expectation of Salvation and Types		
Method of Operation		
Magico–mechanistic	64	1
Religio–spiritual	18	2
Political–social	18	3
Expectation from outside		
Eschatologism	4	4
Chiliasm	12	5
Messianism	11	6
Vitalism	3	7
Hope for goods	76	8
Expectation from own culture		
Syncretism	25	9
Revivalism	9	10
Nativism	21	11
Economic reform	6	12
Origin:		
Internal	17	13
Acculturative	91	14
Actuality		
Extinct	63	15
Latent	38	16
Active	12	17
Personal Leadership		
Prophet–visionary	21	18
Leader–organizer	38	19
Messiah–saviour	4	20
Woman–girl	4	21
Leading team	23	22
Various initiators	5	23
Group psyche	26	24

Effective agencies of motivation and release

Irrational
Dream experience	27	25
Ecstasy	3	26
Influence of drugs	1	27
Instability	4	28

Rational
High Stress situation	59	29
Emergency	16	30
Envy	32	31
Foreign influence	17	32
Contact of civilization	68	33
Cargo-propaganda	11	34
Metamorphosis of culture	8	35
Will to change	12	36

Supporting and fundamental concepts

Available
Cargo mythology	21	37
Materialism	32	38
Magic thinking	85	39
Ancestor cult	30	40
Talent for fantasy	13	41

Added
Psycho–pathology	8	42
Secular misunderstanding	13	43
Religious misunderstanding	18	44
Economic Knowledge	4	45

Additional features of cults

Material
Destruction of goods	13	46
Slaughter of pigs	8	47
Store Houses	13	48
Pits in the grounds	4	49
Expectation of ships	21	50
Magic of imitation	20	51
Increase of production	3	52

Psycho–somatical
Mass psychosis	24	53
Ecstasy	9	54
Trembling of limbs	5	55
Glossolalia	6	56
Sexualism	10	57
Panicking	6	58

Sociological, religious, cultural
Anti-European sentiment	37	59
Anti-taxation sentiment	5	60
Propaganda	22	61
Discipleship	9	62

Quick spreading	22	63
Martyrdom	4	64
Organization	21	65
Military order	10	66
Model villages	5	67
Terrorism	11	68
Striving for unity	10	69
Material sacrifices	14	70
Murder or planning murder	9	71
Feast with meals	11	72
Dancing festivals	16	73
Cemetery assemblies	11	74
Prophecies	6	75
Formation of legends	7	76
Removal of taboos	13	77
Change of customs	9	78

Expectation and goal-orientation

Individual, collective, ideal and materialistic

Natural catastrophe	12	79
The end of the world	5	80
Resurrection of the dead	13	81
Equality of all people	22	82
White colour of skin	4	83
Material wealth	90	84
Satisfaction of needs	23	85
New morality	6	86
Political freedom	25	87
Economical freedom	7	88
National unity	9	89
Eschatological redemption	28	90
Restoration	14	91
Balance of cultures	10	92

Results and consequences

Negative

Depression	42	93
Impoverishment	7	94
Increasing aversion	21	95

Positive

Change of culture	8	96
Economical progress	2	97
Independence	2	98
Increase of self-esteem	15	99
Psychical and mental stability	8	100

Bibliography

Religion and Theology

Barth, K. *The Humanity of God*. Richmond: John Knox Press, 1960.

Bloch, E. *Philosophy of the Future*. New York: Seaburg Press, 1970.

Bultmann, R. *Faith and Understanding*. Edited by R.W. Funk and translated by Louise P. Smith. New York: Harper and Row, 1969.

Cox, H. *Secular City*. New York: Macmillan, 1966.

Gogarten, F. *Despair and Hope for Our Time*. Translated by T. Wieser. Philadelphia: United Church Press, 1970. Originally published as *Verhängnis und Hoffnung der Neuzeit*.

Hermelink, J. *Verstehen und Bezeugen*. München: Christian Kaiser Verlag, 1960.

Luckmann, T. *Invisible Religion: The Problem of Religion in Modern Society*. New York: Macmillan, 1967.

Moltmann, J. *Theology of Hope*. New York; Harper and Row, 1967.

Niebuhr, R. *Pious and Secular America*. Clifton: Augusta M. Kelley Publishers, 1958.

Niebuhr, H.R. *The Meaning of Revelation*. New York: Macmillan, 1967.

Ratschow, C.H. "Die Religionen und das Christentum". Paper delivered at International Congress of Evangelical Theologians at Vienna September 1966. Published as *Der Christliche Glaube*. Berlin: Verlag Alfred Topelmann, 1967.

Sauter, G. *Zukunft und Verheissung*. Zürich: Zwingli Verlag, 1965, and Stuttgart: Evangelisches Verlagswerk, 1965.

Teilhard de Chardin, P. *The Future of Man*. New York: Harper and Row, 1969.

Tillich, P. *Christianity and the Encounter of the World Religions*. New York: Columbia University Press, 1963.

Van der Leeuv, G. *Phänomenologie der Religion*. Second edition. Tübingen: Gerd Mohr Verlag, 1956.

Zahrnt, H. *Question of God*. New York: Harcourt Brace Jovanovich, 1970.

The Sacred and the Profane

Bloch, E. *Man on His Own*. Translated by E.B. Ashton. New York: Herder and Herder, 1970. Originally published as *Religion im Erbe*.

Bühler, A. "Kulturkontakte und Kulturzerfall". *Acta Tropica* 14 (1957):1–35.

Bürkle, H. *Die Reaktionen der Religionen auf die Säkularisierung*. Lecture. Neuendettelsau: Freimund Verlag, 1969.

Dobzhansky, T. *Mankind Evolving: The Evolution of the Human Species*. New Haven: Yale University Press, 1962.

Eliade, Mircea. *Myth of the Eternal Return*. Translated by W.R. Trask. Princeton: Princeton University Press, 1954.

———. *Sacred and the Profane: The Nature of Religion*. Translated by W.R. Trask. New York: Harcourt Brace Jovanovich, 1968.

Evans–Pritchard, E.E. *Theories of Primitive Religions*. Oxford: Oxford University Press, 1965.

———. *Social Anthropology and Other Essays*. New York: Free Press, 1964.

Firth, Raymond. *Themes in Economic Anthropology*. ASA Monograph no. 6. New York: Barnes and Noble Inc., 1970.

Frazer, J.G. *The Golden Bough*. London: Macmillan, 1936.

Hogbin, H.J. *Social Change*. London: Watts, 1958.

Huxley, Aldous. *Doors of Perception*. New York: Harper and Row, 1970.

Huxley, Julian. *Essays of a Humanist*. London: Chatto and Windus, 1964.

Huxley, Julian et al. *The Destiny of Man*. London: Hodder and Stoughton, 1959.

Huxley, Julian. *Evolutionary Humanism*. Dyason Lecture 1953. Melbourne: Australian Institute of International Affairs, 1954.

Jarvie, J.C. *Revolution in Anthropology*. Atlantic Highlands, N.J.: Humanities Press Inc., 1964.

Marsch, W.D. *Hoffen Worauf*. Hamburg: Furche Verlag, 1963.

Marty, M.E. *The Search for a Usable Future*. New York: Harper and Row, 1969.

Mead, M. *Anthropology a Human Science*. Selected Papers, 1939–1960. New York: Van Nostrand Reinhold, 1964.

Rossel, J. *Dynamik der Hoffnung*. Basel: Basileia Verlag, 1967.

Sunden, H. *Die Religion und die Rollen: Eine psychologische Untersuchung der Frömmigkeit*. Bern: P. Haupt Verlag, 1966.

The Religion of the Oppressed

Benz, E. *Dreams, Hallucinations, Visions*. Translated by T.H. Spiers. New York: Swedenborg Foundation, 1968.

Burridge, K.O.L. *New Heaven. New Earth: A Study of Millenarian Activities*. Pavilion Social Anthropology Series. New York: Schocken Books Inc., 1969.

Cohn, Norman. *The Pursuit of the Millenium*. London: Secker and Warburg, 1957.

Festinger, L., Riecken, H.W., and Schachter, S. *When Prophecy Fails*. New York: Harper Torchbooks, 1969.

Firth, R. *Work of the Gods in Tikopia*. Atlantic Highlands, N.J.: Humanities Press Inc., 1967.

Gratus, J. *The False Messiahs*. London: Victor Gollancz, 1975.

Hutten, K. *Seher, Grübler, Enthusiasten: Das Buch der Sekten*. Stuttgart: Quellverlag, 1958.

Lanternari, V. *The Religion of the Oppressed*. London: MacGibbon and Kee, 1963.

Linton, R. "Nativistic Movements". *American Anthropologist* 45 (1943):230–43.

Mead, M., and Schwartz, T. "The Cult as a Condensed Social Process". In *Transactions of the 5th Conference of the Josiah Macy Jr. Foundation*, pp. 85–187. New York, 1960.

Shepperson, George. *The Comparative Study of Millenarian Movements*. In *Millenial Dreams in Action*. See Thrupp, Sylvia.

Thrupp, Sylvia L., ed. *Millenial Dreams in Action*. Society for the Comparative Study of Society and History. The Hague: Mouton and Co., 1962.

Wallace, A.F.C. "Revitalization Movements". *American Anthropologist* 58 (1956):264–81.

Melanesia and Melanesian Cargo Cults

Allan, C.H. "Marching Rule Movement in the British Solomon Islands". *South Pacific* 5 (1951):79–85.

Belshaw, C.S. "Recent History of Mekeo Society". *Oceania* 22 (September 1951):1–23.

Berndt, R.M. "A Cargo Movement in the Eastern Central Highlands of New Guinea". *Oceania* 23 (September 1952):40–65; (December 1952):137–58; (March 1953):203–34.

——. "Reaction to Contact in the Eastern Highland of New Guinea". *Oceania* 24 (1954):190–228; (1954):255–74.

Billings, Dorothy. "The Johnson Cult of New Hanover". *Oceania* 40 (September 1969):13–19.

Bodrogi, T. *Art in North-East New Guinea*. New York: International Publications Service, 1961.

——. "Colonization and Religious Movements in Melanesia". *Acta Ethnographica* 2 (1951):259–92.

Brunton, R. "Cargo Cults and Systems of Exchange in Melanesia". M.A. thesis, University of Sydney, October 1969.

Bühler, A. et al. *Art of the South Sea Islands*. Art of the World Library. New York: Crown Publishers Inc.

Burridge, K.O.L. *Tangu Traditions: A Study of the Way of Life, Mythology and Developing Experience of a New Guinea People*. New York: Oxford Press, 1969.

———. *Mambu.* London: Methuen, 1960.
Christiansen, P. *The Melanesian Cargo Cult: Millenarism as a Factor in Cultural Change.* Copenhagen: Akadamisk Forlag, 1969.
Cochrane, G. *Big Men and Cargo Cults.* Oxford: Clarendon Press, 1970.
Guiart, J. *The Arts of the South Pacific.* Arts of Mankind Series. New York: G. Braziller Inc., 1963.
———. "Culture Contact and the 'John Frum' Movement on Tanna, New Hebrides". *Journal de la Société des Americanistes* 12 (1956):105–16.
Haddon, A.C. *Reports of the Cambridge Anthropological Expedition to Torres Straits* (6 volumes). New York: Johnson Reprint Corp. See volume 1 (1935):46–48.
Harding, T., and Wallace, B. *Cultures of the Pacific.* New York: Free Press, 1970.
Henkelmann, F. *Kukuaik, Story of the Revival Movement on Karkar Island.* Manuscript, copied by Hans and Friedrich Wagner, 16 pages. Lae, P.N.G.: Lutheran Mission Archives, 1942.
Hogbin, H.J.P. *Experiments in Civilization: The Effects of European Culture on a Native Community of Solomon Islands.* New York: Schocken Books Inc., 1970.
Höltker, G. "Die Mambu Bewegung in Neuguinea". *Annali Lateranensi* 5 (1941):181–219.
Inglis, Judy. "Cargo Cults: The Problem of Explanation". *Oceania* 27 (June 1927):249–63.
———. "Interpretation of Cargo Cults: Comments". *Oceania* 30 (December 1959):135–58.
Kiki, Albert M. *Ten Thousand Years in a Lifetime.* Melbourne: Cheshire, 1968.
Lawrence, P. "Cargo Cults and Religious Beliefs among the Garia". *International Archives of Ethnography* 47 (1954).
———. *Road Belong Cargo.* London: Manchester University Press, 1964; and Melbourne: Melbourne University Press, 1964.
Lawrence, P., and Meggitt, M.J. *Gods Ghosts and Men in Melanesia.* 1965. Reprint. Melbourne: Oxford University Press, 1972.
Luzbetak, L.J. "Worship of the Dead in the Middle Wahgi, P.N.G.". *Anthropos* 51 (1956).
Mair, Lucy P. *Australia in New Guinea.* Melbourne: Melbourne University Press, 1971.
Mead, M. *New Lives for Old: Cultural Transformation, Manus 1928–53*, 1956. Reprint. New York: William Morrow & Co. Inc., 1966.
Mühlmann, W., and Uplegger, Helga. "Die Cargo Kulte in Neuguinea und Insel Melanesien". In *Chiliasmus und Nativismus*, edited by W. Mühlmann, pp. 141–64. Berlin: Dietrich Reimer Verlag, 1961.
Oliver, Douglas L. *The Pacific Islands.* Garden City, N.Y.: Natural History Press.

O'Reilly, P. "Jonfrum is New Hebridean Cargo Cult". *Pacific Islands Monthly* 20 (January 1950) and 20 (February 1950).

Poignant, Roslyn. *Oceanic Mythology*. World Mythology Series. New York: Tudor Publishing Co., 1967.

Poirier, J. "Les movements de libération mythique aux Nouvelles–Hébrides". *Journal de la Société des Oceanistes* 5 (December 1949):97–103. Translation: *Movements of Mythical Liberation in the New Hebrides*. Department of Territories, Canberra.

Read, K. "Nama Cult of the Central Highlands, New Guinea". *Oceania* 23 (1952).

———. *High Valley*. London: Allen and Unwin, 1967.

Reay, Marie O. *The Kuma*. Melbourne: Melbourne University Press, 1959.

Rousseau, Madelaine. "L'Océanie devant l'Occident" in *La Musée Vivant*. Paris: L'Art Océanien, 1951.

Salisbury, R.F. "An Indigenous New Guinea Cult". *Kroeber Anthropological Society Paper* no. 18, pp. 67–78. Berkeley: 1958.

———. *From Stone to Steel*. Melbourne: Melbourne University Press, 1962.

Schmitz, C.A. *Wantoat: Art and Religion of the North East New Guinea Papuans*. Atlantic Highlands, N.J.: Humanities Press, 1963.

———. *Oceanic Art: Myth, Man and Image in the South Seas*. New York: Harry N. Abrams (subsidiary of Times Mirror Co.), 1970.

Schwartz, T. "The Co-operatives—ol i bagaripi mani (Manus Island)". *New Guinea Quarterly* 1 (January 1967), p. 43.

———. "The Paliau Movement in the Admiralty Islands 1946–1954". *Anthropological Papers of the American Museum of Natural History*. 49, part 2. New York, 1962.

———. See also Mead, M. and Schwartz, T.

Stanner, W.E.H. *Reconstruction in the South Pacific Islands: A Preliminary Report*. Part I: Papua and New Guinea (with the Vailala Madness or "Cargo Cult"), pp. 31–34. New York: International Secretariat, Institute of Pacific Relations, 1947.

———. *The South Seas in Transition*. Sydney: Australasian Publiciations Comp., 1953.

Steinbauer, F. *So War's in Tarabo*. Neuendettelsau, Bavaria: Friemund Verlag, 1969.

———. "Die Kargo–Kulte als religionsgeschichtliches und missionstheologisches Problem". Thesis, University of Erlangen, Erlangen, 1971.

Thompson, Laura. *Fijian Frontier: Secret Cults, the Water Babies, the Tuka or Immortality Society etc.*, 1940. Reprint. New York: Octagon Books, 1970.

Van de Bruijn, J. "The Mansren Cult of Biak". *South Pacific* 5, March 1951. Translated from Tijdschrift voor Ind. Taal– Land– end Volkenkunde 83 (1949):313–30.

Williams, F.E. *Drama of Orokolo: The Social and Ceremonial Life of the Elema.* Oxford: Clarendon Press, 1940; and New York: Oxford University Press.

——. *Orokaiva Magic.* London: Oxford University Press, 1928; New York, N.Y., 1969.

Worsley, P. *The Trumpet Shall Sound: A Study of Cargo Cults in Melanesia.* Second edition. New York: MacGibbon and Kee, 1967.

The Pursuit of the Millenium outside Melanesia

Aberle, D. *The Peyote Religion among the Navaho.* Viking Fundamental Publications in Anthropology 42. Chicago: Aldine Publishing Co., 1966.

Andersson, Efraim. "Messianic Popular Movements in the Lower Congo". *Studia Ethnographica Upsaliensis* XIV. Uppsala: Uppsala University Press, 1958.

Benz, E. *Messianische Kirchen, Sekten und Bewegungen im heutigen Afrika.* Beihefte der Zeitschrift für Religions– and Geistes–Geschichte no. 10. Leiden: University of Leiden Press, 1965.

Brannen, N. *Soka Gakkai: Japan's Militant Buddhists.* Richmond, Virg.: John Knox Press, 1968.

Dobyns, H.F. and Euler, R.C. *The Ghost Dance of Eighteen Eighty Nine among the Pai Indians of North West Arizona.* Prescott, AZ.: Prescott College Press, 1967.

Fuchs, Stephen. Rebellious Prophets: A Study of Messianic Movements in Indian Religions. Bombay and New York, N.Y., Asia Publishing House, 1965.

Herskovits, M. *Myth of the Negro Past.* Boston: Beacon Press Inc., 1958.

Howard, Helen A. and McGrath, D.L. *War Chief Joseph.* Lincoln: University of Nebraska Press, 1945.

Huxley, Francis. *Invisibles: Voodoo Gods in Haiti.* New York: McGraw–Hill Book Co., 1969.

Kudo, Takuya. "The Faith of Soka Gakkai" in *Contemporary Religions in Japan* 2 (1961). Tokyo: Kokusai Shukyo Kenkyujo.

La Barre, W. *Peyote Cult.* New York: Schocken Books Inc., 1969.

Margull, H.J. *Aufbruch zur Zukunft: Chiliastisch– Messianische Bewegungen in Afrika und in Süd-Ost-Asien.* Gütersloh: Gütersloher Verlagshaus Gerd Mohr, 1962.

Mooney, J. *The Ghost Dance Religion and the Sioux Outbreak of 1890.* Chicago: University of Chicago Press, 1965.

Offner, C. and Straelen, H. *Modern Japanese Religions.* Salesian Technical School, Tokyo. Leiden; E.S. Brill, 1963.

Simpson, G.E. "Jamaican Revivalist Cults". *Social and Economical Studies* V (1956).

Simpson, G.E., ed. *Religious Cults of the Caribbean: Trinidad, Jamaica and Haiti.* Caribbean Monograph Series no. 7. New York: International Publishing Service, 1970.

Sundkler, Bengt G. *Bantu Prophets in South Africa.* Second edition. New York: Oxford University Press, 1961.

Concerning Missions and Church Growth in Contact with Cargo Cults

Beyerhaus, P. *Missions—Which Way?* Contemporary Evangelical Perspectives Series. Grand Rapids: Zondervan Publishing House, 1971.

Kuder, John. "The Cargo Cult and Its Relation to the Task of the Church". Paper presented to the Lutheran Mission New Guinea at Lae, 1964.

Luzbetak, L.J. *The Church and the Cultures: An Applied Anthropology for the Religious Worker.* Techny, Ill.: Divine Word Publications, 1963.

Oosterwal, G. "Cargo Cults as a Missionary Challenge". *International Review of Missions* 56 (October 1967):469ff.

Tippett, A.R. *Verdict Theology in Missionary Theory.* Second revised edition. South Pasadena, Ca.: William Carey Library, 1973.

Vicedom, G.F. *Church and People in New Guinea.* London: World Christian Books, 1961.

Notes

1. F.C. Kamma, "De Messiaanse Koreri–bewegingen in het Biaks–Noem-foorse Cultuurgebied (Ph.D. thesis, University of Leiden 1954), p. 38. *See also* S. Kooijman, "Die messianischen Koreri–Bewegungen auf Neu-guinea", in *Evangelisches Missionsmagazin* (Basel, November 1955), pp. 180–88, citing F.C. Kamma's work.
2. F.C. Kamma, "Messianic Movements in Western New Guinea", *International Review of Missions* 41, no. 162 (April 1952):148–60.
3. *Utrecht Missionary Society Journal* (1887):66, as quoted by P. Worsley in *The Trumpet Shall Sound*, 2nd ed. (New York: MacGibbon and Kee, 1967), p. 132.
4. Kamma, "De Messiaanse Koreri–bewegingen" pp. 59–100; also cited by Kooijman, 1955, p. 183.
5. Kamma, "Messianic Movements", p. 154.
6. A.C. Haddon in E.W.P. Chinnery and A.C. Haddon, "Five New Religious Cults in British New Guinea", *The Hibbert Journal* 15, no. 3 (1916–17): part II: 455–63.
7. Copland King, "The Baigona Cult", *Papua Annual Report*, (1912–13), Port Moresby, Appendix A, pp. 154–55.
8. *Steyler Missionsbote*, 1932–33, p. 108. (Printed news-sheet or messenger of the missionaries of the *Societas verbi divini* [Society of the Divine Word] previously at Steyl in Holland now at St. Augustin near Bonn, West Germany.)
9. Hans Wagner, "A Field Study of the Bongu-Buged Circuit" (Paper read at the Lutheran Mission New Guinea Field Conference, Wau, PNG 1964), p. 17.
10. Wagner, ibid., p. 34.
11. K.O.L. Burridge, *Mambu, A Melanesian Millenium* (London: Methuen and New York: Humanities Press, 1960), p. 12.
12. P. Lawrence, *Road Belong Cargo* (Melbourne: Melbourne University Press, 1964), pp. 147ff.
13. Wagner, "Field Study of Bongu–Buged Circuit", p. 63.
14. Wagner, ibid.
15. F. Wagner, "The Outgrowth and Development of the Cargo Cult" (Paper read to the Lutheran Mission New Guinea Field Conference, Wau, PNG, 1964), pp. 7–14.
16. Wagner, ibid., p. 21.
17. Herwig Wagner, "Die grosse Erwartung, Phäenomene des Kargo Kultus in Neu Guinea und Ansäetze zu seiner Ueberwindung". (Lecture delivered at Neuendettelsau, Bavaria, 1968.)
18. C. Laufer, "Psychologische Grundlagen religiöeser Schwarmgeist-bewegungen in der Süedsee", *Kairos*, no. 1, (1959):153.

19. Theodore Schwartz, *The Paliau Movement in the Admiralty Islands 1946–54*. Anthropological Papers of the American Museum of Natural History, New York, 49, part 2, 1962, pp. 211–421.
20. Schwartz, ibid., p. 256.
21. See *Pacific Islands Monthly*, (April 1965):37.
22. Theodore Schwartz, "The Cooperatives", *New Guinea Quarterly* 1, no. 8 (January 1967):36–47.
23. Caspar Luana (pseudonym), "Buka, a Retrospect", *New Guinea Quarterly* 4, no. 1 (1969):15. A similar story was told to the author in 1966 when he visited Buka.
24. Luana, ibid., p. 13.
25. Luana, ibid., pp. 15–20.
26. Luana, ibid.
27. Don Marsh, "The Surprising Gospel of John Frum", *Pacific Islands Monthly* 32, no. 10 (October 1968):87.
28. J. Graham Miller, "Naked Cult in Central West Santo", *The Journal of the Polynesian Society* 57, no. 4 (December 1948):330–41.
29. Miller, ibid., 331–32.
30. *Les Missions Catholiques* (1919), p. 127, as cited by J. Blanc, *Histoire Religieuse de l'Archipel Fijienne* (Toulon, 1926), pp. 179–81.
31. *See* Table 1 and bibliography.
32. A.R. Tippet, "For Uppsala to Consider", *Church Growth Bulletin* (Oakland, Pasadena: Institute of Church Growth, Fuller Theological Seminary, School of World Mission, 4, no. 5, May 1968), p. 10.
33. P. Beyerhaus, *Humanisierung—einzige Hoffnung der Welt?* (Salzuflen, West Germany: MBK—Mäedchen Bibelkreis Verlag, 1970), pp. 73ff.
34. As a basis for comparison with later statistics (see *Pacific Islands Yearbook* 1977) the following figures for the population and Christians are quoted from the *Pacific Islands Yearbook* (Sydney: Pacific Publications, 1968). Europeans, Indonesians, Indians, Chinese, mixed races or other non-Melanesians are not included in the figures.

		Population		
		Total		Christians
Fiji		202,176		200,000
New Caledonia	approx	50,000		25,000
New Hebrides		4,968	approx.	3,000
British Solomon Islands		142,740	approx.	70,000
Papua		586,208	approx.	300,000
Territory of New Guinea		1,562,153	approx.	1,017,000
West Irian		728,000		300,000
Total		3,276,245		1,915,000

35. See glossary.
36. For example, see note 12.
37. H. Strauss, "Der Cargo Kult", *Junges Neuguinea*, (Neuendettelsau: Neuendettelsauer Lutheran Mission, 1970) 144.
38. P. Christiansen, *The Melanesian Cargo Cult, Millenarism as a Factor in Cultural Change* (Copenhagen: Akadamisk Forlag, 1969) pp. 114–18.
39. Schwartz, *The Paliau Movement*, p. 219.
40. Manfred Curry, *Schlüessel zum Leben* (Zürich: 1949, second edition 1969) published by Medizinisch-Bioklimatische Institut which was founded by Manfred Curry in Riederau, Ammersse/Oberbayern, West Germany. An earlier publication is "Bioklimatik", 1946. Curry's work is continued. English translations are apparently unknown.

41. J. Sterly, "Heilige Mäenner und Medizinmänner in Melanesien". (Ph.D. thesis, University of Köln, 1965), p. 418.
42. In ancient times the Papuans had been created from the flesh of the big, man-eating lizard Waran and the Dutch from its fat. Then two ancestors of the Papuans journeyed as spirit beings by aeroplane to the far west. There they settled and developed the two great ways of salvation by which life may grow happy. One ancestor became the mother of God and thus she created the new religion; the other became Queen Wilhelmina, mother of the Dutch government, and thus the originator of western standards of living. The arrival of the first white men had not been seen as something totally new, but as a return of the mythical world of salvation. The European often conceives cargo cults as syncretism. For the Melanesian they are only a natural continuation of what has been. Hans Nevermann, *Die Söhne des Tötenden Vaters, Dämonen und Kopfjäger Geschichten aus Neu Guinea*, (Kassel, Erich Roeth Verlag, 1957), p. 23.
43. Sunden, *Die Religion und die Rollen: Eine psychologische Untersuchung der Fröemmigkeit* (Bern: P. Haupt Verlag, 1966).
44. Sterly, *Heilige Mäenner*, p. 418.
45. H. Sunden cites Jean Lhermitte, *Les Hallucinations*, Paris, 1936.
46. Sterly, "Heilige Mäenner", pp. 212–16.
47. Sunden, *Die Religion und die Rollen*. pp. 48–50. Sunden refers to *The Doors of Perception*, Aldous Huxley (New York: Harper and Row Publishers, 1970).
48. Sterly, *Heilige Mäenner*, p. 218.
49. F. Steinbauer, "Der Religiöese Bezug im Cargo–Kultkomplex", *Evangelische Missions Zeitschrift* 26, no. 4 (November 1969) 211–29.
50. Sunden, *Die Religion und die Rollen*, pp. 1–7 elaborates the subject with several examples.
51. Van der Leeuw, *Phäenomenologie der Religion*, second edition (Tüebingen: Gerd Mohr Verlag, 1956), especially in the chapter "Epilegomena". *Also* Hermelink, Jan, *Verstehen und Bezeugen* (Müenchen: Christian Kaiser Verlag, 1960), pp. 22–34.
52. Hermelink, *Verstehen und Bezeugen*, p. 23.
53. *Worte des Vorsitzenden Mao–Tse–Tung*, a translation from the English: *Quotations from Chairman Mao Tse–Tung* (Peking: Foreign Language Press, 1967), p. 209.
54. H. Cox, *Stadt ohne Gott*, fourth edition (Stuttgart: Kreuz Verlag, 1968), pp. 30–31.
55. Translated from H. Zahrnt, *Die Sache mit Gott* (Munich: Christian Kaiser Verlag, 1966), p. 34.
56. A. Van der Heuvel, "Saekularisierung als Freiheit und Buerde", *Oekumenische Diskussion* I, no. 2: 73.
57. Ibid., p. 71.
58. *Oekumenischer Pressedienst*, (May 1970), p. 8. (*Oekumenischer Pressedienst* is published in Geneva by the World Council of Churches, the World Alliance of Young Men's Christian Associations and Young Women's Christian Associations and the World Student Christian Federation. English edition is *Ecumenical Press Service*.)
59. H. Bürkle, *Die Reaktion der Religionen auf die Saekularisierung* (Neuendettelsau: Freimund Verlag, 1969), p. 30.
60. *Lutherische Rundschau* (Stuttgart: German Headquarters of Lutheran World Federation, April 1970), pp. 196ff.
61. Some German representatives of this line of thought are G. Anders, H. Plessner, A. Portmann and T. von Uexkull.

62. T. Dobzhansky, Julian Huxley and H.J. Muller are suggested as important representatives of this view.

63. This concept is used in the biochemistry of cell research. It means that the division of a cell and the information which it receives for its development is steered by a so far not controllable centre. By our traditional, theological concepts this can only be expressed as transcendent. Therefore I do not introduce a new concept but accept what is already a concept for the scientific knowledge.

64. P. Worsley, *The Trumpet Shall Sound*, Second edition (London: MacGibbon and Kee, 1968.

65. The Native Marketing and Supply Service company has developed from mission work of the Lutheran Church in 1958–59 and is self-supporting since that time and works with profit. It enjoys the confidence of the population.

66. Following the English text and the Kâte original. Missionary W. Flierl had prepared the draft which was accepted by the 5th Synod of the Evangelical Lutheran Church in New Guinea on 5 October 1964. It reads as follows:
Declaration Concerning Cargo Cult
Translation from Kâte by Dr W. Flierl

As a member of the Church of Lord Christ on the basis of His Holy Word, I state with full conviction:
1. All things on earth supporting human physical life, now in existence and currently emerging, have been provided by God my Father on my, His child's, behalf.
2. In order that I may continually reap the benefits of what He has provided, He ordered that I work diligently with my mind and my hands, "in the sweat of my face".
3. Therefore, clinging to God with my heart, I am to do prayerfully the work He has assigned to me, and whenever through His blessings I reap the fruits of my labour, to make use of them with thanksgiving.
4. It is completely impossible that money and goods, or cars and machines, or any physical commodities, are obtainable from dead ancestors, or from empty space, or from inside the mountains, or out of lakes.
5. Therefore, praying to the dead, making preparations for expected goods in cemeteries or dug-outs or any other places, quivering of the body, babbling (i.e. speaking in tongues), or suspecting the whites of concealing from us the real origin of (fabricated) goods are nothing but abject perversities.
6. Recognising all these things as foolish, reprehensible and do away with them.
7. Those who assert (or believe) to have received messages from the dead or from the spirits or angels, in dreams or while awake, are victims of Satanic deception.
8. Therefore, relying on the power of the Lord, I shall reject any advice or instructions by such people, and report their activities to the church circuit authorities.
May the Lord help us to remain united in upholding this confession until cargo cult ideas have vanished.

Amen.

67. P. Potter (General Secretary of the World Council of Churches in 1977). "Präesenz und Solidaritäet". Lecture given at the Deutscher Evangelischer Missionstag, Bad Liebenzell, 1967.
68. This subject is nearly always avoided. In church circles human love between members of different races or nations still seems taboo. Exactly in this area we can prove how strongly we believe in solidarity. Why does it practically never happen that children of missionaries marry someone out of the group of their early friends? Why do we sneer when a well educated Papuan marries an Australian girl? Why is the majority displeased when an Italian surveyor prefers to live with the family of his dark friend rather than stay in a hotel? Such cases show how biassed we are and how little our words about solidarity mean in actual life.
69. Neither horses nor donkeys did exist in Melanesia. The only domestic animal was the pig. Therefore the story of Jesus' entry into Jerusalem on a donkey can be translated only while critically screening certain theological points of view. Similarly we have to deal with "wine", the "leaven", or the "sacrificial lamb" or with "wheat". These originally were as alien and incomprehensible concepts as the word "thanks". Either we import the English words and leave it to the phantasy of the individual and to the education in the community what should be understood by them, or we apply kindred native words which alter the meaning decisively. That is true also for the concept of God. In East New Guinea one says Anutu for God. But Anutu used to be a mountain spirit. He dwelt in the hinterland of the coast. If he moved earthquakes resulted. We should not be surprised if even today features of Anutu affect the biblical picture of God. The ideals which a man preserves are more deeply rooted than a rational discussion would allow us to suspect. These ideals or archtypes are effective in our culture. We should know from one thousand years of Christian history that such original images of God cannot be transcended within one generation.
70. In the course of history many changes have taken place which affected attitudes towards human problems. For instance consider attitudes to slavery and obedience to authorities at the time of St. Paul and today; the importance attached to food laws in the early church, in the Middle Ages or in the twentieth century; or the emancipation of women at different periods in history; the disputes about the Eucharist from the time of the Reformation on; or even the change in comprehension of the divinity in the Old Testament. At times, quite obviously, God's Spirit creates new criteria in His church for changes in society; yet the church does not suffer damage by the change.
71. The solemn praise of God in the Gregorian church music is, not only in its form but also in its content, different from the worship of God by dancing mountain tribes in New Britain or in Africa. The Heliand epic of the Teutons by no means corresponded to the standard of the canonic gospels. The representation of Christ in paintings or sculpture as a dark-skinned African or as an Asiatic teacher of meditation designates not only a formally changed reception of the message in a different, cultural frame but indeed beyond that a somewhat changed notion of reality. Unless we want to see the history of the church only as a history of heresies we cannot but think in the categories of an ever new revelation challenging human beings. Amongst illiterate nations where preaching is often not controlled, the meeting with the Gospel obviously reacts upon the Gospel itself. Thus concepts are coined which remain effective even when new formulations have long become current.

72. J. Drechsler, *Das Wirklichkeitsproblem in der Erziehungswissenschaft* (1959), p. 21.
73. H. Henz, *Ermutigung* (Freiburg, 1964), p. 18.
74. Ibid, pp. 116ff.

Index